TRAFALGAR

TRAFALGAR

Napoleon's Naval Waterloo

RENÉ MAINE

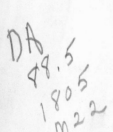

CHARLES SCRIBNER'S SONS

NEW YORK

Translated from the French by

RITA ELDON *and* B. W. ROBINSON

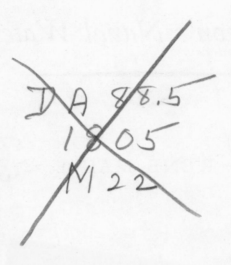

CONTENTS

CHARTS

PREFACE

THE APPEARANCE of a book dealing with a naval encounter in the era of sail and of "wooden walls", now that we are at the dawn of the atomic navy, may perhaps be matter for surprise. But the Battle of Trafalgar, whose 150th anniversary was celebrated in 1955, was much more than a dramatic clash between two fleets. It rang down the curtain on a vast enterprise with which Napoleon had been threatening England for two years—Invasion.

For this reason the history of the war at sea between 1803 and 1805, an episode all too often neglected in the great Napoleonic panorama, has gained in our day a new significance and an unexpected importance. There is in fact a striking parallel between the events of those years and those that we ourselves lived through between 1940 and 1945.

When, on July 2, 1940, Hitler decided to launch his "Operation Sea-Lion", he was simply reliving the former dreams of Napoleon: to break England by throwing an army across the Channel and invading her very soil. The means envisaged were certainly different: 155 steamships, 1,722 barges, 471 ocean-going tugs, and 1,160 motor-boats were to replace the Emperor's 2,000 oar-driven sloops. Hundreds of aircraft were to take the place of the hot-air balloons which, in the pages of periodicals, contemporary visionaries brought to the support of the Grand Army. But the point of departure was the same— an enlarged Boulogne camp. And the underlying motives were identical—to overthrow England before an alliance could open a second front. In the end Hitler, too, failed from having undertaken the war with insufficient strength on the sea and in the air to give him absolute control of the Straits of Dover, even for twenty-four hours. He met his first Trafalgar in the air, and then on all the seven seas, where he lost one by one the finest units of his fleet, until finally the Allies turned the tables, crossed the Channel, and themselves made a successful landing.

It is said that history repeats itself, a proposition supported by the events of 1803-1805. In the light of what happened in 1940 those events take on a fuller meaning for us to-day.

We can tell now, in retrospect, the exact moment when Hitler's Germany lost the war. It was on September 15, 1940, when the R.A.F. inflicted on the Luftwaffe its first great defeat, above the Channel. Two days later Hitler decided to postpone *sine die* his "Operation Sea-Lion". On October 15 he finally cancelled it, despite the protests of Field-Marshal von Brauchitsch, who calculated that he could have ten divisions on English soil in six days, and sixteen in eighteen days.

In the same way, as I think this book will make even more clear, we know the precise moment at which the French Empire received its real death blow. It was not on June 18, 1815 at Waterloo: it was on October 21, 1805 off the little Spanish cape called Trafalgar; and in memory of that battle French and English sailors to this day wear a black cravat round their necks; the latter mourn for their leader who fell in the thick of the fight, and the former mourn for their shattered illusions.

Paris   R. M.
1954-1955.

I

WAR IS DECLARED

"AT AMIENS," Napoleon was to say in St Helena, "I believed in all good faith that France's fate and mine had been decided."

His optimism did not last long. Once the first flush of enthusiasm had passed, it soon became evident, even to the least informed of Frenchmen, that the Treaty of Amiens on which the victor of Marengo was banking to found the glorious destiny of France was no more than a halt in the pilgrimage of war.

The truth was that despite the moving pleas of Fox, English opinion, powerfully worked upon by an active war party, could not resign itself to accepting the consequences of a treaty which did not merely hound the English out of the Mediterranean but also left France mistress of Belgium and set the final seal upon her political and economic ascendancy on the Continent. Every day City stockbrokers, merchants and shipowners bitterly denounced the colonial ventures of the First Consul in San Domingo, Guadeloupe and India; the resurgence of the French fleet, whose budget had just been considerably increased; and the vast public works up and down the country, such as the Nantes-Brest canal, the Oureq canal and the Simplon highway. All these things, they maintained, served only to increase French military and commercial power.

On the surface, however, Malta remained the only bone of contention. Even if, contrary to all expectations, Bonaparte had been willing to go back on the pacts into which he had entered, and had agreed to surrender the island to England, war would still have been inevitable: only if France had renounced all her claims under the treaty and had immediately evacuated Belgium—only then might it have been averted.

*

Three days after a stormy interview with Lord Whitworth, the British Ambassador to France, the First Consul presided at the opening assembly of the Legislature. It was February 21, 1803. On the subject of Franco-British relations, he said that in England there were two parties struggling for power. "One was responsible for the peace treaty and seems determined to maintain it; the other has sworn implacable hatred against France. So long as the issue of this debate remains uncertain there are a number of measures which prudence prompts the Government of the Republic to adopt. Five hundred thousand men must and will be ready to defend and avenge her. Whatever the outcome of the political struggle in London, England will not succeed in forging new alliances and the Government can say with pride that without such support England could not stand up to France."

News of this speech reached England at the same time as a note asking the Cabinet for a clear statement on the evacuation of Malta. Strong feelings were aroused. On March 8, King George III replied in a message to Parliament which, far from calming public opinion, inflamed it still further.

"His Majesty," the document proclaims, "thinks it necessary to acquaint the House of Commons that, as very considerable military preparations are carrying on in the ports of France and Holland, He has judged it expedient to adopt additional measures of precaution for the security of His Dominions. Though the preparations to which His Majesty refers are avowedly directed to Colonial service, yet, as discussions of great importance are now subsisting between His Majesty and the French Government, the result of which must at present be uncertain, His Majesty is induced to make this communication to His faithful Commons, in the full persuasion that, whilst they partake of His Majesty's earnest and unvarying solicitude for the continuance of peace, He may rely with perfect confidence on their public spirit and liberality, to enable His Majesty to adopt such measures as circumstances may appear to require, for supporting the honour of His Crown and the essential interests of His People."

George III's message was received at the Tuileries on March 11. It had an electrifying effect. "Napoleon," wrote Stendhal, "has been called treacherous. He was on fact no worse than fickle." In this emergency he cast aside the character of First Consul and, in a moment, became a new man. This was no longer Bonaparte: it was Napoleon, the Emperor. According to Thiers, the mind that had been wholly devoted to peaceful labours the preceding day needed no more than a second to adjust itself to the single-minded pursuit of war. Did the British accuse him before the world of contemplating aggression? Very well! They would see what had never been seen before: the Continent closed to England from Denmark to the Adriatic, and England herself invaded, overrun, crushed and enslaved by a vast and invincible army.

Already a stream of orders was pouring out setting in motion a whole world, lulled to sleep by what Bainville called "the illusion of Amiens". Napoleon's exceptional mind automatically excluded anything that was not "the destruction of England". He hatched out vast plans with disconcerting speed and meticulous precision, taking details in his stride. An inventory was to be made of all existing naval resources, the coast was to be put in a state of defence, troops were to be deployed to complete the sealing off of Europe; Hanover, Portugal and the Gulf of Taranto were to be occupied immediately upon the outbreak of hostilities; Louisiana, the least secure of the French possessions, was to be sold immediately to the United States; envoys were to be despatched to the courts of Prussia and Russia to inform them of the march of events and of their possible consequences.

On March 13, forty-eight hours after the publication of George III's message in Paris, a reception was held at the

Tuileries for the ambassadors of foreign countries. Though the date had been fixed long before, the diplomatic corps came out in full strength, all being anxious to see how Bonaparte—who was rumoured to be in a towering rage—would greet the English ambassador.

The scene surpassed all expectations.

Striding rapidly across the floor past the waiting diplomats in their gold braid and decorations the First Consul, scowling blackly, made straight for Lord Whitworth. He challenged him in a quivering voice.

"Have you any word from England, my lord?"

And then, not waiting for an answer:

"So you want war?"

"No, general," said the English ambassador calmly. "We are too conscious of the advantages of peace."

"So you want war?" continued Bonaparte as though he had not heard. "We have fought each other for ten years and now you want us to go on for another ten?"

He was trembling with fury.

"How dare a certain person say that France was rearming? A certain person has been deceiving the world. There is not a ship in our ports, everything seaworthy has been sent to San Domingo. The only existing fighting ships are in Dutch waters and everyone has known for the last four months that they are intended for Louisiana. A certain person has said that there is a dispute between France and England. I know of none. I only know that the island of Malta has not been evacuated in the prescribed time, but I don't imagine that your Ministers wish to break the sworn word of the English nation by refusing to carry out a solemn treaty. At least they have not yet said so. Nor do I suppose that by your war preparations you wish to intimidate the French people: one can slay them, my lord, intimidate them never!"

Lord Whitworth, though stung to the quick, answered with great composure: England was not seeking to intimidate France, she wished only to live with her in perfect understanding.

"In that case," thundered Napoleon, "you must honour treaties. Woe betide those who do not!"

He strode round the silent circle, stopping in front of the Russian ambassador to tell him that as England did not observe her engagements, treaties would in future have to be "put in mourning". He dumbfounded the Swedish minister by declaring brutally, with reference to some recent incident, that Sweden had outlived the age of Gustavus Adolphus and had sunk to the rank of a third-rate power; and then, regaining possession of himself and becoming very much the man of the world, returned towards Lord Whitworth with a smile to enquire after the health of his wife.

Such a scene virtually amounted to a declaration of war. For another two months, however, Talleyrand and Lord Whitworth did their utmost to arrive at a compromise. But England still had no intention of evacuating Malta; and Bonaparte had lost confidence in the peace by which, only a few weeks before, he had set such store.

One day Talleyrand said to him:

"After all, the English have got Malta. You will not wrest it from them by declaring war."

Bonaparte answered simply:

"That may be so. But I refuse to surrender so great an advantage without a struggle; I shall fight for it and I hope to bring the British to such a pass that they will be obliged to surrender Malta and more. Besides which, of course, once I set foot at Dover it will be all up with these tyrants of the seas. Moreover, since we are bound to clash sooner or later with a people that cannot abide the glory of France, the sooner the better. Our national morale has not yet been blunted by a long spell of peace; I am young and I would rather get it over now; the English are in the wrong; I have made up my mind; they shall not keep Malta!"

Thus the die was cast. On May 12, 1803 Lord Whitworth left Paris; on the 16th the French ambassador in London was officially informed of the declaration of war and on the 18th

the first shots echoed in the Bay of Audierne in an exchange
between the English schooner *Doris* and the French lugger the
Affronteur.

The last act in a rivalry, already over a century old, was
about to begin.

*

The French and the English had been almost uninterruptedly
at war for a hundred and fourteen years; a hundred and fourteen years during which the sea had been the scene and, indeed,
the principal stake in their fierce struggle.

War had broken out in 1689 when England, having eliminated first Spain and then Holland—rival claimants to naval
supremacy—had joined the famous League of Amsterdam
which had been organised by William of Orange against
Louis XIV.

It is impossible to assess the historical significance of the
Battle of Trafalgar without retracing, at least in outline, the
main stages in the great conflict of which Trafalgar was the
outcome.

In 1689 France which had not existed as a sea power only
thirty years before was the proud possessor of the finest battle
fleet in the world. Thanks to the work of two great *commis*,
Colbert and his son, the Marquess of Seignelay, she had available 120 ships against England's 106 and Holland's 95. Moreover, she was fortunate enough to possess in Tourville one of
the ablest sailors of the time.

At this period conditions of naval warfare were undergoing
radical transformation.

Men-of-war had been increasing steadily in size and tonnage
since the preceding century. Whereas sixteenth-century vessels
had a displacement of 1,500-2,000 tons, carrying 500 men and
80 guns, Tourville's *Soleil Royal* had a tonnage of no less than
2,700, carried 1,200 men and was armed with 110 guns discharging a broadside of 1,386 lb. of shot.

Tactics, too, had changed. Whereas formerly they were left

to the discretion of the captain, they now conformed to a strict code of laws which stifled all independent action.

In the first half of the seventeenth century, when two fleets met, each attempted to annihilate the other in detail, first cutting the enemy's line at several points. This was the method used by admirals such as Blake and Tromp. But in 1689 caution was the order of the day. One rule had priority over all others: keep your line of battle intact. Initiative was proscribed. The commander-in-chief could alone decide the course of action. A naval battle thus became an amazing parade, with the rival fleets, after a slow succession of manœuvres to get a favourable wind and to approach within range (about 500 yards), aligning themselves with mathematical precision and sailing on opposite tacks, raking each other with gunfire, fiercely or negligently, as the fancy took them. The English fired straight into the enemy's hull in order to breach it and cause the maximum damage to men and guns. The French, on the other hand, aimed at dismasting in order to paralyse their opponents. But since methods of aiming were rudimentary in the extreme (they merely sighted along the barrel), there was often more sound than effect.

"Do you know what goes by the name of a naval battle?" Maurepas used to ask when he was Minister of the Marine under Louis XV. "Some manœuvring, an encounter, an exchange of gun-fire followed by the withdrawal of both fleets, and when it is all over the sea is as briny as it was before."

It was no more than the truth. These too well regulated aquatic ballets seldom achieved the purpose for which they had been mounted at such expense. They had their virtuosi none the less and among these Tourville was outstanding.

As others played the harpsichord, so Tourville played the line. No one could equal him in the art of controlling a fleet of several dozen ships stretching out over a line of ten to twelve miles. But he was fettered by the inviolable doctrine and never forgot Louis XIV's counsel of prudence. He was not and could never be the man who won decisive victories by putting bold plans into action without regard for the rules.

He missed a wonderful opportunity on July 16, 1690 off Beachy Head when he could have destroyed an Anglo-Dutch fleet of 13 ships of the line which his own outnumbered.

Two years later he received orders to embark 20,000 soldiers at Le Havre and La Hogue and make a surprise landing on English soil. London got wind of the operation. He found himself facing the same opponents, this time north-east of Barfleur; but conditions were no longer the same: he had 44 ships, the Anglo-Dutch fleet 99. It was May 29, 1692. After an indecisive engagement lasting all day, the battered French fleet was obliged to run for shelter in the nearest ports with the allies in close pursuit. Three French vessels, one of which was the *Soleil Royal*, were destroyed by fire-ships under the very guns of Cherbourg and 12 on the beach at La Hogue where they had run aground.

The loss of 15 men-of-war was not a catastrophe for a fleet of 120. But, as Michelet has pointed out, although it appeared insignificant, the unfavourable outcome of the battle of La Hogue had a decisive influence on the course of history. It gave Louis XIV and the greater part of his people an antipathy for anything to do with the sea.

Overnight, the King abandoned the fleet to his Minister under whose direction it no longer put out to sea in disciplined formations but confined itself to energetic commerce-raiding, which was then graced with the title of "economic naval warfare".

This new move had precisely the opposite effect to the one intended. Far from weakening England it drove her to increase still further her naval power as a security for her commercial power. The French fleet, on the other hand, suffered not only from inaction and from the bad habits it had acquired (piracy cannot be practised with impunity), but from the growing embarrassment of the Royal Treasury. It fell under distaff influence and soon ceased to count in the war.

From the beginning of the war of the Spanish Succession the

naval superiority of England was established beyond doubt. The English took possession of Gibraltar, key to the Mediterranean. Fifteen years later they were in a position to challenge French colonial supremacy in the Seven Years' War.

In 1756, at the outset of a war which was to settle for many years "the future of England and of the world", Colbert's navy was no more than a memory. From a fleet of 135 capital ships in 1696 it had dwindled to a mere 60, all equally ill-equipped, usually entrusted to inefficient officers and manned by crews who had been assembled without any discrimination. Inexorably, disaster followed upon disaster. Having been repulsed in India, Canada, Senegal and Guinea, France set her last hopes on an invasion of England. But it was too late. Before the invasion force could embark the fleet had been destroyed.

This time France could meditate at leisure upon the meaning of the expression "mastery of the seas". In 1764, at the signing of the Treaty of Paris, she was left with no more than thirty-odd ships all more or less unseaworthy. But the lesson had been learnt. Shocked by the humiliation of defeat, individuals, corporations, towns and provinces began organising collections to enable the king to rebuild the battered fleet. Never before had national enthusiasm been so spontaneous and sincere. When the American War of Independence broke out in 1778 France had built up her fleet to 80 ships.

It was indeed a miracle. Naturally enough, it was not long before the idea of an invasion of England once again began to possess the French mind.

"With 40 men-of-war and 60,000 men," declared Count de Broglie, "we would be certain of success."

But the project had to be abandoned and so had the idea of recapturing Gibraltar. The restored fleet was still too young to challenge an enemy whose training was meticulous and whose equipment was beyond praise.

At this period, the sailing ship had reached its peak of perfection. It had been stripped of the rich ornamentation fashionable in the previous century and had become more efficient due to the introduction of copper-lined bottoms. Armaments had been standardised and reinforced and now consisted of a minimum of 74 or 80 guns in two-deckers, or 118 in the case of two- or three-deckers.

The frigate, a new type of fast light craft, was beginning to appear at this time. It was designed to scout for the heavier man-of-war and to carry out secondary missions. Finally, though the rigid strategy still had the force of law, its effectiveness was beginning to be seriously questioned by younger officers. Among them was Suffren, the Frenchman operating in Indian waters; but the honour of being the first to make a definite break with tradition belongs to Admiral Rodney, again an Englishman.

On April 12, 1782 Rodney, operating in the Caribbean Sea, met a French fleet commanded by Count de Grasse between Guadeloupe and the des Saintes Islands. At the instance of his chief of staff, Rodney cut across the French line breaking it at two points. This opened up the possibility of combat at close quarters and revealed the effects of concentrated artillery fire: five French ships were captured and de Grasse was taken prisoner. Rodney's success would have been even more complete if he had not been so stunned by his own audacity as to allow the bulk of the French squadron to slip away.

Despite this defeat, which was partly offset by the final victory of the American colonists, France had reason for satisfaction at the end of the War of Independence. She had shown that in spite of appearances the struggle for naval supremacy was not yet over and that England would once again have to reckon with her. Her efforts to keep her fleet in good condition, which were to cost her another 380 million francs from 1784-1789, had not been in vain. In a world tired of war, she was able at last to share in the general prosperity.

On September 26, 1786 a commercial treaty with England—forerunner of identical treaties with the United States, Switzerland and Russia—put an end to the economic war between the two countries which had lasted nearly three-quarters of a century.

Though Anglo-French rivalry, the root of so many evils, seemed to have abated, the peace which was the dream of merchant and philosopher alike was far from being assured.

On the eve of 1789, Jacques Bainville has written, France and England were living in a state of precarious equilibrium. All were aware that it could be upset at any time by the action of either side.

It was the French Revolution that tipped the scales. The occupation of Antwerp by the *sans-culottes* on November 13, 1792 caused an explosion in England. She had shown ever since the time of Louis XIV that she considered the presence of the French at the mouth of the Scheldt to constitute the most serious threat to her commerce and security. The inevitable war broke out on February 1, 1793.

At no other moment in their naval history had the French been less ready to give battle. Shorn of its leaders and left to the mercy of the revolutionary committees, their navy had fallen into indiscipline and neglect. The first pitched battle (June 1, 1794) ended in a cruel setback: of the 26 French ships taking part, seven were lost. Six months later the Brest squadron found itself unable to weather a sudden squall, and lost a further six vessels.

The *Convention*, appalled by the evidence of such helplessness, found but one answer. It proceeded categorically to condemn the classical formations of standard naval practice as "useless displays of naval power flattering only personal pride" (*sic*) and, like Louis XIV, pinned its hopes entirely on the tactics of isolated commerce-raiding. But the more realistic *Directory* took care not to fall into the trap. At all costs it was determined to make use of those French ships which were still serviceable. Lazare Hoche was entrusted with the task of making a landing in Ireland thereby stirring up disaffection among the Irish, sworn enemies of their English overlords. It was a good plan. Unfortunately, when the fleet which had somehow been assembled finally took to sea (January 1797) it was dispersed by bad weather more effectively than if it had come under enemy fire. Not one soldier landed on Irish soil; but two warships and three frigates were lost at sea.

The only hope of rectifying the situation lay in France's allies, Spain and Holland. Alas! One month after the Irish adventure the English routed the Spaniards off Cape St Vincent. Seven months later they crushed the Dutch at Camperdown, destroying 11 of their 16 ships.

It was too much. The possibility of winning a pitched battle had to be excluded. Once again the idea of striking at the heart of England came to the surface. But a new method was envisaged.

*

Two years earlier, in 1795, a lieutenant of Flemish origin named Muskeyn, on the strength of experiences gathered in Sweden during the Russo-Swedish war, had suggested to the French authorities the possibility of employing a new type of naval craft in the North Sea and in the English Channel. He had in mind flat-bottomed boats propelled by either sail or oar, armed with guns mounted near water-level. According to Muskeyn they were easy to handle and could outclass the average men-of-war, not only in fire power and mobility, but also in their general manœuvrability, especially in coastal waters too shallow for ships of the line.

It must be admitted that the first trials, which were carried out on the Belgian coast, had not exactly been conclusive. But certain engineers were optimistic and Pierre Forfait, the foremost among them, had even shown enthusiasm.

In spite of obvious defects, these armed launches came finally to be regarded as perhaps the only possible means of conquering England, for they alone could carry an invading army across the North Sea on to her very soil.

The failure of the attempted landing in Ireland removed the last vestiges of doubt.

In July 1797 the *Directory* gave orders for the construction of a fleet of landing craft at Calais and Boulogne.

Nine months later 294 launches and 1,307 barges capable of transporting 70,000 men and 6,000 horses had been assembled in the North Sea ports ready for the attempt. But Bonaparte had already changed his plans. On May 19, 1798 he emerged from Toulon at the head of a fleet of 400 sailing ships and turning his back on England scudded before the wind towards Egypt.

It seemed as though fortune might favour him at last. But two-and-a-half months later, on the evening of August 1, Rear-Admiral Nelson, suddenly appearing between the lines of the French fleet at anchor in Aboukir Bay, near Alexandria, destroyed it almost entirely: only two ships out of 13 escaped.

This new disaster, which was indeed more serious than the one of La Hogue, upset all calculations. In the following three years the French battle fleet, blockaded at Brest by a powerful British squadron cruising permanently off Ushant, was not to be seen in the Mediterranean.

Was France, the mistress of the Continent, finally to renounce her natural right as a naval power and yield to *force majeure* without a last struggle?

In the confused minds of the French a landing on English soil seemed once again the only possible way out.

The first landing fleet had been left to the mercy of the weather since 1798. In the spring of 1801 Bonaparte gave the order that it should be overhauled and that its complement should be made up to 2,000, placed under the command of Rear-Admiral Latouche-Tréville.

There could be no doubt that Bonaparte was fully aware of the serious risks involved in an invasion of England. He had himself written to the *Directory* in 1798 that "it would not only be a bold but a dangerous step to take without first gaining control of the sea".

In 1801 France was no more mistress of the sea than she had been in 1798. Was Bonaparte's real purpose, in deciding to restore the Boulogne fleet, merely to undermine English morale, already badly shaken, according to reliable reports, by the prolonged struggle?

At all events, when word reached London of what was afoot on the other side of the Channel there was a considerable stir. His Majesty's Government at once undertook new coastal defences, raised militias and drew up a plan for the evacuation inland of the inhabitants from the most vulnerable areas. As these measures did not appear to have reassured public opinion, it recalled Nelson and solemnly entrusted him with the defence of the island.

Nelson, already famous after his inspired attack at Aboukir Bay, had just won a second brilliant victory by destroying the Danish fleet at Copenhagen. In August 1801 he attacked Boulogne, full of fire and fury, but was severely punished by the guns of the coastal batteries and of the fleet. He suffered some losses and was forced to retire in dismay.

Another attempt a few days later was no more successful.

In face of this twofold setback, England was profoundly disturbed, and felt that perhaps this was the moment to reconsider her position. As Bonaparte was only too ready to "talk" it was easy to come to an understanding. On October 1, a preliminary agreement put an end to hostilities. Six months later the final peace was signed at Amiens.

It was March 27, 1802.

The event was joyfully welcomed on both sides of the Channel. After so many quarrels and so much bloodshed it seemed that the two nations had concluded a marriage of convenience and would at last be able to abandon themselves to the joys of life. But the honeymoon was to be brief. They had thought that there would be peace for a hundred years. Actually, it was no more than a few months' truce, an armistice which was to be broken—scarcely had its first anniversary been celebrated—by an exchange of gunfire between the lugger *Affronteur* and the schooner *Doris*. This was in the Bay of Audierne, on May 18, 1803.

II

PLANNING THE INVASION

WHAT WAS the state of the French navy at the opening of this last act of the drama?

Despite successful reforms undertaken since 1800 (such as the establishment of naval districts and naval prefects) and despite the laying down of new ships (30 in 1802 alone), the fleet would still have had scant chances against the British in May 1803. The programme of expansion still had a further eighteen months or two years to run when the renewal of hostilities broke in upon it. In all, the French could muster a dozen line of battleships immediately, increase this number to about 30 in September and to 55 or 60 in the course of 1804. This was little enough, for England already possessed 60, could count on 101 by the autumn and 189 the following year (including those out of commission), plus 226 frigates and 274 corvettes. On May 17, twenty-four hours after the declaration of war, the British deep-sea fleet commanded by Cornwallis was in position blockading Brest; three days later Nelson left for the Mediterranean. Thus the French fleet from the start found itself confined to its bases and condemned to remain there for some time by its hopeless inferiority.

Not only in ships did France fall short of England: a far greater drawback was her lack of real sailors, men who in all ranks of the service had a feeling and taste for their calling.

Despite seaboard conscription for the navy, seamen of quality were hard to find and inevitably crews had to be made up of conscripts chosen haphazardly and trained after a fashion in the roads. Three-quarters of them quaked at the thought that some day, perhaps, they might put to sea.

Certainly, it would not have been impossible to school these novices and eventually to turn them into first-class sailors if competent officers had been there to give them guidance and inspiration. But good officers, too, were lacking. A great purge of impostors and drones who had entered the service by way of the Revolution had brought back into service a host of officers of the Ancien Régime supposedly brilliant but in fact as second-rate as the men they replaced. Professionally, they had not benefited from the lessons taught them by Rodney and Suffren but went on clinging obstinately to the out-of-date strategy in which they were steeped: socially, their caste outlook had remained unaffected by the events of '89. They had no comprehension of the grandiose schemes of their master, and he was equally incapable of understanding them. Their talk of winds, currents and tides merely irritated him and he refused to believe that ships at sea could not manœuvre like battalions on the parade ground. With a few exceptions these officers were to bear the main responsibility for the failure of the imperial navy.

"I spent all my time looking for the man with a flair for the Navy without ever finding him," Napoleon confessed at St Helena. "There are specialised and technical factors in this profession which blocked all my schemes. Whenever I put forward a new idea I was told: 'Sir, it is impossible.'—'And why?' 'Sir, the winds wouldn't allow it and then there are the calms, the currents . . .' And I was stopped short. How could I carry on a discussion with people whose language I could not speak? To listen to them, one would think that one had to be born in the navy to know anything about it. I often told them that they exaggerated; that if I had done no more than the crossing to India with them I would on return have undertaken to be as familiar with their business as with my battle-fields. *If, instead of having to negotiate obstacles I had met in the navy a man whose mind was in harmony with my own and who had anticipated my ideas, what results could we not have achieved!* But throughout my reign I looked in vain for the man who could rise above routine and think creatively!"

The judgment is severe but true, in the final analysis. Admittedly, it could be argued that Napoleon, being a man of lightning decisions and accustomed to their immediate execution, could never grasp the basic fact that in naval matters there is no such thing as improvisation, that the navy is the product of great patience; it is a difficult plant to rear and bears fruit slowly. Nevertheless, at a time when thousands showed aptitude in military careers, when the army could pride itself on having thrown up from the ranks several dozen exceptional leaders since 1792, the French navy remained sterile and incapable of furnishing the country with even the handful of able men whom she needed even more desperately than ships of the line.

Let us briefly pass in review the men who ruled the French navy after the breach of the Treaty of Amiens.

On October 1, 1801 Bonaparte had placed Rear-Admiral Denis Decrès at the head of the navy.

Decrès, who was born in 1761 and had entered the service in 1779, was one of the survivors of the battle of Aboukir. As he had been in command of the light squadron, he had succeeded in escaping disaster and had reached Malta with Rear-Admiral Villeneuve. Three months later he had distinguished himself aboard the *Guillaume-Tell*, in an heroic engagement with three English ships of the line. Some people thought him a seasoned technician who knew his job. In fact he was jealous of his privileges, hard on his colleagues and averse to all new ideas. He lacked not only imagination and intelligence but, what is worse, confidence in France's naval power. The blow of Aboukir had stunned him. From that moment he became convinced that the English fleet was invincible and he would declare unhesitatingly that the only way to get the better of it was "to drive the English to despair by keeping our ships of the line in port and thus deprive their fleet of an enemy". But circumstances required an inspired leader with bold ideas and a flexible mind; for Decrès to have professed such views at such a time showed clearly enough what type of man he was.

"Decrès never used his mind," Napoleon said at St Helena. "He carried out the strict minimum of his duties; he would walk, but was not prepared to run. He should have spent half his time in the ports and on fleet exercises—I would have made allowances for it. But being a courtier he was afraid of losing his portfolio by prolonged absences."

He did in fact keep it until the waning of the Empire, which shows that his back bent easily before Caesar, and also that Napoleon—unless he was accessible to the most servile flattery—had no one else to put in his place.

There was a real absence of vitality throughout the navy, and, all things considered, Decrès may well have been the best man after all. That this absence of vitality was indeed real can be further proved by a catalogue of the naval leaders who stood behind Decrès—the vice-admirals.

In May 1803 there were six vice-admirals: Thévenard, Truguet, Villaret-Joyeuse, Martin, Rosily and Bruix.

Count Thévenard, naval prefect of Toulon, was 70 years old. He had been Minister of the Navy for five months in 1791, but was now devoting himself entirely to scientific studies. Among other things he was trying to calculate the dimensions of Noah's Ark "from the number of animals of all kinds which had been shut up in it".

Truguet, Councillor of State and future Commander-in-Chief of the Brest squadron, was 51. He had entered the navy in 1765 and been seriously wounded in the American war while saving the life of d'Estaing at the battle of Savannah. On January 1, 1792 he had been promoted *capitaine de vaisseau* and, six months later, rear-admiral. Discharged and imprisoned in 1794, he had been set free at the fall of Robespierre and was shortly afterwards appointed Minister of Marine and of the Colonies (November '95 to July '97). He was a valuable officer; when in 1797 Bonaparte had been looking for a "young and intelligent" admiral to command the first fleet destined to invade England, he had singled him out. But Truguet, unlike Decrès, was not flexible. Having become—at least provisionally[1]—a convinced republican, he was soon to create a stir by his opposition to personal power. When the First Consul called a plebiscite to establish his position as Emperor (April 1804), Truguet alone in the entire navy dared to swim against the current.

"I implore you to keep the august title of First Consul," he exclaimed to Bonaparte. "The lustre you have shed upon it makes it greatly superior to that of king or emperor."

To which the enraged Caesar replied (May 25, 1804):

"I cannot but be displeased by the inactivity of the squadron under your command. Your men-of-war are idle. The enemy is neither contained nor harassed. Action and results are what I am entitled to expect from you, not fine phrases and promises."

Truguet was soon to pay a high price for his act of republican loyalty: he was relieved of his command and, moreover, his name was struck off the lists of the Council of State and the Legion of Honour.

Villaret-Joyeuse, captain-general in command of Martinique, was 55. He had transferred to the navy from the police as the result of a duel in which he had killed his opponent. He could boast of having been in India with Suffren. His name was also linked with the great events of 1794 when it had been his task to protect, with the Brest fleet, the entry into France of a grain convoy from the United States. He had then clashed with Lord Howe's English squadron, had lost eight ships of the line —including the *Vengeur*—but had finally effected the safe

[1] We say "provisionally", as Truguet, after his dismissal by Napoleon, returned to duty in 1809 under the Empire and also served Louis XVIII after 1814. For the record we note that he was given the broad ribbon of the Legion of Honour at the first Restoration on September 2, 1814. On the 24th of the same month he was made a Count and after the Hundred Days—during which he remained in office—he was appointed Commander-in-Chief at Brest. He received the Cross of St Louis on October 21, 1818, was made a peer of France on March 5 of the following year and promoted Admiral on November 19, 1831. Finally, on October 30, 1832, he received the baton of a Marshal of France at the hands of Louis-Phillipe in token of his rank of Admiral.

passage of the convoy. He was not incompetent but at the same time he was not outstanding. Furthermore there could be no question of moving him from the post he occupied in the West Indies where he was rendering very good service.

Martin, naval prefect at Rochefort, was 51. Born at Louisburg in Nova Scotia, he had entered the navy the hard way. He began as an able seaman, served for a while as a navigating specialist and was later commissioned. In 1793 he was promoted rear-admiral, then in 1796 vice-admiral, commanding the Mediterranean fleet without much distinction from 1794 to 1797. Since then he had remained in Rochefort first as a commander and then, from 1801, as naval prefect. He could be reckoned out of the running for active service at sea.

Rosily-Meros, at 55, had a similar career to Martin's. Having entered the Navy at 14, he had served all over the world—with La Motte-Picquet in America, with Kerguelen in the South Seas, and with Suffren in India—and since 1795 had been Director and Inspector-General of the admiralty office of maps and charts. In spite of a brilliant career of rapid promotion (lieutenant at 30, captain at 36, rear-admiral at 45) he had rarely been in command of an operational force, and it seemed that his true vocation lay in the field of hydrography.

Finally, Bruix, the last on the list, was undeniably the first in character and intelligence. He was born in San Domingo in 1759 and so was 44 at this time.

He had volunteered for the navy in 1778, and rapidly attained the highest honours: he became a lieutenant at 27, member of the Naval Academy at 32, captain at 34, rear-admiral at 38, Naval Minister at 39, and vice-admiral at 40. The representatives of the people of Brest degraded him on October 24, 1793, but nine months later restored him to his rank and detailed him for duty as major-general in the naval force under Villaret-Joyeuse. As major-general, he also took part in the Irish expedition of 1797 under Morard de Galles and Hoche. The latter, who normally had no love for naval men, sang his praises so enthusiastically that in the same year he was gazetted rear-admiral, and appointed Naval and Colonial Minister on April 28, 1798. Next year, with the rank of vice-admiral, and still retaining his ministerial post, he emerged from Brest with 27 ships, and succeeded in regaining control of the Mediterranean for a period of several weeks. He was a man of quick reactions, and his outlook was balanced and sound. Unfortunately his health was bad, and he was forced to quit the fleet in 1802 to take a long rest. It was said that he was worn out; fate decreed the shortest of careers for the only man among the great admirals of France who was capable of outstanding service to his country.

*

Such was the disturbing state of the French navy when the curtain rose on the final act of the struggle between France and England.

In control was a soldier—Bonaparte (for in the final count he was its real chief)—constitutionally and temperamentally incapable of understanding an arm of the service that seemed to him too clumsy and slow to be effectively deployed, and which had the serious fault of depending all too often on the vagaries of the elements rather than on the human will. At the master's side was, for the sake of appearances, an admiral—Decrès, a man devoid alike of imagination and enthusiasm, but who had an occasional idea of what had to be done. He shouted, raged, grumbled and was invariably obsequious. Behind this Minister were six vice-admirals: one in his dotage, one about to be cashiered, a third serving in the West Indies, two acting purely as administrative officials, and the last, who alone could have taken command of a grand fleet, in such weak health that his services could not long be counted upon. Behind these admirals, again, came a disorderly tribe of officers carried over from the monarchy, as deaf to the call of fame as they were opposed to new ideas and still reeling under the disaster of Aboukir. They inspired no more confidence in the nation than in the men who served under them. Finally, on the lowest rung of the ladder, were the casual able seamen, recruited with the utmost difficulty, rough, demoralised, undisciplined and without a spark of patriotism. The last straw—there were no ships, or practically none.

Nevertheless, France had to fight: more than that—she had to fight on the sea, since England was once again her enemy.

At the news that the Peace of Amiens had been broken, a great wave of patriotism swept over the length and breadth of France. The people knew that the war would be long and hard: they knew the courage and strength of their adversary. But national honour and interest demanded a firm and confident front. Had not the American war demonstrated that, given equal forces, France, already invincible on land, could hold England in check on the sea? No doubt there was a lack of ships and seamen. . . . But at the helm was a man of whom everything could be expected, and whose genius justified the hope that many miracles might be accomplished if only every Frenchman lent his aid in achieving the impossible.

With the same impulse that followed the Treaty of Paris in the time of Louis XV, but with even greater enthusiasm, every parish, every city, every department and every corporation and association in France contributed its quota to the fitting-out of the fleet.

When the department of Loiret imposed on itself a levy of 300,000 francs to build a corvette, Paris replied by offering a warship of 120 guns, Lyons donated one of 100, Marseilles one of 74, Bordeaux one of 80 and the Senate one of 120. The department of Côte d'Or arranged for the casting of 100 guns of large calibre, that of the Rhône offered one-eighth of its taxes, that of Nord gave a million francs, that of Lot-et-Garonne thousands of yards of sailcloth. More modest groups contented themselves with the offer of simple corvettes, or, like the towns of Verdun, Foix, Countances, Moissac and Bernay, and the associations of employees in finance and commerce, simply gave flat-bottomed boats to help in the invasion of England.

For the idea of invading England—of carrying fire and sword into the island itself—had become once more the supreme motive force, a cause to which, in a gigantic effort of many months, everything was to be enthusiastically sacrificed.

None the less, the precedents were hardly encouraging. Nobody could have forgotten the trial efforts or projected plans of Louis XIV in 1689 and 1692, of Count Maurice de Broglie in 1765 under Louis XV, and in 1777-1779 under Louis XVI, the "Irish adventure" of Hoche in 1797, the first attempt to build an invasion fleet in 1798, and the second in 1801. Some remarks of Bonaparte himself were in people's minds. In 1798 he had said that "to launch an invasion of England without control of the sea is the rashest and most difficult operation conceivable"; and to Lord Whitworth in February 1803, "An invasion of England, my lord, would be a piece of uncommon daring." On the other hand, where Julius Caesar and William the Conqueror had been successful, the one with 800 ships and two legions, the other with 750 ships and 12,000 men, why should a man like Bonaparte fail—the greatest soldier of all time and with enormous resources at his disposal?

The break with England occurred on May 16, 1803. On the 20th Bonaparte convened the Senate, the Legislative Chamber and the Tribunate, to communicate to them the documents setting forth the origin of, and responsibility for, the conflict. All three bodies approved his action and loaded him with panegyrics.

"Citizen First Consul," cried M. de Fontanes, president of the Legislative Chamber, "the people of France have been victorious in order to secure peace; like you, they desire peace, but like you they never shrink from war. England may think herself well bastioned by the sea, but does she not realise that from time to time the world witnesses the birth of those rare beings whose genius effects what had previously seemed impossible?"

In the Tribunate Daru went even further:

"We can conquer the King of England's European possessions whenever we choose, and, once our feet are planted on
the island soil, England's power is overthrown: she can only
wound us slightly, but we can pierce her to the heart!"

Thus the note was struck, and a great shout of hope re-
sounded throughout France, which was taken up like a war-
cry in every valley and plain:

"Our legions have crossed the Alps; a mere strait cannot
hinder their conquest of England; a day is enough to carry
them over to the panic-stricken beaches!"

Bonaparte was already in action: on May 24 Forfait, the
engineer, was appointed Inspector-General of the national
invasion fleet, under the direct orders of Rear-Admiral
Decrès, the Minister of the Navy.

*

Pierre Forfait, who had been responsible for the invasion
fleets of 1798 and 1801, knew his business and the task before
him. At his command, thousands of men began a life of high
adventure, whose vicissitudes, even to-day, make a romantic
story unequalled in history.

The starting-point of the expedition was to be the same: it
was confined to the coast between Ostend to the north and
Etaples to the south, and in the centre of it was Boulogne,
the port from which Julius Caesar had set out for Britain with
800 ships on the evening of August 26 in the year 55 B.C.

As Bonaparte wished to make the crossing under cover of a
long winter's night, Forfait had to put at his disposal by
December 23, 1803, 1,300 ships, of which 1,000, transports for
men and stores, were purchased in many quarters, and 300
were specially constructed as protective craft.

Five types of vessel were to be used, which the engineer had
designed and worked out in advance:

(i) the Barge (*prame*) flat-bottomed, rigged as a corvette,
armed with 12 twenty-four pounders or 20 thirty-six pounders,
and manned by 38 soldiers and seamen.

(ii) the Gun-sloop (*Chaloupe canonnière*) rigged as a brig, armed with 3 twenty-four pounders and an eight-inch howitzer, and manned by a crew of 22 seamen and 130 soldiers.

(iii) the Gun-boat (*Bateau canonnier*) rigged as a lugger, armed with 1 twenty-four pounder and 1 eighteen-pounder, and manned by a crew of six sailors and 100 soldiers.

(iv) the Pinnace (*Péniche*) also rigged as a lugger, armed with 2 light howitzers, and manned by a crew of five sailors and 66 soldiers.

(v) the skiff (*Caique*) or tender of a man-of-war, armed with 1 twenty-four pounder and manned by 20 men.

Planned for a single purpose, a calm crossing of the Channel under cover of a moonless night, these little ships—the barges measured no more than 115 feet and the pinnaces 59 feet—should, according to their advocates, form an irresistible force. Some people could already see them, flanked by fishing-boats or transports requisitioned for the carrying of stores, making a victorious landing, one misty morning, on the shores of England. Of course, a start had still to be made with their construction, and, once constructed, they had to be conveyed to the point of embarkation, where their armaments could be fitted, and their crews trained to handle them.

In fact, everything had still to be done. Nothing but broken hulks remained from the invasion fleet of 1801, sunk in the mud, sand or shingle. At the end of May, Bonaparte ordered that everything possible should be salvaged from these shells, and that wherever possible they should be repaired or reconditioned. He gave Forfait the freedom of the forests in the Boulogne area; from Russia and Sweden he ordered timber to make the hanging-knees, of which there was no supply in France, together with masts, copper, hemp and pitch, all these to be shipped to Holland, and transported by river and canal through the Low Countries to Boulogne.

Couriers left Paris daily to set in motion the wheels of this gigantic enterprise, and every day new dockyards were opened wherever ship-building was possible—on the banks of the Rhine, the Meuse, the Scheldt, the Gironde, the Somme, the Loire, the Oise, and even the Seine in the heart of Paris, where a thousand workmen made their hammers ring from the Rapée to the Invalides.

All along the coast, trees were being felled, whilst inland workshops began once more producing guns, pistols and swords. While General Saint-Cyr was off to occupy the Gulf of Taranto, while General Mortier pressed on into Hanover, while the expert Monge travelled to Liège to supervise the casting of big guns, and General Marmount toured the found-ries of Douai and Strasbourg to arouse the zeal of the workers, long coloums of men from the garrisons of the east and south were marching towards the northern sea-ports: Ostend, Nieuport, Dunkirk, Gravelines, Calais, Ushant, Ambleteuse, Boulogne, Étaples. . . .

But the naval men were without exception sceptical ("mon-strous idea, paradoxical absurdities, ill-founded and fore-doomed conceptions," Decrès said), and without exception opposed to the plan, as they had always been to anything that did not conform to their antique principles of tactics and strategy. At the same time they were unequal to making any kind of original suggestion and, for that reason, were forced to give in when the affronted Bonaparte turned upon them the full force of his prodigious personality. Necessity forced him to sacrifice his dreams of expansion in far-off lands; he sold Louisiana to the Americans for 80 million francs, cut his losses in San Domingo, and recalled his cruiser squadrons to Europe except for frigates and light craft. At the same time he ordered all available vessels at Toulon, Rochefort, Lorient and Brest to be armed; commissioned fresh units in the dockyards of Genoa, Cherbourg and Flushing: extracted effective assistance from Holland and Spain; raised the army's strength to 480,000 men; saw to the reinforcement of coastal defence and decreed the formation of six vast reserves of man-power, deployed from the Texel to the Pyrenees, the first near Utrecht, the

second at Ghent, the third at St Omer, the fourth at Com-
piègne, the fifth at Brest and the sixth at Bayonne. . . .

"The whole world," wrote Thiers, "was affrighted at the
preparations for this gigantic conflict between the two most
powerful empires of the world."

This was only a beginning. Hour by hour Bonaparte aimed
higher and enlarged his vision still further: without retracting
anything from his initial plan, he was forever altering its
details. He harried Decrès: "Every river must be utilised for
shipbuilding", and he harassed Forfait, for after asking him to
complete 1,300 vessels by December 23 at the latest, he now
demanded double that number by September 23: "Time is
precious, Mr Inspector-General", and, doubtless finding that
progress was not rapid enough, he decided to proceed to
Boulogne, the nerve-centre of the whole undertaking, and
hurry things along in person.

On June 23, 1803, thirty-seven days after the outbreak of
war, the First Consul left Paris for Boulogne, arriving there
on the evening of the 29th; he was greeted by an enormous
crowd who strewed his path with flowers, and raised innumerable pyramids of foliage in his honour. He was preoccupied
as he listened to the torrent of panegyric poured upon him by
the Prefect of the Pas-de-Calais: "To humble in the dust the
rash disturbers of the tranquillity of both worlds, and to establish peace on the earth at last, God created Bonaparte, and then
He rested." He made a long tour of the harbour with Decrès,
Forfait and Bruix, and obtained detailed information on the
stage reached by the various undertakings he had ordered: the
building of new quays, the making of a semi-circular pool,
the construction of a dyke to check the local river, and of a
sluice to enable the channel to be deepened. At dusk he was
still going over the dockyards and arsenals; he ordered work to
stop on the foundations of the camp for the future army of
Boulogne, and on the emplacements of the batteries for the
defence of the harbour and town, demanding instead that three
forts should be built well out in the roadstead itself. Finally he

selected a residence—a castle at the Pont-de-Brique—and a look-out post on the cliffs at l'Ordre, against his future visits.

Forty-eight hours later he was on the road again to continue his inspection at Calais, Dunkirk, Ostend and Antwerp. At the beginning of August he returned to Paris by way of Brussels, Liège, Namur and Sedan, full of confidence and satisfaction. Before he left Boulogne, he had the pleasure of seeing some of the gun-sloops drive off two English frigates that had come too far inshore. This first move would doubtless make the English think.

*

When the preliminary steps had been taken, the purchases completed and the work of construction begun, a decision had to be made on who was to shoulder the task of preparing the invasion fleet for battle. A young and dynamic commander was required, with no misgivings on the success of the venture. In 1801 Rear-Admiral Latouche-Treville had held this post, but he had since left for San Domingo, and as he was still away, Bonaparte turned to the most brilliant of his available vice-admirals, Eustache de Bruix, and offered him the command of the invasion fleet.

Although seriously ill (according to Thiers he was worn out with pleasure-seeking and suffered from tuberculosis) and although he had recently scouted the very idea of an invasion fleet, Bruix accepted. His appointment was officially announced on July 15, 1803. Hardly had the new commander taken over his post than he received a letter from Decrès reminding him of his duties.

"The First Consul's intention is that the invasion fleet shall be kept in a state of continuous activity by which it will at once gain practice and make itself useful."

In plain language this meant no relaxation: follow the example of Bonaparte, maintain the alert at all points, let nothing escape you, and let no detail be neglected.

Even in the Tuileries, Bonaparte followed the preparations

in the minutest detail. "A large number of barrels have wooden hoops: the water escapes! 400 of them must be hooped with iron . . . this matter is of the gravest importance! See to it without delay." He was for ever retouching, modifying and enlarging his plan. The final composition of the invasion fleet was to be as follows:

54 barges in 2 divisions (the different vessels of the expedition were marshalled in sections of 9 units, 3 sections forming a division).

324 gun-sloops in 12 divisions, each sloop being accompanied by a pinnace.

432 gun-boats in 16 divisions, each one being likewise accompanied by a pinnace.

108 skiffs in 4 divisions.

81 armed fishing-boats in 3 divisions.

300 fishing-boats to carry non-combatants and their supplies.

100 fishing-boats adapted as horse-transports.

Altogether a total of 2,155[1] vessels, which were to convey to the coast of England:

115,000 men, of whom 77,000 were infantry, 11,000 cavalry and 4,000 gunners.

11,000 horses.

450 field-guns with 200 rounds each.

14,000,000 cartridges.

Several hundred tons of provisions and stores.

The projects of 1798 and 1801 had been left far behind! It was not the numbers of ships and men that the First Consul intended to use that made the strongest impression on observers —in fact, nobody could estimate the size of the fleet with any certainty—but rather the scale of the preparations, the manner

---

[1] The composition of the invasion fleet varied from time to time. The list given above is taken from a memorandum dated September 10, 1803; it differs somewhat from another—that usually quoted—amounting to 2,008 vessels, which is fixed by a memorandum dated August 22 of the same year. Either may be accepted; in the last resort the differences between them are trifling; in fact the number of gun-sloops and gun-boats is exactly the same in both.

in which they were organised, and, also, the ardour displayed by the whole French nation.

The coast of France had become one vast dockyard, and her interior, an arsenal and a barracks; she continued with extraordinary enthusiasm to respond to the call of the man of the hour. Gifts towards the fleet continued to pour in, and the collections amounted to millions.

"Our best-beloved kings, and those most worthy to be so, saw nothing like it," noted a contemporary writer. Indeed, as Louis Madelin has justly observed, "the project captured the imagination and flattered the hopes of the nation". It was discussed loudly and with pride; night after night countless minds occupied themselves by torchlight with a hundred different ways of crossing the Channel, even (as witnessed by contemporary prints) in hot-air balloons, or on foot by means of a tunnel dug beneath the waters of the strait.

However, everyone was aware of the difficulty and dangers of the enterprise, and there were many who refused to see anything in the opening moves beyond a novel method of intimidation calculated to bring to his knees an enemy already crazed with fear.

For England, though at first she had not appeared to take the French intentions seriously, was now showing unmistakable signs of alarm. At different points along the coast the haunting fear of a landing had become such that the appearance of certain friendly ships, not immediately identified, had been enough to create a real panic. Addington's feeble Ministry was unable to meet the crisis and succeeded only in intensifying the general state of nerves. Along the coast towers had been built and mounted with guns; whole villages had been evacuated and, inland, camps and fortifications had been erected. Under pressure from the Opposition, the Government soon proposed the embodiment of an army of 50,000 men to be employed only within the Kingdom. But public anxiety continued to increase, and on July 27 the Prime Minister asked for, and obtained from Parliament, an authority to call up for armed service every man between the ages of 17 and 55.

When news of this mass conscription reached the French, and when they learned that the Right Honourable Mr Addington had appeared in the Commons in his Volunteer's uniform, that Pitt had been made a colonel, and that Fox, despite his generous proportions, was undergoing training as a private, they did not miss the joke, and Bonaparte was the first to laugh.

This was a serious psychological error. If the English had been made to look ridiculous, they were not going to be slow to demonstrate their firm decision to defend their liberty and independence to the utmost. Before the end of December 1803 their army, composed of professional soldiers, militia and volunteers, had reached a strength of 700,000 or more than six times the effective troops concentrated at Boulogne.

"One active division," relates Thiers, "was deployed from the Isle of Wight to the Thames Estuary. A signal system of fires lighted along the coasts was established to give the alarm at the first appearance of the French. Specially designed waggons were built for the express purpose of conveying troops at top speed to any threatened area. In short, on the English side of the strait as well as on the French, extraordinary inventiveness was exercised in devising new methods of attack and defence, in overcoming the forces of nature, and in harnessing them to the proper side."

Naturally enough it was on the open sea that the English, not over-confident of their effectiveness as make-shift soldiers, placed their brightest hopes. For on the open sea watched and waited the best English admirals, ready to swoop upon any vessels that tried to emerge from the French ports. In the North Sea was Keith, at the Channel approaches Cornwallis; in the Mediterranean was the greatest and most popular of them all, the admiral who already had one victory over Bonaparte's fleet to his credit—the one-eyed and one-armed Horatio Nelson.

III

NELSON, THE IMPLACABLE

FORTY-FIVE years earlier, on September 29, 1758 the Hon. Catherine Suckling, wife of the Reverend Edmund Nelson had given birth to her fourth son in the rectory of Burnham Thorpe, Norfolk. He was a delicate little thing scarcely able to breathe. They called him Horatio and rushed him to the font on the tenth day, lest he die unchristened.

Contrary to all expectations, the child lived and, without being robust, grew to boyhood in the normal way, though inclined to prefer his own company and to keep others at a distance. When not at school or in church he used to launch little paper boats of his own making in the local streams. He would spend many silent hours watching these frail vessels; almost invariably some unexpected obstacle caused them to capsize before they had made the course.

In a place where everything was connected with sailors and the sea such a game was only natural. However, one evening in December 1770 when he was no more than twelve years old, a chance incident revealed that young Horatio's vision extended beyond his own parish boundaries.

Taking advantage of the absence of his father who was at sea (his mother had died three years before) he had opened the local newspaper. After reading it for some time he cried out to his elder brother:

"Look here!"

He pointed to five lines buried in naval reports announcing that their uncle, an officer in His Majesty's Navy, had just been appointed to command the *Raisonnable*, of 64 guns.

He was wild with excitement.

"Pray write to Uncle," he said to his brother, "and tell him that I want to serve under him!"

Thinking it was only a whim of no consequence, his elder brother took him at his word. His uncle's answer arrived three weeks later; it was written in all seriousness:

"What has poor little Horatio done that he, being so weak, should be sent to rough it at sea? But let him come, and if a cannon-ball takes off his head, he will at least be provided for!"

Thus in the spring of 1771 the "captain's servant" (midshipman Horatio Nelson) aged twelve and a half, embarked at Portsmouth on the *Raisonnable*. As soon as it put to sea he had his first experience of sea-sickness—a complaint which was to dog him throughout his career.

He had a difficult start.

The *Raisonnable* having been put out of commission after five months, his uncle sent him to the West Indies aboard a merchantman. After this Horatio took part in a Polar expedition, then sailed to the East Indies. He came home ill and disillusioned and did not leave again until the American War. In 1777 in his twentieth year he was commissioned and obtained his first command.

He now seemed to be on the right road. But five months of fighting on the Nicaragua river so completely exhausted him that he had to be repatriated once more. He reappeared on the far side of the Atlantic only after a spell in the Baltic. The Admiralty deemed no doubt that the best way of curing his fever was to expose him to extreme cold. He was in Canada towards 1782, in the West Indies, in New York, too, where the future William IV, who was serving in the Navy, met him and was struck by his curious appearance:

"He was the youngest and shortest captain I had ever seen; he had a full-laced uniform; his lank unpowdered hair was tied in a stiff Hessian tail of extraordinary length; the old-fashioned flaps of his waistcoat added to the general quaintness of his figure. Altogether he was a somewhat eccentric figure. I had never in my life seen anything like it."

It was not long before it became clear that the world had never seen anything like it, either.

In the autumn of 1783, Nelson, who had returned to England, decided to take a holiday in France to learn the language. He did not go beyond Saint-Omer where he succumbed to the charms of an English clergyman's daughter whom he could not marry for lack of money. He came back to London disgusted with the French ("I hate their country and their manners") and, the following spring, took command of a frigate on cruising duty in the West Indies. It was his last campaign as a bachelor. There he married, at the beginning of 1787, Mrs Fanny Nisbet, a young widow and mother of a child of three. And so the curtain fell on his adventurous youth.

*

"We shall be a happy couple, and if not, the fault will certainly be mine."

The newly married couple landed in England in June 1787. Nelson soon discovered that by attempting to bring to heel certain notorious West Indian law-breakers he had made bitter enemies, some of them in the Admiralty itself.

He thus lost favour in high places so that there was nothing left for him to do but to shut himself up at Burnham Thorpe with his wife and wait for better days, trying his hand at farming and, above all, nursing his rancour and disillusionment. There could be no hope of early release.

This lasted for five years, five years of humiliation and despair. The Admiralty never even answered his letters. "It is my firm and unalterable determination never again to set my foot on board a King's ship." But just when there seemed no hope left, a message came from London that released him from his purgatory. It was January 1793 and England was recalling all her sons to the colours to fight revolutionary France. The first was Horatio Nelson, the rebel. He was appointed to the

Agamemnon of 64 guns. It formed part of a squadron under the orders of Admiral Hood and was assigned to the Mediterranean.

Goodbye, Fanny!

"Our country has the first demand for our services; and private convenience or happiness must ever give way to the public good. Duty is the business of a sea-officer: all private considerations of sentiment must give way to it, however painful. It is a sad thought, but so it must be. . . ."

From the first days of his command Nelson had warned the midshipmen of the *Agamemnon* that there were three things which they must always bear in mind:

1. Obedience to orders.
2. The obligation to consider as a personal enemy any man who spoke ill of the King.
3. The necessity to hate the French as one hates the devil.

The ship duly arrived in the Mediterranean and Nelson was instructed to take dispatches to Sir William Hamilton, His Majesty's Ambassador at the Neapolitan court.

Sir William was 64. He was justly famous on several counts. First, because he occupied an important post; second, because he had enriched the British Museum with antique vases discovered at Pompeii, thereby also enriching himself; third, because he was the fortunate husband of a woman whom the great Romney used to call the "divine lady" and whom he had painted as a Bacchante, as Circe, Cassandra and Ariadne.

Having met Nelson, Sir William insisted on accommodating him at the Embassy. He informed his divine lady:

"We are having a guest this evening, Captain Nelson. He is a little man who cannot boast of being very handsome, almost bald, but I'm sure he will one day astonish the world."

Thus on that very evening at supper, the captain of the *Agamemnon* met the woman to whom, together with the pursuit of glory, the remainder of his life was to be dedicated.

Emma Hamilton was at this time in her late twenties. Her stormy past had left no traces, though she had been in turn tavern wench, chambermaid, servant to a doctor, mistress of a seafarer, principal star of a curious impresario who organised public exhibitions of "plastic beauty", Romney's model, and "companion" of Sir William's nephew who eventually sold her back to his uncle. On the contrary, she had reached the full flower of her beauty which had blossomed out and ripened in the six years since Goethe had met her on his way through Naples:

"Sir William has found the most perfect object that art or nature can devise: a beautiful woman. She is a young English-woman of twenty who lives in his house; she is very beautiful and well made. He has had fashioned for her a Greek dress which suits her to perfection. When she wears it she lets her hair fall on her shoulders, puts on one or two shawls, and goes through a series of attitudes, postures and expressions till one fancies oneself in a dream. . . . She is by turns serious, sad, pro-vocative; she withdraws, entices, repels and then runs wild. One follows her in her metamorphoses. . . . The old knight has given himself body and soul to this lovely creature. . . ."

Nelson with his weathered face and red hair, was dazzled. He hardly dared to look upon this voluptuous vision. How-ever, as he spoke of war and the French, he saw in the two large eyes suddenly fixed on him an extraordinary expression, which had the hard glitter of intense hatred. . . .

To Fanny:

"Lady Hamilton has been wonderfully kind and good. . . . She is a young woman of amiable manners who does honour to the station to which she has been raised."

He took to sea again, sailing to Corsica to destroy the garrisons of the Republic. He fought at Bastia and then took part in the siege of Calvi. A trying siege under a relentless sun, on rocky soil with French cannon-balls ricocheting as they struck the stones. On July 12, 1794 one of these fell not far from Nelson, and like others, made the sand and pebbles fly:

"I've been hit," he cried, raising his hand to his right eye. He was not only hit: he was blinded.

"An infallible power, good and kind, has lessened the force of the blow by which you lost your eye and we thank the hand that spared you," wrote the Reverend Edmund Nelson from Burnham Thorpe. The Admiralty, on the other hand, remained strangely silent and Horatio, tortured by physical suffering, soon let out a terrible cry of anger and pride:

"For services in which I have been wounded others have been praised who, at the same time, were actually in bed. They have not done me justice. But never mind, *I'll have a gazette of my own.*"

Never before had he so thirsted for honour or longed for rest:

"I assure you I shall return to the plough with redoubled glee," he wrote to Fanny.

Months passed, spring returned. In March 1795 the French fleet finally sailed from Toulon to relieve Corsica, and the British squadron went to intercept it. It could have been the occasion of a decisive English victory, for the French ships were being handled by worthy fellows many of whom were having their first sight of the sea. But Admiral Hotham, who had taken the place of Hood, was as lacking in dash as the French were in training. It took him no less than three days to finish off two sail of the line which had been damaged and isolated from the bulk of the Republic's fleet.

Nelson who, for his part, had acted well, came out of the action in a fury: "I wish to be an admiral. I should very soon either do much, or be ruined: my disposition cannot bear tame and slow measures. Had I commanded our fleet either the whole French fleet would have graced my triumph, or I should have been in a confounded scrape."

Impatient as ever!

Luckily Bonaparte had entered the lists and the war was only just beginning.

The blockades of Genoa and of Leghorn were obscure and wearisome tasks for a man burning with a desire for outstanding achievements—for a gazette of his own.

For another year the English Mediterranean squadron, latterly commanded by the intractable Sir John Jervis, lay in wait for an eventual sortie of the French fleet stranded at Toulon, and tried to delay the advance of Bonaparte in Italy. Then, suddenly, in September 1796 Spain's entry into the war forced the British fleet to fall back on Gibraltar. At one stroke the inland sea was once again under complete control of the tricolour.

The English were not slow to take their revenge. On February 14, 1797 Jervis was sailing southward with 15 ships of the line off Cape St Vincent when he came upon a Spanish fleet sailing in two groups, 18 ships of the line on one side and nine on the other, the latter far behind, being becalmed.

Jervis at once scented an easy prize. He swiftly thrust his ships between the two enemy blocs, drove the weaker to his left, the larger to his right, and as the latter were heading north, tacked and sailed in pursuit.

At this precise moment an unexpected incident took place. Nelson, who was commanding the *Captain* in the rear-guard at third position from the rear of the line, noticed that the Spanish admiral was bearing up before the wind from north to east in an attempt to rejoin his nine separated ships by out-flanking the British fleet. Ignoring Jervis's orders he at once wore ship, slipped between the two ships behind him and threw himself on the three leading Spanish men-of-war, the *Santissima Trinidad* of 130 guns, the *San-Joseph* of 112 and the *San-Nicolas* of 80. It was a terrifying encounter. Two hours later, despite friendly assistance, the *Captain* had lost sails, rudder and shrouds. Nelson thereupon put himself at the head of his men and hurled himself aboard the *San Nicolas* with the cry—"Death or Victory". In a few minutes he had settled the matter and, still followed by his roaring crew, dashed in to attack the *San-Joseph*, another Spanish ship of the line lying on her opposite beam. He reached it just as it was striking its flag under the fire of the *Prince George*. No matter: "I received the swords of the vanquished Spaniards and which, as I received I gave to one of my bargemen, who placed them, with the greatest sang-froid, under his arm."

By evening four Spanish ships of the line were in British hands and the rest were fleeing in disorder towards Cadiz. It was a great success for Jervis who, with 15 ships, had not hesitated to attack 27. But it was an even greater one for Nelson for whom the crews gave three lusty cheers after the battle.

This time Horatio held glory in his grasp. And to make sure of not letting it slip through his fingers he at once composed his own panegyric for the attention of the Admiralty. When he had done so he whispered discreetly into the ear of a colonel leaving for London his preferences in the matter of rewards. To wit: he hoped to wear on his person some honourable decoration to attact people's attention and act as a recognition of his services.

His wishes were gratified beyond all expectations. He had been promoted rear-admiral just before the battle. Now he received the Order of the Bath. His name was all over the gazettes, the broadsheet ballads and in theatrical declamations echoing through the length and breadth of England. The Reverend Edmund Nelson wept for joy and gave thanks to the Lord with a loud voice. Only Fanny, being but a simple woman and horrified by the cruel demands of war, failed to appreciate the grandeur of the occasion. "You have done desperate actions enough," she wrote. "Now may I—indeed I do—beg that you never board again. Leave it for Captains." It was as though she had a presentiment of misfortune.

*

Off Cadiz, the month of July was so hot that Sir John Jervis (created the Earl of St Vincent after the battle) saw fit to relieve the nerves of certain over-excited crews by sending them under Nelson's orders to attack Santa Cruz on the island of Teneriffe.

On August 24 Nelson anchored before the sleeping town. The night was so stormy that the boat containing the first landing party was dashed against the mole. Instead of being taken by surprise, the sentinels were awakened by the men in the water. All the bells of Santa Cruz began to peal, rousing the population who rushed to arms. A few minutes later as a second landing party approached the mole, a cannon-ball fell on the boat carrying Nelson, who collapsed.

"I am a dead man!"

His right arm was shattered. He was brought bleeding alongside his ship. His sailors wanted to hoist him on deck themselves.

"Let me alone," he said: "I have yet my legs left and one arm!"

He took hold of a rope and twisted it twice round his left arm: "Hoist!"

Having reached the deck he hailed a seaman:

"Tell the surgeon to make haste and prepare his instruments. I know I must lose my right arm so the sooner it is off, the better."

He walked firmly down to the surgeon's cabin leaving a trail of blood behind him.

"Get on with it."

He took off his coat and shirt, and stretched himself out on the wooden table. The candles smoked. The surgeon sweated profusely. He brought a small saw towards the shattered shoulder. The saw moved backwards and forwards, and soon made a shrill sound as it bit into the bone.

At the patient's request they threw the dead limb out of a porthole into the sea.

In the days that followed, Jervis received the first letter written by Nelson with his left hand:

"I am become a burthen to my friends and useless to my Country . . . I go hence and am no more seen. I hope you will be able to give me a frigate to convey the remains of my carcase to England. A left-handed admiral will never again be considered as useful therefore the sooner I get to a very humble cottage the better and make room for a better man to serve the State."

He returned to England racked with pain. For many weeks he had to obtain from laudanum the peace which his ill-sewn and ill-healed wound denied him. But in his unhappiness beside the tender Lady Nelson he had the consolation and pride of feeling that his greatness was undiminished. The Government had granted him a pension of £1,000 a year; the Norwich museum was showing the swords he had taken from the Spaniards. As soon as he was able to appear in public the City of London gave him the freedom of the City and the King invited him to court. All these consolations healed the bleeding wound only to open another which Fanny dreaded most of all. Whilst the invalid was recovering, the distant war not only continued but seemed to be gaining momentum. It was said that at Toulon the French were arming a vast fleet on which to embark a gigantic army under the command of Napoleon himself; strange flat-bottomed boats were observed massing on the Boulogne beaches; there were rumours of a possible landing in Devon, in Ireland or in India.

Nelson could not stand it any longer. The following spring he asked the Admiralty to allow him to return to active service. On May 4, 1798 he entered the Mediterranean at the head of three men-of-war, four frigates and a sloop. His mission was both delicate and exciting: to find out what was afoot in Toulon.

At first it seemed as though he might have spared himself the trouble. He had scarcely reached the French coast when a vicious north-west wind—the very wind for which Napoleon had so long been waiting—drove him towards the coast of Italy and scattered his squadron. He was forced to take shelter in a Sardinian port. Before the damage to his ships could be made good and he could put to sea, the ponderous French armada was already on its way to Egypt having no enemy to fear.

The chase did not begin until June 7, 18 days after the French had set sail. Off Barcelona Nelson collected a reinforcement of 11 ships of the line which had been detached from Gibraltar on Admiralty orders. He was unable to reconnoitre owing to the disappearance of his frigates in the storm and sailed straight for Naples. There he was told that the French fleet had rounded Sicily. Through his old friend Sir William Hamilton he tried in vain to obtain food and water for his squadron from King Ferdinand IV, popularly known as "Big Nose".

Luckily there was Emma. In '93 the "divine lady" had met Queen Maria Carolina, sister of Marie-Antoinette, and, having become her confidante, had without difficulty imbued her with her own hatred of the French. And she had not forgotten the ex-captain who had, by the fortunes of war, become one-eyed, one-armed and a rear-admiral. Just as Nelson, in desperation, was about to weigh anchor he received a letter full of promises ("Ever yours, Emma") assuring him that the queen would do everything in her power to open the Neapolitan ports to him.

In a more cheerful mood he made for Syracuse. As ill-luck would have it, only Big Nose's orders had arrived and the port remained closed to the squadron. However, he learned that the French had taken Malta without having to strike a blow, and had then left in an easterly direction—Palestine or Egypt. He therefore put to sea forthwith, and, passing close to Bonaparte's fleet without realising it in the night of June 22, arrived in Alexandria first (June 28). Finding the port empty of course he sailed up to Syria, came back by Crete and finally returned to Syracuse on July 19 with nothing to show for it.

"The Devil's children have the Devil's luck!" he roared. "I

cannot find . . . where the French fleet are gone to. All my ill fortune, hitherto, has proceeded from want of frigates!"

But he, too, had the Devil's luck: this time, thanks to Emma's efforts, Syracuse opened its stores to the famished squadron. The revictualling took five full days. At dawn on July 25 Nelson turned towards Egypt once again, after writing to Sir William and the "divine lady" that next time they saw him he would "return either crowned with laurel or covered with cypresses".

The climax had taken long to build up, but it broke swiftly. At two o'clock in the afternoon on August 1, 1798 the French fleet of 13 warships was anchored in line three miles off the coast in the bay of Aboukir, east of Alexandria. To its surprise and alarm, the English squadron suddenly appeared on the horizon. Before there was time to recall the numerous working parties which had gone ashore and before Admiral Brueys, the Commander-in-Chief, could consult his lieutenants Ganteaume, Decrès and Villeneuve, to decide whether to fight at anchor or under sail—no one was expecting action before the next day—Nelson, driven by a strong north-north-west wind, was within range.

He had a clear plan: he would first overwhelm the advance guard and the centre with two line of battleships to one; then deal with the rear-guard which could not go into action without sailing to windward.

His ships were already approaching their objectives, aglow with the last rays of the setting sun, when Captain Foley, who was leading the attack from the Goliath, discovered that he could sail between the coast and the French vessels. He plunged at once into this narrow passage and, dragging his anchor, closed with the third warship of the enemy line. The four consort ships behind him followed suit, each settling for a particular enemy. Nelson, who was in sixth position, understood his lieutenant's manœuvre in a trice. To complete it, he brought the rest of the fleet round to the seaward side thus sandwiching the French fleet between them.

The battle began at half-past six.

By the next morning the French squadron had ceased to exist, save for two ships of the line and two frigates which had succeeded in escaping, as the conquerors were too exhausted to give chase. Nine ships of the line had been captured, two destroyed; 1,700 men, including Admiral Brueys, were lost—killed or drowned—1,500 were wounded, and more than 2,000 had been taken prisoner.

In a single night Nelson and his lieutenant had inflicted on the French navy the most bloody disaster in its history.

*

It was a sort of apotheosis for Nelson—who only a short while before had prayed Heaven that he might some day have a gazette of his own.

When the news became known the King made him Baron of the Nile and of Burnham Thorpe, the Commons voted his family a pension of £2,000, the Lord Mayor of London ordered a salute to be fired in his honour, the Tsar of Russia sent him his portrait set in diamonds, and the Grand Turk despatched an ambassador to him bearing a sable coat and the most beautiful aigrette from his turban. As for the "divine lady", she merely offered him "the keys of heaven":

"I fainted when I heard the joyfull news, and fell on my side and am hurt. I shou'd feil it a glory to die in such a cause. No, I wou'd not like to die until I see and embrace the Victor of the Nile. . . . For God's sake come to Naples soon. . . . My dress from head to foot is alla Nelson. . . . My earrings are Nelson's anchors; in short we are be-Nelsoned all over."

This time Horatio could consider himself gratified—gratified beyond all hopes and, also, perhaps, beyond reason.

The triumph at Aboukir was in no small measure due to Nelson's tenacity in pursuit; to his courage during the engagement—he had been wounded in the head by a burst of grapeshot—and to the authority with which he had welded his squadron into a homogeneous, integrated force. But it was

Captain Foley's bold and intelligent initiative which, in the final count, decided the issue of the battle.

"We are a band of brothers," Nelson liked to say, in speaking of his lieutenants.

Brothers before and during the battle, no doubt. But afterwards? It must merely be observed that, as though by accident, Captain Foley's name appeared neither in Nelson's official report, nor in the accounts circulating among the public and inspired by him.

The admiral alone, considering the situation *"with an ardent and penetrating mind"*, had been *"struck by the fact that where an enemy ship could float, one of ours could drop anchor."*

Truth, like Emma, was be-Nelsoned.[1]

*

The *Vanguard* dropped anchor in Naples on September 22, nearly two months after the battle. Big Nose, the Queen, Sir William and Emma were there to cheer him and the crowd gave him a delirious welcome. The "divine lady", seeing her hero with his head still swathed in dressings and bandages, cried "O God, is it possible?" and fainted, as foreseen. After which scene the carnival began.

"Our hearts and our hands must be in a flutter: Naples is a dangerous place and we must keep clear of it . . ." wrote Nelson. "It is a country of fiddlers and poets, whores and scoundrels."

He spoke truer than he knew. Within a month Naples and its King, with Emma's help, had completely bewitched him. He was no longer Horatio Nelson, Baron of the Nile in the service of His Majesty, but Horatio Nelson, Baron of the Nile, in the service of Ferdinand King of Naples.

It was indeed a ludicrous episode. Anything that was not the "protection" of Naples had ceased to matter in the eyes of the

---

[1] It was only from 1800 onwards that the rôle of Foley began to be mentioned, but the public had to wait for the appearance of General Napier's account in 1837 before the true picture emerged.

victor of Aboukir. He paid little attention to Malta and even less to Bonaparte, though the latter could scarcely be expected to remain in Egypt for ever, given the opportunity to sail back unmolested. In Italy the French were only 15,000 strong. King Ferdinand, having received an assurance from Nelson, his guardian angel, that if the French attacked he would not leave the town, launched an army of 35,000 men against them. As there was no opposition on the way, the fiery Neapolitan army reached Rome. At court people were saying that the men would get to Paris. But, when 3,000 French troops suddenly appeared, they took to their heels in disorder. Half the men threw their muskets into ditches, the others hurried back to Naples where the revolution broke out. King Ferdinand, Maria Carolina and Sir William were forced to flee by an underground tunnel leading from the palace to the sea and just had time to jump aboard the *Vanguard* which set sail at once for Palermo.

There, after this annoying interruption, court life resumed its carefree course. Nelson played cards till dawn, pressed his suit on Emma under the sympathetic eye of the magnificent ambassador and listened to the flatteries of King Ferdinand. All was going well in the best of all possible worlds. In London, however, both Fanny, who had been discreetly advised, and the Lords of the Admiralty were of a totally different opinion. The first intimation of their displeasure fell like a whip lash: Earl St Vincent had been obliged because of ill-health to give up the command of the English forces in the Mediterranean at the very moment when the French fleet from Brest had reappeared, reinforced by a Spanish squadron. Without even bothering to answer Nelson who had offered to take his place, he delegated his powers to Lord Keith. Nelson acknowledged the blow by assembling his ships of the line and preparing to pursue the allied fleet. But at that moment he received a joint appeal from Emma, the King and Queen and Sir William, begging him to complete the liberation of Naples which had been partially freed by the "resistance" after an Austrian defeat of the French army. Nelson was faced with the choice between duty—the pursuit of the Franco-Spanish fleet—and love—a return to Vesuvius.

On June 24, 1799 the *Vanguard* dropped anchor once again in the bay of Naples.

*

Facilis descensus. . . .

Ever since he had become involved in the Neapolitan farce the glorious Nelson cut a somewhat ridiculous figure. The part he was now about to play was even less heroic.

The last Neapolitan revolutionaries had been assured that they would be given their liberty and a safe passage to Toulon, if they so desired. The assurance was given them in an agreement with representatives of King Ferdinand signed five days before the *Vanguard's* arrival and ratified by the captain of a British warship. Nelson would not admit it. The "divine lady" whom the sight of the tricolour threw into a fury (and this was the very flag the rebels displayed), spurred him on. He first made them capitulate and gave them in return a formal pledge that the armistice would not be violated; then, making them believe that they were boarding ships bound for France he simply handed them over to King Ferdinand's vengeance. Three days later he set up aboard his ship and on his own authority, a Neapolitan tribunal extraordinary. In two hours it had condemned to death the leading revolutionary, Admiral Prince Caraccioli, an old man of seventy who had served in the English navy and with whom Nelson was well acquainted. The latter confirmed the verdict himself and twice refused to go back on his decision. At five o'clock in the evening the wretched Caraccioli was hanged on the fore-yard of the frigate *Minerva* under the very eyes of the delighted Emma.

Order was thus restored after this momentary interruption, and festivities were resumed with intensified enthusiasm. On August 1 the anniversary of the battle of Aboukir was celebrated in grand style with an abundance of singers and musicians. Afterwards the happy band returned to Palermo. King Ferdinand, in a disarming gesture of gratitude, made "the invincible Nelson, defender of the two Sicilies" a duke handing over to him the town of Bronte and its dependencies—a mere trifle bringing in a revenue of some £3,000 a year.

Meanwhile, Lord Keith, the new Commander-in-Chief of the Mediterranean fleet was vainly issuing repeated calls to order:

"Leave Sicily and report to Minorca!"

But Nelson turned a deaf ear.

"I think it right not to obey your Lordship's orders. . . . I have no scruple in deciding that it is better to save the Kingdom of Naples and risk Minorca than to risk the Kingdom of Naples to save Minorca."

The storm was brewing.

In mid-October Nelson learnt, not without some embarrassment, that Bonaparte had quietly left Egypt and had succeeded in returning to France. Four months later Keith came in person to tear Nelson away from the pleasures of Palermo and take him to Malta where 3,000 besieged Frenchmen were still holding out. He now had the good fortune to capture the *Généreux*, one of the two ships of the line that had escaped from Aboukir Bay, and it seemed as though the Baron of the Nile was indeed himself again. But less than four weeks later he left his ship, the *Foudroyant*; and on the pretext that his health would not permit him to go on any longer he returned to Emma at Palermo. It was an unfortunate decision: in his absence the *Foudroyant* accounted for the *Guillaume-Tell*, which had also escaped with the *Généreux* from the Battle of the Nile. The Admiralty made this the occasion of inviting him to return to England. The Foreign Office, for its part, had already "liquidated" Sir William without more ado.

But some ties are not easily broken. One fine morning, November 6, 1800, the trio landed in England. As might have been expected, the journey across Europe had made them more ridiculous than ever. In every town they passed, Nelson's undignified bearing—he was covered in ribbons and decorations—and Emma's vulgarity scandalised their fellowcountrymen.

The good people of England, however, were not so particular. They came in crowds to witness the landing of their idol and did not hesitate to drag his carriage up from the quayside on to the London road. In the capital itself there was a furore. Nelson, quite unruffled, warmly introduced "his dear friends, the Hamiltons" to Fanny and the Reverend Edmund Nelson who was standing beside her.

But very soon Nelson had to face the ugly facts. When the occasion was not an official or popular function the court, the gentry and his old friends gave him a cool reception. Eyes turned away in disapproval at the approach of the hero of Aboukir—"that poor man, a prey to his own vanity, weakness and stupidity", according to Jervis. Nelson was exasperated. "I would stay abroad for ever," he declared. But there was Fanny to consider and, to make matters worse, Emma was pregnant.

Shortly afterwards an unexpected event further complicated matters. Czar Paul I, at the instigation of Bonaparte, had set up the Armed Neutrality League to oppose British interference with the sea-borne trade of the Baltic Powers and especially the right of search. When Denmark joined this League, the Admiralty set about reorganising its northern forces. On January 1, 1801 Nelson, to his surprise, found himself promoted vice-admiral and appointed to the command of the reserve squadron.

He had scarcely the time to breathe a sigh of relief. The next day Fanny, tired of her false position, left their home banging the door behind her. On the 29th, whilst Nelson was already on board his flagship at Plymouth, Emma gave birth to a girl whose Christian name was to be Horatia.

*

At the beginning of March Nelson received instructions to

go to Yarmouth. Relations with Denmark were decidedly not improving and a fleet of 23 of the line, 11 frigates and numerous sloops and brigs was concentrating there in readiness for an expedition to restore order in the Baltic. Nelson expected to be put in command of this fleet, but the Admiralty, whilst still in need of his services, was not prepared to overlook his private life. It was therefore under the orders of Sir Hyde Parker, a notoriously incapable but dignified old man, that the fleet put to sea on March 12 making for Copenhagen.

As soon as he arrived in the Kattegat on the morning of the 20th Parker sent the Danes an ultimatum—a choice of submission or war. They proudly rejected it, and war became inevitable.

The squadron's task was an arduous one. Copenhagen is built on a strait, called the Sound, which connects the Kattegat to the Baltic. Opposite the town this strait is divided into two channels by a sandbank of considerable length. To make an attack on the Danish capital a position would therefore have to be established in the inner channel, called the King's Deep. This was the first difficulty. But there were others. The Danes, a resolute people, had not waited to be shot at before organising their defences. At its northern extremity, that is to say, at the point where the most serious threat might be expected, the King's Deep was protected by a fort mounting 68 guns, and a number of ships including two of the line; all along the channel were posted 37 vessels of various kinds which had been transformed into floating batteries and thus constituted a fortified line mounted with 628 guns. These ships were covered from the rear by shore batteries. Finally, the entire male population had been mobilised and were ready to meet any attack.

Faced with this situation Sir Hyde Parker called a council of war. He made no secret of the fact that he considered a frontal attack an extremely hazardous operation and that it would be far preferable to wait in the Kattegat until the Danish fleet and its allies should emerge. Nelson on the contrary was in favour of immediate action. He proposed an assault on the city itself, but not frontally, from the north, since that was the quarter where the defences were strongest—Fort Trekoner and the warships. His plan was to approach from the rear, by sailing up the King's Deep and attacking from the south. This operation was certainly not a simple one, for the channel was narrow and difficult to negotiate without the aid of local pilots or the most accurate charts. But if successfully carried through, Nelson maintained, it would certainly result in the annihilation of three-quarters of the Danish defences.

Parker had the good sense to trust the judgment of his subordinate. On the evening of the 30th the fleet entered the Sound and anchored beyond the shoal off Copenhagen. On the morning of April 2 Nelson rounded the southern tip of the shoal and began to sail up the King's Deep with 12 ships of the line, 18 frigates, bomb-ketches and corvettes. The rest of the fleet remained inactive to the northward, since the wind was in the south, favouring Nelson. There was not a sound. The English warships advanced relentlessly towards the batteries. Three ran aground. Even so, at ten o'clock the first shot was fired.

After the battle Nelson wrote: "Here was no manoeuvring: it was downright fighting."

Indeed it was. For three hours the two sides blazed away at each other at almost point blank range. The Danes did not flinch. It seemed as if the whole nation was manning 600 guns determined to fight on to the last drop of their blood. Nelson saw at a glance how matters lay. As he paced the quarterdeck of the *Elephant* a cannon ball cut through the main mast showering him with splinters. He remarked to a young officer:

"This might well be the last day for many of us. But, mark you, I would not be elsewhere for thousands."

Sir Hyde Parker was well out of harm's way, but had begun to feel uneasy. About one o'clock he had signal No. 39

[cease fire] run up. On board the *Elephant* a lieutenant dashed up to Nelson:

"Sir, the Commander-in-Chief has run up No. 39!"

Nelson appeared to have heard nothing, continued his solitary pacing, and then returned to the lieutenant:

"Acknowledge it."

He walked a few paces more:

"Wait! Is our No. 16 [engage closely] still flying? It is? Mind you keep it so."

He then noticed Captain Foley, in command of the *Elephant* (Foley of Aboukir), and said to him:

"You know, Foley, I have only one eye: I have a right to be blind sometimes."

He put his telescope to the eye that had long been blind, directed it out to sea, where Parker lay, and cried:

"Really, I do not see this damned signal 39!"

By about two o'clock the Danes began to give signs of exhaustion. They had suffered enormous losses. Several of their batteries had surrendered; others lay gutted. Still, no decision had yet been reached, for the English fleet had also suffered badly. The frigates had obeyed Parker's order and retired from the action, where they had been very roughly handled. Several ships of the line were severely damaged. Fresh Danes were coming up to replace their fallen countrymen, and to continue the fight in such conditions would probably have been to court disaster, the more so as, in emerging from the channel, the English would have had to pass under the fire of the undamaged fort at its northern extremity. Nelson was well aware of all this. Filled with a sudden inspiration, he called for pen and paper, and, upon the top of the rudder-housing, he wrote straight down:

"To the Brothers of Englishmen, the Danes.

"Lord Nelson has directions to spare Denmark, when no longer resisting, but if the firing is continued on the part of Denmark, Lord Nelson will be obliged to set on **fire** all the floating batteries he has taken without having the power of saving the brave Danes who had defended them."

Though couched in these magnanimous terms, the message was in fact little better than blackmail. When the letter was written, he ordered it to be carefully sealed, saying to the secretary who brought the wax and taper: "At this juncture we must not act hastily: everything must go according to rule."

Half an hour later the Danes sent a representative to ask for detailed terms, and firing ceased. This was what Nelson had been waiting for. Under the truce that followed he weighed anchor, and his squadron sailed out of the channel. He had 943 men killed or wounded, and the Danes 1,600. He was worried: "Well, I have fought contrary to orders," said he, as he left the *Elephant* to go aboard Parker's flagship. "Perhaps I shall be hanged. Never mind; let them!"

However, he was not hanged. For by the threefold merit of boldness, courage and intelligence—boldness of plan, courage in action, and shrewd intelligence at the critical moment—he had won one of his most dramatic victories, and indeed one of the most astonishing in naval history. Denmark signed the armistice within the week.

For three more months Nelson sailed the northern seas to complete the breaking up of the Armed Neutrality League. It was only on July 1, his mission accomplished, that he returned to England and to Emma—at last! No campaign had ever seemed so long. All he wanted now was to rest and end his days in peace, far from the importunate Fanny, who was still writing to him, and at the side of the only woman who had truly understood him: "I have a horror of all praise but what comes from you," he said.

But this was the time when Bonaparte was assembling an invasion fleet at Boulogne. England had more need than ever of the man who had twice already, at Aboukir and Copenhagen, checked the diabolical designs of this nightmare general.

Besides, this time it was not only the Admiralty that called him to fresh labours; it was the united voice of a nation in agony who looked to him as its brightest hope of dispersing the most serious danger it had ever faced.

On July 27, 1801, less than a month after his return from the Baltic, Nelson put to sea again to defend his native island. On August 2 he attempted to bombard Boulogne: the attempt failed. On the 15th at night he returned to the charge, launching about fifty sloops against the ships guarding the invasion fleet, in an attempt to set them on fire: this also failed.

All England felt a great sense of disillusion. Was Nelson finished, or was the French invasion fleet more formidable than had been supposed?

The British Government was not sorry to sign the preliminaries to the Peace of Amiens, on October 1.

*

"Peace at last, and may God bless us!"

Never had Horatio Nelson been happier than in that autumn of 1801. At Merton, in Surrey, he had bought a small farm stocked with turkeys, poultry and ducks. The quartet hurried off there, Emma, Sir William, Horatio and Horatia (his "adopted daughter" as she was called in society), eager for the rustic pleasures of quietness and simplicity.

At Christmas-time Fanny tried to pit her poor worn-out heart against this paradise: "I now have to offer for your accommodation a comfortable warm house. Do, my Dear Husband, let us live together. I assure you, I have but one wish in the world, to please you."

Nelson returned the letter "opened in error but not read". What did Fanny matter, what did the world matter to him when Emma was there, and Horatia, and that splendid fellow Sir William who went fishing from morning till night?

However, if the truth must be told, life at Merton was not so simple or quiet or rustic as Nelson liked to picture it, after sailing the seven seas for more than thirty years, courting adventure. Emma "the farmer's wife" was strangely similar to Emma "the ambassador's wife". She had the same expensive tastes, the same urge to dazzle all eyes, the same desire to be seen everywhere. Every day guests followed guests, dinners succeeded suppers, and tea-parties came hard upon garden-parties, to the great detriment of Nelson's weary eye, his ruined digestion, and, above all, his purse.

And then, away from Merton, that other life went on, always full of threats despite an apparent return to serenity and calm. On March 27, 1802, the Peace of Amiens was finally signed. Contrary to expectation, the Viscount of the Nile and of Burnham Thorpe (for Nelson had been made a viscount after Copenhagen), received the news with feelings of humiliation and contempt:

"It is a test," said he, "and this test will soon shatter our illusions."

He was morose and melancholy, full of troublesome misgivings, as though he felt that the happiness he had so earnestly hoped for would be of only short duration. In April his father died. He took it very hard, and a tour in Wales did little to soften his grief.

In the autumn Sir William's strength began to fail. In the spring he took to his bed and never got up again. One morning he took Nelson's remaining hand and said: "You are the most loyal of friends, and the most upright character I have ever met." Then he turned to Emma, "You are a model among wives."

His head sank: he was dead.

It was April 5, 1803.

Horatio and Emma looked at one another. Had the hour come at last when they could go and hide their love at Bronte under the Italian sky, far from the hurly-burly, far from foggy England, and far from that society that was already beginning to gossip again? "Now what will they do? Pray tell me how Her Ladyship can live with the hero of Aboukir, at least in an honourable manner?"

War supplied the answer. A month earlier the famous, the "everlasting" Peace of Amiens had also entered the land of shadows.

Late in April the Admiralty appointed Nelson Commander-in-Chief of the Mediterranean Squadron.

At dawn on May 18, leaving Emma in tears, the one-armed admiral took the road for Plymouth, and found there waiting for him the finest ship from which he had ever flown his flag, the *Victory* of 100 guns.

IV

TOULON—THE KEY

THE YEAR 1803 was now in its last quarter, and at Boulogne everybody was working with intensified enthusiasm.

At the beginning of September, while 36,000 men under the orders of General Soult were beginning to raise an enormous wooden hutted encampment on the shore, Admiral Bruix established his headquarters as commandant on the cliffs of l'Ordre. This was a large barracks commanding a view of the roadstead and harbour, near which there was soon to be a somewhat similar building reserved for the use of Bonaparte himself.

Every day couriers brought innumerable orders to the commandant of the invasion fleet, orders dictated by his indefatigable master in the Tuileries during long and often sleepless nights. What was uppermost in the First Consul's mind was the men's training.

"My army must be amphibious at all times," he kept repeating, and in order to produce these "sailor-soldiers" he created the naval battalion of the Guard; conversely, he had the grenadiers and light infantry, already in camp at Boulogne, put to the oars on every possible occasion, so that the troops might feel at home on the sea.

"Seventy-five men to a pinnace will row for two or three hours daily. The men must row in the harbour, on board both pinnaces and gun-boats: they are not to enter the roadstead."

However, despite the effort expended both in Paris and on the actual beaches, time was slipping by, winter was coming on, and the grand enterprise was taking shape all too slowly. Not only was construction well behind schedule, but so many difficulties were still cropping up that Bonaparte decided he must make a personal visit to take stock of the situation.

Arriving at Boulogne unexpectedly on November 4, 1803, he immediately went up to his residential barracks and, surveying the scene below him, listened to Bruix's explanations. At his feet the endless thatched roofs of the army encampment, divided in two sections to the right and left of the harbour, covered several miles. Its thoroughfares were given evocative names such as Valmy, Jemmapes, Campo-Formio and Marengo. While many hundreds of men were still at work on this gigantic barracks, others were building the roadstead forts, digging out the approach-channel, and finishing off the semi-circular pool, whose construction had been decided upon five months earlier, at the time of the "Little Corporal's" first visit. Further off, engineer units were at work among the coves of Ambleteuse and Wimereux making two harbours to relieve congestion in the main base when the time came.

But only when the time came. For it must have been clear to Bonaparte that the invasion fleet was still very far from completion. Scarcely a hundred craft could be counted in the Boulogne roadstead, though some of those had indeed covered themselves with glory by driving off several English patrols during the months of July, August and September. But more, many more—were required. It was, in fact, plain that from now on all idea of a descent on England during the winter was out of the question. Even if preparations were to be complete by the spring, there was not a moment to be lost.

Faced with these facts Bonaparte, contrary to all expectations, showed no annoyance. But he did decide to stay on at Boulogne—in the end he spent thirteen days there—in order to rekindle enthusiasm and encourage activity by his presence in person. The letters he wrote at this time from his headquarters on the cliffs of l'Ordre merit attention:

To the Consul Cambacérès (November 5, 1803):

"At one o'clock on Wednesday afternoon I arrived at Boulogne harbour, on a completely unexpected visit. I viewed with the utmost interest all the works and preparations in connection with this great expedition and was still there at midnight.

"I am 'billeted' in the middle of the camp on the seashore, whence one can measure at a glance the distance between us and England."

To the same (November 7, 1803):

"I spent the whole of Sunday visiting the many harbours of Ambleteuse and Wimereux, and in exercising the troops there. Progress is being made.

"I have just converted a barracks into a naval arsenal. I have to arrange everything down to the last detail.

"I spent several hours inspecting troops, man by man, and in personally satisfying myself of the state of the various active units. What I still have to do here will take me several days."

To the same (November 9, 1803):

"I spent part of last night putting troops through night-operations, which can sometimes be effectively used by well-trained and disciplined men against mass-conscripts."

To Admiral Bruix (November 9, 1803):

"It is absolutely essential that the rate of construction at Ambleteuse should be trebled. Two thousand five hundred workmen will be provided by the army. Work on the dredging of Boulogne harbour must also be speeded up, and the number of workmen doubled."

To the Consul Cambacérès (November 12, 1803):

"I spent the whole of yesterday at the harbour, on board ship and on horseback. That is to say that I was soaked the whole time. At this time of year one can get nothing done without braving the rain. Fortunately for me, I find it highly beneficial, and have never felt better."

To General Augereau (November 12, 1803):

"I have been here ten days, and I have grounds for hope that within a reasonable space of time I shall reach the goal that all Europe looks to. We have ten centuries of wrongs to avenge."

To the Consul Cambacérès (November 16, 1803):

"My dear Citizen Consul, the Naval Minister arrived the day before yesterday. I have spent the last three days in the camps and in the harbour. Everything here is beginning to move in the right direction.

"From the high ground at Ambleteuse I saw the coast of England, as clearly as you can see the Calvary on Mount Valerien from the Tuileries. I could see houses and movement. The Channel is a mere ditch which will be crossed when we have the courage to make the attempt.

"The Seine at Paris must have risen considerably. It has rained incessantly here. From here to Saint-Malo we have more than two hundred vessels, either in the roadstead, or on the point of sailing to join us. I am hoping for the arrival of a division to-day."

To Citizen Chaptal, Minister of the Interior (November 16, 1803):

"I am satisfied with the morale of the workmen both on land and sea."

The recipients of these letters could not fail to be impressed by their tone of resolute optimism. Yet during his stay at Boulogne Bonaparte could not but have noted that the execution of his orders was several months behind schedule: *he had also become firmly convinced that the invasion fleet could never make an attack on England unprotected, even if surprise were achieved, without running into disaster; and that by this circumstance it was already damned in advance.*

*

It has been said, and rightly so, that in spite of the obvious confidence of Forfait, and certain others, the First Consul had never had much faith in the sloops, as a means of opening up a passage by force. He preferred to think that their success would depend either on a momentary withdrawal of the English cruisers to their bases, or on a squall driving the cruisers out to sea, or even on a calm keeping them immobile.

In any case, since the end of the summer of 1803 he had begun to make a serious reassessment of his position. Nobody knows whether this was due to his own reflections, or to the persuasions of his admirals, who had always opposed the plan. It is worth noting, however, that on September 5, Truguet, commanding the Brest squadron, had sent him a pitiful letter charging him not to go out and expose, in such an enterprise, "his person and his reputation".

In any case, this visit to Boulogne was a decisive event. Having seen for himself,[1] Bonaparte clearly realised that the little vessels whose praises he had so often heard were nothing but clumsy unmanageable tubs, moving with equal difficulty under oar or sail, low in the water with their load of guns, themselves difficult of use, and incapable of riding even a moderate swell. On November 5, shortly after the invasion fleet had, for the first time, been drawn up bow to stern across the roadstead, an English detachment made its appearance. Though the engagement was short, the invasion fleet had the best of the exchange of gunfire. But there was bad weather the following day, and five vessels ran ashore, while the remainder were dispersed like chaff.

This spectacle, and the similar one of the sloops approaching from neighbouring ports, unable for the most part to make harbour unless they hugged the coast the whole way, quickly made it clear to the First Consul that it would be impossible for the invasion fleet to cross the straits except in fine weather —that is to say, only in the summer months from May to October. It was also clearly impossible to keep the small

[1] This visit was all the more effective for having taken place in winter, for Bonaparte could thus see that the North Sea was no mill-pond, and that the elements had to be reckoned with continuously. To document our account, we may observe that Napoleon Bonaparte was in residence at Boulogne directing the operations planned against England at the following times: February 10, 1798; June 29 to July 1, 1803; November 4 to 17, 1803; January 1 to 5, 1804, July 19, 1804; during August 1804; August 3 to September 2, 1805; the above dates are quoted by M. Fernand Nicolay (*Napoléon au camp de Boulogne*, Paris, 1907) from the research undertaken by M. Lefebvre, a native of Boulogne.

vessels permanently in position in the roadstead: any hope of achieving surprise was ruled out.

Neither Boulogne, nor Calais, nor Dunkirk—far less Ambleteuse, Étaples or Wimereux—was equipped to shelter, in case of necessity, more than a hundred vessels each tide. To leave the invasion fleet at anchor in the roadstead with sails set ready to move off at the first signal, was to expose it to mortal danger at the first onset of bad weather: if a few vessels could be saved here and there, how many would be destroyed? Conversely, if almost the whole fleet remained concentrated in harbour, it would be impossible for more than a hundred vessels to sail out on each tide. Even with conditions at their best, a minimum of five days would be required to line them all up ready to move. It is hardly necessary to add that the English, alerted at the first sign of movement (they had organised a remarkable spy-service) would immediately make profitable use of this delay to concentrate their squadrons in the straits.

Thus the question arose whether, even in the most favourable conditions—that is to say, with support for a time from the coastal batteries—the invasion fleet could hope to get the better of the British men-of-war. The rational answer was "no". There was only one way to hold the English force in check and so facilitate the crossing of the sloops, and that was to oppose them with a force of like strength. In other words, the French Grand Fleet must either be concentrated in the North Sea on the day fixed for the enterprise, or else used as a bait to lure the greater part of the English force after it, far away from the Channel. Alternatively the problem could be put in this way: the invasion fleet must be given, by a judicious use of the Grand Fleet, what it could never gain on its own account: MASTERY OF THE SEA.[1]

We have come a long way, indeed, from the original plan!

[1] In the same way in 1944 the Anglo-American forces, setting out from the British Isles in their assault on "Fortress Europe", could not have crossed the Channel except as masters of both sea and air.

Bonaparte left Boulogne on November 17, 1803. He had scarcely re-entered Paris when he wrote a letter to Rear-Admiral Ganteaume, naval prefect of Toulon, which clearly reveals his uneasiness. It should be noted at this point that Honoré Ganteaume, formerly chief-of-staff to Brueys at Aboukir, enjoyed a measure of Bonaparte's confidence, for it was he who brought him back secretly from Egypt, on board the frigate *Muiron*, in 1799.

This is the key passage of the letter:

"I have just come from Boulogne where activity is intense, and by the middle of Nivôse (January) I hope to have assembled 360 gun sloops, 500 gunboats and 500 pinnaces. [As we shall soon see, Bonaparte was much too optimistic.] Each pinnace is to carry a 36-pound howitzer, each boat a 24-pounder gun, and each gun-sloop three 24-pounders. Let me know your opinion of this fleet. Do you think it will convey us to the shores of Albion? It will carry 100,000 men. *Eight hours of darkness, if conditions are favourable to us, would decide the fate of the universe.*"

Ganteaume's reply was prompt:

"In the last analysis I consider the expedition of the invasion fleet as being, if not impossible, at least extremely risky. Its only chance of success lies in some unforeseen major contingency."

But immediately afterwards, having expressed regret that everything had not been sacrificed to the building of the ships of which France was now in such desperate need, the admiral added:

"Even to-day I regret never having been put in command of a light squadron with a roving commission, such as the one I asked for at the end of last year. Perhaps it might not have been impossible, though certainly very difficult, to sail up the Channel unexpectedly, make various feints to put the enemy off the scent, and then take by surprise the cruiser squadron stationed off Boulogne—I presume it consists of no more than a few warships and frigates—driving them from the Channel not for eight hours only, but for forty-eight. This scheme, I repeat, would be a very bold one, and extremely dangerous, but I think naval men would not consider it impracticable.

"To attain this object two alternative movements could be tried: either to sail round the north of England, or to enter the Channel with a brisk following wind, skirting the Scilly Isles. For the first alternative the weather must be less rough than at present, and the ships thoroughly well provisioned, for it would be a long round trip."

The effect of this letter upon Bonaparte was what might have been expected. Never had a naval man forestalled his thoughts so well, or understood them so perfectly. His reply of December 7, was almost ecstatic:

"You have partially sensed my design. I shall explain it to you personally. I need not tell you that secrecy is essential."

And so, point by point in that surprising succinct style of his own, he set out his plan—or rather submitted it to the admiral's judgment.

The point was to wrest from the English, *for a given period*, the control of the North Sea, and so allow the invasion fleet to cross. This was to be achieved by "moving" the units available—nine ships of the line and five frigates at Toulon, seven of the line and three frigates at Rochefort, and 20 of the line at Brest—into a concentration sufficient for the purpose.

There were three possibilities:

1. The Toulon squadron would sail on January 11, picking up the Rochefort squadron en route, off Cadiz or Lisbon; they would proceed together to Boulogne without putting in anywhere and, their mission accomplished, make for the mouth of the Scheldt or Cherbourg.

2. The Toulon squadron would sail on January 11, proceed to the island of Aix, put to sea again, together with the Rochefort squadron, and follow its course as foreseen above.

3. The Rochefort squadron would sail on January 11, reaching Toulon on the 10th of the following month, and the two

squadrons, setting sail from the Mediterranean port in March, would appear off Boulogne in April.

In all three cases the Toulon squadron must act in such a way as to give the English a false idea of its actual destination, and make them think it was starting for Egypt, so that Nelson, the Commander-in-Chief in the Mediterranean, would be waiting for the French at Alexandria. The Brest squadron, in its turn, must dupe the British with an appearance of sailing for Ireland, so as to keep Admiral Cornwallis occupied—he was then stationed off Ushant—or even to draw him after them, thus making him lose the substance for the shadow.

"Which is the best idea of the three?" asked Bonaparte, adding, "At the end of February I shall be at Boulogne with 130,000 men, 2,000 pinnaces, gun-sloops and gun-boats,[1] and with batteries of 2,000 24-pounders and more than 1,000 howitzers. If our squadron is then forced to an engagement off Boulogne (which God forbid!), we can give it good and powerful support. Étaples, Boulogne, Wimereux and Ambleteuse are the only four ports we have where the winds are the same—they are all close together—and given favourable conditions, all we need ask is that the squadron should be there *for twelve hours.*"

Once again Ganteaume replied by return courier "according to his lights and his experience".

His preference was for the second alternative, with rendezvous off Rochefort. He considered the suggested diversion to be created by the Brest squadron as a further possibility. On the other hand, he thought that the arrival of a force of 24 ships of the line (the Toulon and Rochefort squadrons combined) "in such a confined space as the Channel, and among them, doubtless, some second-rate and slow-moving vessels" could not long remain unknown to the English. He felt it would be a better plan to form a light squadron of the fastest-sailing ships of the Toulon and Rochefort squadrons, which could appear unexpectedly in the Straits, take the English

[1] Once again, Bonaparte was deceiving himself.

watchdog cruisers by surprise and even destroy them, and thus ensure a crossing for the invasion fleet. This operation, he repeated, would secure a period of not eight, but forty-eight hours.

Lastly, he was categorical on the amount of support that the invasion fleet might provide. "I have no hesitation in informing you that in my view artillery support from the sloops and gunboats is an illusion, in the event of the squadron being forced into an engagement off Boulogne."

Such were the sentiments of Ganteaume the technician. Without coinciding exactly with those of the First Consul, they agreed with them on one fundamental point: both recognised that the key to the whole vast enterprise lay not at Boulogne, as had so long been thought, but at Toulon, and that in the last resort all would depend on the action of the fleet stationed there.

That brought up, once again, a problem of command—the choice of a leader.

On December 30, 1803 it was announced that Rear-Admiral Latouche-Tréville, who had returned from the West Indies three months before, was promoted vice-admiral and appointed Commander-in-Chief of the Mediterranean squadron.

V

DEATH OF TWO ADMIRALS

NEW YEAR'S DAY 1804 dawned in an atmosphere of rejoicing. For the third time within the space of a few months, Bonaparte was inspecting his fleet. Four hundred flat-bottomed boats, drawn up by divisions, were lined up in the inner and outer harbour, with their crews at battle-stations.

The spectacle was not without grandeur. There was no doubt that the state of the fleet had improved since November. But there was also no deceiving the eagle eye of the First Consul: in spite of the efforts made it was still, as in November, well below expectations. At the present rhythm of work, there could be no hope of more than 600 vessels being available in February, and 700 to 800 at the beginning of spring. Many of the fortifications had still to be completed: a thousand questions of detail, settled on paper, still awaited practical solution; the embarkation of horses, the training of a small corps of interpreters speaking perfect English (this was one of the First Consul's ideas), the working-out of a system of signals between sloop and sloop, the familiarisation of the soldiers with nautical terms, and so on.

Bonaparte continued to fulminate:

"Citizen Lebrun. . . . You will set out immediately for Saint-Valéry-sur-Somme; you will take note of the workmen employed on each sloop: you will make sure that all warlike stores, rigging, and ordnance are present and correct. . . ."

"General Savary. . . . You will start this day for Flushing; you will proceed thence to Bruges, and thence again to Liège; from Liège to Mézières, and from Mézières to Paris: you will visit the foundry at Liège and the two dockyards on the Meuse at Liège and Mézières. . . ."

"Rear Admiral Decrès. . . . I observed at the arsenal that the blacksmiths were idle because they had no forges. I have ordered the artillery to supply four, which will be delivered at the arsenal to-morrow before eight o'clock in the morning. I was distressed to see that whilst a large number of cloths had been used for 800 horses, no steps had been taken to provide a simple tent for the protection of the workmen or to set up a mast-makers' shop. . . ."

This latest inspection lasted five days.

Meanwhile, at the other end of France, an official carriage was travelling at top speed. It exhausted successive teams of post-horses, as it brought the First Consul's surest hope from Toulon, M. de Latouche-Tréville.

Vice-Admiral de Latouche-Tréville was the son of a *chef d'escadre* (rank of the pre-Revolution navy equivalent to Rear-Admiral) and the nephew of a lieutenant-general in the marines. He had entered the Navy in 1758 at the age of thirteen, and, after gaining his promotions with the greatest gallantry on active service, he and Bruix had become the best French sailors of their time. He was one of those men—rare at all times—whose energy could be counted upon to carry out successfully the able plan Bonaparte had constructed. It was he who had held Nelson in check off Boulogne on August 2 and 15, 1801. Although much wasted by fever, he was burning to repeat his success, especially as the Admiralty had given Nelson the task of keeping watch on the Mediterranean squadron.

The First Consul instructed the vice-admiral to hold himself ready to sail out of Toulon after January 21. On the 14th Latouche-Tréville hoisted his flag on the *Bucentaure* of 80 guns and reviewed his force, consisting of seven sail of the line and six frigates. These appeared to be in good trim, but in reality they were perfectly filthy, and commanded by officers who thought more of living ashore than afloat, and manned by crews with a sorry notion of naval service. All the more vigorously did the admiral take in hand the task of setting his house in order. During the following days he redoubled practice in getting under sail, clearing the decks for action, and coming to anchor, driving his frigates to chase to the farthest point of the outer anchorage the English frigates that had been on guard there for months.

When these facts reached the ears of Nelson, he could not hide his contempt:

"He was sent for on purpose," he wrote to the Admiralty, "as he beat me at Boulogne, to beat me again; but he seems very loth to try."

But some days later, when his frigates reported growing activity in the French squadron, he began to be disturbed. He wrote to friends: "Monsieur La Touche . . . is ready, and, by their handling their ships, apparently well manned; but I command, for Captains and Crews, such a Fleet, as I never have before seen; and it is impossible that any Admiral can be happier situated. M. Latouche frequently ventures outside his station. If he will get abreast of Porquerolles I will try what stuff he is made of . . . I am satisfied he meant nothing but a gasconade; but am confident, when he is ordered for any service, that he will risk falling in with us, and the event of a Battle, to try and accomplish his orders."

Most assuredly Latouche-Tréville was not a man to fail in his duty. But contrary to all expectation, and to the great detriment of Nelson, glued permanently to his poop, the end of January came, and then the end of February, and still the Toulon fleet had received no orders to hoist sail.

The truth was that so many component parts were still missing from the immense machinery conceived by Bonaparte that nobody was in a position to say when it could be set in motion. Decrès, the Minister, had brought out of the dockyards every available vessel, but the Brest squadron was short of men, and five ships of the line under the command of Gourdon remained shut up in Ferrol, unable to gain Rochefort, where they had been expected since November. So far as the invasion fleet was concerned no more than 1,273 vessels, out of the 2,000 provided for, had been completed by March—completed but not concentrated, for not one of those built in the sea-ports had succeeded in entering the Channel.

Vainly did Forfait arouse the anger of Decrès by inveighing against the lack of enterprise shown by the commanders of the sloops. Vainly too, did Bonaparte bluster against admirals who, like Truguet at Brest, complained of not being able to recruit crews. Only the army was ready, proudly completing its bar-racks at Boulogne, Calais and Flushing, and zealously carrying on its training under the distant but watchful eye of the master.

"General Ney . . . make your division practise rowing on board the pinnaces and gun-boats too. Let me know the distances a gun-boat and a pinnace can travel in half an hour, driven by oars, with no sail, and when the tide is flowing."

It is a remarkable fact that despite all the difficulties encoun-tered, enthusiasm never waned. On the contrary, every day, from every camp, every workshop and every arsenal came tokens of loyalty and confidence to be poured out at the feet of the man who had brought France to the threshold of the greatest adventure in her history—the very man whom even now the forces of counter-revolution and treason, led by Pichegru, Cavondal and Moreau, were seeking to overthrow.

On March 21, before the first light of a spring morning, the volley of a firing squad rang out in the direction of Vincennes, and the Duc d'Enghien fell dead.

Four days later Admiral Ganteaume, outstripping even the quickest-moving opportunists, presented a motion to the electoral college of the Var over which he presided. Apart from the ruthless punishment of conspirators, he called for a constitutional system designed to consolidate and perpetuate "for the country's good" the powers of the First Consul and of his family.

Two months later, on May 18, 1804, Bonaparte became Napoleon I.

*

It was natural that this crossing of the Rubicon should delay still further that other crossing, perilous in a different sense, with which England had so long been threatened. But the idea was far from being abandoned. Even though domestic matters had for the moment pushed it into second place, the delay thus caused was no matter for regret.

"In his impatience to put his vast design into execution," Thiers has written, "Napoleon had considerably exaggerated in his own mind the possibility of being ready by the end of 1803."

No word could be truer. Even in April 1804 the preparations for the expedition continued to run into serious obstacles. The most notable were lack of funds—new resources had to be tapped to balance a budget that had soared to 800 millions (for year XII, from September 1803 to September 1804) from the 619 of the previous financial year. Even more serious was that chronic complaint, lack of ships of the line.

Whilst England, on January 1, 1805, had 83 battleships in commission, with 13 other ships larger than frigates, the French main high seas fleet, on which depended, in the last resort, the success or failure of the operation, had available only a meagre effective strength, and it was all blockaded: eight line of battleships at Toulon, one at Cadiz, five at Ferrol, five at Rochefort, and 20 at Brest.

To attempt mastery of the sea—even for only a few days—in such conditions, was to display a singular boldness or, rather, a singular degree of folly. Did Napoleon aim at merely bluffing the English, as in 1801? Or did he, on the contrary, believe—and that with the utmost sincerity—that his lucky star would once again bring within his grasp the seemingly impossible? Or, having gone too far to withdraw, did he think the preparations should be continued against some new development, and, if there was none, did he envisage a time in the distant future when France would come through toil and sweat to brave the adventure at last?

Writing to Decrès on April 21 on the subject of laying the foundation stone of the arsenal at Antwerp, he let slip this admission: "We have no navy, and we cannot be considered to have one until we have a hundred ships of the line. These we must have five years from now."

He returned to the charge on April 28: "To-day I am signing a decree on naval construction. I shall accept no manner of excuse. Have reports made to you twice weekly on the orders you give, and see that they are carried out: if emergency measures are required, let me know. . . ."

"It will be obvious to you that my intention is to launch a wide programme of ship-building. Before Vendémiaire, year XIV (September 1806) I wish to have 26 ships of the line afloat. Of course their launching will above all depend upon whether or not peace is declared between now and then. . . .

"Our main dockyard must be at Antwerp. It is only there that the *revival* of the French navy can become a possibility in a few years.

"Before the year XV (1807) we must have a *hundred* ships of the line."

Do these two letters reveal to us what the Emperor really thought? They do not. "Napoleon was fickle," Stendhal said.

*

The very day after the proclamation of the Empire, the great army chiefs began reaping their rewards: fourteen generals on active service were promoted marshals—Jourdan, Berthier, Masséna, Lannes, Ney, Augereau, Murat, Brune, Bessières, Mortier, Moncey, Soult, Davout and Bernadotte. Four generals who had become senators—Kellermann, Lefebvre, Sérurier, and Pérignon—were proclaimed honorary marshals.

On May 30 came the turn of the navy. Three rear-admirals took the rank of vice-admiral: Decrès the Minister, Ganteaume the Naval Prefect of Toulon, already ear-marked for the command for the Brest squadron in place of Truguet, who was thought too much of a republican and too flabby, and Pierre de Villeneuve, in command of the naval forces at Rochefort. It is worth emphasising that these three men were bound together by a common memory of the tragedy of Aboukir, to which their names were indissolubly linked. Not only had they vehemently urged their commanding officer before the battle to fight at the anchorage, but they had played conspicuous parts in the action itself, Ganteaume as chief-of-staff to Admiral Brueys, Decrès as commander of the light squadron, and, above all Villeneuve. He was responsible for the rear-guard, but had left the greater part of it to sink under Nelson's blows without attempting to intervene. All three, as we have already noted in the case of Decrès, and as we shall soon see with Ganteaume and Villeneuve, were afterwards oppressed with a sense of inferiority vis-à-vis the British fleet. And it was certainly no minor paradox of the Emperor's promotions of May 30 that this trio, who carried the stigma of defeat, and were personally convinced that they had witnessed the final collapse of the French navy, were suddenly raised to the highest honours.

Meanwhile, freed from direct personal anxiety, Napoleon resumed his labours. After May 25, when Ganteaume went to take over his command at Brest, he had determined upon a "final" plan, based entirely on the ideas he had hammered out during the winter: Latouche's squadron, sailing from Toulon and misleading Nelson as to its actual destination, was to make the Atlantic, endeavour on its way to take with it the single man-of-war blockaded at Cadiz, make a wide circuit of Cape Finisterre, and gather up on the high seas the Rochefort squadron under Villeneuve. Then, when Ganteaume, emerging from Brest, was harassing Cornwallis, it would take advantage of the first favourable wind to press forward into the Channel.

At the beginning of July Latouche-Tréville had raised the strength of his squadron to 11 warships. Ganteaume had given encouraging signs of activity in hastening the fitting out of his detachment, and the first ships of the Batavian flotilla, built at Flushing, had arrived at Ostend. The Emperor thought, or appeared to think, that the moment had come.

He wrote to Latouche-Tréville on July 2, 1804: "Let me know by return courier the day you will be able to sail, making allowance for weather: inform me of the enemy's activity and the position of Nelson.

"Consider the mighty enterprise you are charged with. . . . I have already made you one of the chief officers of the Empire, Inspector of the Mediterranean coasts, but I am greatly desirous that the operation you are to undertake will justify me in raising you to such a height of honour and reputation that you will have nothing left to wish for.

"The Rochefort squadron of 5 of the line and 4 frigates is ready to sail: it is opposed by no more than 5 enemy ships.

"The Brest squadron consists of 21 of the line.[1] These have just started out to harass Admiral Cornwallis, and to compel the English to concentrate a large battle fleet in the area. The enemy is also maintaining 6 line of battleships off the Texel, in order to blockade the Dutch squadron, which comprises 5 of the line, 4 frigates, and a convoy of 80 other craft.

"Between Étaples, Boulogne, Wimereau and Ambleteuse, we have 270 gun sloops, 534 gun-boats, 386 pinnaces—a total of 1,200 vessels with 120,000 men and 10,000 horses on board. *If we can control the Straits for six hours, we shall control the world!*

"If you hoodwink Nelson he will make for either Sicily, or Egypt, or Ferrol. In my opinion he will certainly appear off Ferrol. . . . The best course would appear to be to pass that point well out to sea; then arriving off Rochefort you will have a squadron of 16 ships of the line and 11 frigates;[2] after

---

[1] This figure is theoretical; the real position was that Ganteaume, due to lack of men, had no more than half a dozen of the line fully armed and effective.

[2] Napoleon's meaning is: "The combination of the force anchored off this port (5 of the line and 4 frigates) with your own, will give you in all a squadron of 16 warships and 11 frigates."

that not a moment must be lost in making Boulogne—do not anchor anywhere—either making a wide circuit of Ireland, or else carrying out the first plan.

"Our Brest squadron will have the support of an army ashore. Its sails will be set day in day out, so that Cornwallis will have to keep well in shore if he is to prevent its getting out.

"For the rest, I await the plan you have promised me by return courier, in order to settle my ideas on this operation, which is certainly risky, but which, if it succeeds, will bring us such immense rewards. . . .

"I consider it preferable to take advantage of a favourable *mistral*[1] and carry out our operation before winter. Assuming that you could leave before the 10th Thermidor [July 29], it is improbable that you would be off Boulogne before September—when the nights are already reasonably long, and bad weather does not last."

Hardly had the Emperor despatched this letter than he sent an equally urgent message to Admiral Bruix, Commander-in-Chief of the invasion fleet: "The invasion fleet consists of over 1,800 vessels, of which more than 700 are concentrated at Boulogne, 290 at Étaples, 340 at Wimereaux and 437 at Ambleteuse. I am not including the 20 barges, which must be stationed in whichever port offers the most advantageous conditions, and the least degree of inconvenience to their starting out.

"Accordingly I wish you to inform me of your opinion on the following questions:

1. Can the number of vessels that have been brought to each port be accommodated there?

2. Can these vessels sail out of the ports on two tides?

3. Finally, would it be better to increase the number of vessels at Étaples, and reduce them at Boulogne, or to increase those at Calais?"

Judging by these two letters, it seems that this time Napoleon was resolved to take his chance. A fortnight later,

[1] A north-west wind in the Mediterranean. (Translator's note.)

moreover, on July 19, 1804, he burst upon Boulogne like a bomb. He was saluted by the guns of the vessels lying broad-side on and by those of the harbour batteries: he made several pinnaces move out into the anchorage and go through gunnery practice against the forts guarding the inner harbour approaches; and he reviewed the army, drawn up on shore in battle order. He appeared delighted, and wrote to Marshal Brune:

"I have round me here 120,000 men and 3,000 pinnaces and sloops: give them a favourable wind and they will hoist the Imperial Eagle over the Tower of London!"

But he added, as if to himself: "Time and Destiny alone can tell what the outcome will be. . . ."

Time and Destiny . . . it was indeed not difficult to see that upon them alone, in effect, depended the course events would take.

The day after his arrival, without consulting Bruix, Napoleon ordered a general review of the whole line. The sea was rough and a gale was threatening. When he heard of it, the admiral declared point-blank that, loth as he was to cross the Emperor's wishes, circumstances were such that the review would not take place. Napoleon turned on him like a madman:

"Obey me!"

"Sire, I will not obey!"

"You are insolent, sir!"

He had a riding-crop in his hand, and he raised it; it looked as if he would strike. Bruix turned pale, stepped back a pace, and put his hand to his sword:

"Take care, Sir!"

For several seconds the two men glared defiantly at one another motionless, while members of the suite stood petrified with fright. Napoleon flung away his riding-crop:

"The review!" he cried.

The only course was to yield. But Bruix had turned on his heel, so his second-in-command, Rear-Admiral Magon, gave the order to move, and the fleet began its evolutions, making for the open sea, and tossing on the swell. Before an hour had passed, the wind reached gale force, and a storm of unusual violence broke, driving sloops, pinnaces, and gun-boats towards the shore. Amid the roll of the thunder, under a sky streaked with lightning, rose the terrified cries of the soldiers. Rolled over by the heavy seas, the small boats capsized. Rescuers ran along the beach, throwing out lines and life-buoys to the men cast overboard—and foremost among them was Napoleon, soaked to the skin, feeling it a point of honour to redeem his blunder.

All the afternoon and throughout the night the struggle continued against the forces nature had let loose. When at last dawn broke the sea was calm once more, but it was found that a dozen craft had been smashed against the cliffs, and that 200 sailors and soldiers[1] had perished in the disaster.

The Emperor was no doubt not very proud of himself. All the same he wrote to Josephine: "The wind freshened considerably during the night, one (*sic*) of our gun-boats in the anchorage dragged her anchor and ran on the rocks a league from Boulogne. I thought all was lost, both men and material, but we succeeded in saving everything (again *sic*). It was a magnificent sight: guns firing alarm-signals, fires burning up and down the shore, the sea raging and roaring; I was racked all night with anxiety whether the poor wretches would be saved or whether we should see them perish. My spirit was suspended between Ocean, Night and Eternity. At five o'clock in the morning all became light, all had been saved, and I went to bed feeling as if I had had some fabulous and heroic dream. I might have thought that I was alone in the Universe had I not been drenched through and too exhausted to think of anything but sleep."

We may be sure that details of the incident were soon known in England through the host of spies she maintained on the coast. There was talk in London of 400 casualties. The *Annual*

[1] Thus far the reports of witnesses. The official report, written by Marshal Soult, addressed to the Minister of War, and dated July 22, 1804, gives the limited figures of 8 vessels wrecked and "about 50" casualties.

Register did not spare its sarcasm: "Bonaparte has been shown that English shot and English ships are not the only things he will have to face on the day he launches his immense Armada across the Channel. . . ."

But no matter: at this juncture the Emperor's confidence remained unshakable. From the castle of Pont-de-Briques by night, and from his cliff-top barrack by day he poured forth orders, exhortations and threats, crouched over his maps and statistics, wearing out his secretaries, spurring on his generals, and shaking up his admirals. His thoughts flitted from Boulogne to Ostend, where the Batavian detachment was gradually gathering; from Ostend to le Havre, where a mere handful of light craft had arrived from the Atlantic; from le Havre to Paris, for he must certainly have been thinking of Josephine and the approaching ceremony; and lastly from Paris to Brest and Toulon, where his fondest hopes were embodied in Ganteaume and Latouche-Tréville. . . .

On July 25, to the day, having succeeded in fully arming 5 ships of the line and 3 frigates, Ganteaume ventured to nose out into the Iroise. But not for long. As soon as he saw the English making towards him, he put about and returned to the shelter of the harbour. He did not come out again for the rest of the year!

Latouche-Tréville, who had a little more luck and a great deal more daring, scored a distinct success. Two of his frigates, patrolling off the Hyères Islands, were about to be cut off by Nelson's cruisers, when he set sail forthwith and proceeded resolutely to their assistance with eight of the line. The English were out-numbered and withdrew out of hand . . . followed by the withering scorn of the French press, in which the affair was eagerly reported, not without exaggeration. When Nelson read that Latouche had pursued him "till nightfall", he fell into a black rage. He wrote to his brother:

"You will have seen Monsieur La Touche's letter of how he chased me and I *ran*. I keep it; and, by God, if I take him, he shall *eat* it!"

This adversary, whom he had kept in the field of his telescope for six months, without ever an opportunity to go ashore and relax, made Nelson positively ill.

"I shall chase him to India," he proclaimed.

He was not to be put to the trouble.

*

After a stay of twelve days at Boulogne, during which he had weighed and estimated every contingency, Napoleon wrote to Decrès on August 2, 1804:

"It is my desire that you dispatch post-haste a special courier to Toulon to infirm General Latouche that, in view of the fact that a number of units of the invasion fleet have found it impossible to join up, I have judged that a month's postponement will be all to the good, especially as the nights will be getting longer. . . ."

Once more it was put off, due to the fact, admitted by the Emperor himself, that the fleet was still far from being complete, and perhaps also to some gloomy foreboding.

In any case, Napoleon did not seem in the least put out. After having reviewed in turn the possibilities of winter, spring and summer, he returned to the conclusion that, everything considered, the autumn was still the most favourable season for the project, and that he must have patience and wait for it. Moreover, he spoke no more of returning to Paris, but, to maintain his troops in good heart and to keep them exercising, he ordered a repetition of that spectacle that was to become a byword in history and legend—the distribution of crosses of the *Légion d'Honneur*.

This day of celebration was truly an immense occasion, for 100,000 men were there to cheer their "Little Corporal" to the echo, whilst a detachment of the invasion fleet from le Havre entered the harbour at Boulogne under the fire of the English cruiser squadron. The date was August 16. Hearts were intoxicated and energies galvanised—if indeed that had still been necessary.

In England meanwhile the implacable Pitt had returned to power. He had just launched into battle "St George's Cavalry",[1] in the form of an extraordinary loan of two and a half millions sterling "for use on the Continent" to rally Europe against the Emperor. Russia indeed was already making overtures to Prussia and Austria. But facing England was this army unique in its power, its discipline, and its fierce attachment to a single man.

For a few hours the uncertain course of events was forgotten in the distribution of crosses and eagles. But, as Napoleon himself had said, all depended on Time and Destiny. And Destiny now took a hand. For on August 20, 1804 on board the *Bucentaure* in the roadstead of Toulon, Vice-Admiral Latouche-Tréville, who had been confined to his bed for a week, died from a fever he had contracted in the West Indies.

*

The news caught Napoleon as he was setting out for the Rhineland (he was anxious to see for himself what was afoot on France's eastern frontier). Twenty-four hours earlier the Boulogne fleet had brilliantly repulsed an attack by the English cruiser squadron, in which the latter, apart from material damage, lost 80 men killed and wounded.

It was a hard blow.

On August 28, 1804 the Emperor wrote to Decrès from Saint-Omer: "Not a moment must be lost in posting an admiral capable of commanding the Toulon squadron. . . . There are only three possibilities: Bruix, Villeneuve or Rosily. You may sound Bruix. I think Rosily has the will for it, but he has done nothing for fifteen years. At all events an early decision must be made."

After writing this letter he left Saint-Omer for Aix-la-Chapelle and Mayence, having given orders that the death of Latouche-Tréville should be hushed up for a time, so that

---

[1] English money, so-called from the design of a mounted St George on the reverse of the gold coins. (Translator's note.)

London should not be able to turn it to account. He was troubled in spirit, racked with doubt and dilemma. No less so were his immediate assistants. Thus at this very moment Bruix, of whom he was thinking in his carriage, was writing from Boulogne to M. de Talleyrand "for his eye alone":

"During the Emperor's stay here, I experienced much trouble and fatigue, as well as a few vexations. His Majesty seemed dissatisfied with what I had done: I am by no means certain of the opinion he may have formed of my zeal and devotion. This is not surprising: among the thousand and one things that had to be done here, his attention was only drawn to the small number that remained undone. All the difficulties I had overcome were quickly passed over. His Majesty's eye was concentrated only on those that might perhaps appear to have been neglected or forgotten. . . .

"You must judge, my dear Talleyrand, from all that I have just said, how sorely my heart has been vexed and what a miserable situation I am in, both now and for the future. My health, which has been maintained only by my courage and desire to serve the Emperor, is going rapidly downhill, and it may be that I am fated not to be justly appreciated by the Emperor until I am dead. . . ."

Tragic and prophetic words! A few weeks later he arrived in Paris for the coronation of a master whose favour he feared he had forfeited. He too took to the bed from which he was never again to rise up.

Latouche-Tréville died at the moment he was expected to sail (and he could have done so the more easily as Nelson's exhausted squadron had relaxed its vigilance); Bruix felt and announced the near approach of death. It was under this double omen that the great naval drama of the Empire was about to begin.

VI

THE CAMPAIGN OPENS

On September 2, 1804 Napoleon arrived at Aix-la-Chapelle. Since his visit to Boulogne, his mind had been incessantly preoccupied by the death of Latouche-Tréville and by the equivocal attitude of the European powers. Even before going to meditate before the tomb where Charlemagne had lain for a thousand years, he received Count Cobenzl, the Austrian Ambassador, in the palace. He had come to assure Napoleon that the Emperor Franz desired nothing more than to live at peace with France, and that he had no intention of objecting to Napoleon's assumption of the title of Emperor. But at the same time the Russian chargé d'affaires was leaving Paris. Although no actual rupture had followed his request for a passport, the situation needed the most careful watching.

On September 4 Napoleon wrote to Decrès: "It is impossible to forecast what may happen here in the next two or three months. *Cancel all our northern projects and put everything possible into storage.* Let me know what the dangers are and what is the best course of action. But do nothing unless I have personally approved the steps you consider should be taken."

This meant that the preparations for invading England were to be abandoned, but only provisionally, for Napoleon immediately decided to convert the temporary camp of Boulogne into a *permanent* naval and military establishment to serve his political purposes at any given moment during the war—no longer only at a precise date fixed in advance.

He explained himself in a further letter to Decrès: "So far, we have thought of the invasion fleet in terms of an *expedition*;

from now on we must treat it as a *fixed establishment*, and pay the greatest attention to all its permanent elements. It will not be administered along naval lines."

So Napoleon's orders were carried out; the enormous war-machine was trimmed, mulled over, cut up and reassembled at distant points (at Aix-la-Chapelle to begin with, then at Cologne, Coblenz or Mainz); it was recast to make it more flexible and less costly. The invasion fleet was divided into seven detachments of 108 vessels each: two at Étaples (the left wing); four at Boulogne (centre and right wing); and one at Wimereux (in reserve). This did not include the Batavian squadron, and some 500 unarmed craft organised in 30 divisions for the transport of horses, guns and stores.

At this time Decrès was busy in Paris arranging for a successor to the ill-fated Latouche-Tréville.

Bruix was eliminated, as being indispensable at Boulogne; Rosily had been for too long out of touch with events; Decrès finally turned to Pierre de Villeneuve, in command of the Rochefort squadron, and, to replace him, decided on Rear-Admiral Missiessy, Ganteaume's second-in-command at Brest.

The two admirals had been summoned by the Minister during the first fortnight of September. A few days later a courier brought to Napoleon at Aix-la-Chapelle the following historic letter from Decrès:

"Sire,

"Vice-Admiral Villeneuve and Rear-Admiral Missiessy are here with me.

"I have spoken to the former about the grand plan. . . .

"He listened coldly, and said nothing for a few moments. Then, with a calm smile, he remarked to me 'I am expecting something of the kind; but before they can be accepted, such plans have to be complete. . . .' You will permit me to write down for your benefit the actual words of a reply made in a private conversation, because it will give you a clearer picture of his reaction to my approach. He went on to say 'It would

not take me four hours to join up with the first ship;[1] with
the other five and my own detachment, I shall have forces
enough. My luck must hold, and to prove it, I will accept the
task.'

"We spoke of the route to be followed, and on that subject
he is of Your Majesty's opinion. He only noticed adverse
possibilities to the extent of showing me that they did not put
him off. Nothing daunted him in the whole project.

"His position as a high-ranking officer—a vice-admiral—
has completely transformed him. All his fears have faded
before a vision of future glory, and in the end he said 'I am
entirely at your disposal' in a tone and with a gesture suggesting
a calm and final decision.

"He will proceed to Toulon as soon as Your Majesty has
been good enough to let me know that you have no other
orders for him."

This passage is followed by a few reflections on Missiessy—
discontented at not having been promoted vice-admiral, discontented at not being given command of the Mediterranean
squadron, and finally ordered to report to Rochefort within a
week. But he was not an essential factor: the essential was
Pierre de Villeneuve, that "lucky man" to whose appointment
Napoleon was about to give full ratification with the most
disastrous results to the French navy.

*

Pierre-Charles-Jean-Baptiste-Sylvestre de Villeneuve was 41
years of age. He was born at Valensole, in Provence, on
December 31, 1763, and entered the navy in his sixteenth year.
As a nobleman, he was degraded in November 1793, but rein-
stated in May 1795. At the time of which we are speaking,
therefore, he had 24 years' service behind him.

---

[1] In plain language: the *Aigle* which was then at Cadiz: similarly "with
the other five and my own detachment" means "with Missiessy's five of
the line (the Rochefort squadron) and the ten under my command at
Toulon."

Until Aboukir his career had not been in any way outstanding. We only know that during the American war he had distinguished himself as ship's ensign, especially at Tobago, before Saint-Christophe and in Les Saintes Islands; that he was promoted lieutenant in 1786, and *capitaine de vaisseau* in 1793; but this position had not been one of any importance until his return to favour with the authorities. It was thus that he was appointed, in succession, major-general at Toulon and commander of the line of battleship *Peuple-Souverain*; in the spring of 1796 he was raised to the rank of commodore, and promoted rear-admiral six months later.

It is always dangerous to judge from appearances. Lithographed portraits of Rear-Admiral Villeneuve that have come down to us show energetic features and a firm wilful chin under a perruque of the old fashion, carefully set and powdered. The fact was that, granting him a good appearance and his share of physical courage, he had neither the will-power nor the energy the artists have endowed him with—the stuff of which great commanders are made. He was withdrawn and diffident, timorous in the extreme, a prey to doubts, irresolute and incapable of making a quick decision or of assuming the least responsibility. "He is a coward not at heart, but in spirit," Admiral Jurien de la Gravière said of him. This is a fair verdict. Aboukir, where he commanded the rearguard, showed Villeneuve "the coward in spirit", remaining inactive throughout the battle, not daring to go to the assistance of the doomed fleet, for fear that his movement might be interpreted as an attempt at flight, and finally deciding to withdraw in order to take refuge at Malta with two ships of the line and two of the frigates of Decrès. At Malta, on the other hand, a few months later, there was revealed (as was the case with Decrès) the Villeneuve of true-tempered courage, no "coward at heart", holding out in an epic siege, and only yielding under weight of numbers.

Logically speaking, the Aboukir episode should have done Villeneuve almost irreparable harm. Instead, it helped him.

The mere fact that (although by flight) he had succeeded in snatching four vessels from Nelson's grasp filled people with enthusiasm. "Here at least," they said, "is a French seaman different from the rest. The English could neither catch nor kill him!"

He thus reached the height of fame—at which he had never aimed—and may ·have ended up by believing himself in his "luck". At all events the account of his interview with Decrès points in that direction.

Napoleon's attitude remains to be explained. Most certainly the Emperor was not unaffected by the legend of the "lucky man". Doubtless, however, he had not been entirely convinced by it, and even less by the excessive enthusiasm manifested by Decrès. He was too good a judge of human nature not to have realised that Villeneuve could never truly replace Latouche-Tréville. But he was pressed for time and had to choose when there was in fact no choice; he had therefore no alternative but to approve the appointment of Villeneuve to the command of his leading squadron. Only, as a precaution, he began a complete revision of his plans.

*

At Mainz, on September 27, 1804, Napoleon communicated to his Ministers of War and of the Navy the outcome of his latest cogitations.

The whole previous plan, hinging on the manœuvre of Latouche-Tréville, had been shelved, and had been replaced by a chain of operations involving the active participation of the three squadrons of Toulon, Rochefort and Brest, while the invasion fleet at Boulogne awaited its auspicious moment.

His proposals fell under four heads:

1. The Toulon squadron (Villeneuve), taking on board 7,000 men under the command of Generals Lauriston and Reille, and being the first to set sail from France, would make for the west coast of Africa to relieve Senegal and destroy the English factories there; proceed thence to the conquest of St Helena,

and thence again to the Caribbean to join up with the Roche-fort squadron. The combined force would then take possession of Dutch Guiana, which had fallen into the hands of the English, and at the same time carry assistance to San Domingo.

2. The Rochefort squadron (Missiessy), taking on board 4,000 men under the command of General Lagrange, and setting sail from France after Villeneuve, would make straight for the West Indies, reinforce Martinique and Gaudeloupe, raid Dominica and St Lucia, and then, joining up with the Toulon squadron, would act in conjunction with it, as indicated above.

3. On the return journey, the united force would lift the blockade of Gourdon's squadron at Ferrol, and complete the operation by returning with the latter to Rochefort.

4. Finally the Brest squadron (Ganteaume), on which this time the chief rôle devolved, would set sail unexpectedly thirty or forty days after the other two had left home waters. Those latter, he thought, would draw off the English cruisers at their heels; and meanwhile Ganteaume's squadron would disembark an army corps of 18,000 men in Ireland, under the command of Marshal Augereau. It would then sail into the Straits of Dover, make for Cherbourg, and there await news from Boulogne, so as to cover the crossing of the invasion fleet. If on arrival off Boulogne contrary winds were encountered over a period of several days, and the squadron was obliged to pass the straits, it should make for the Texel. Seven Dutch warships and 25,000 men on board under the command of Marmont would be found there, and these were to be convoyed to Ireland.

Villeneuve was to leave France on October 12, Missiessy on November 1, and Ganteaume on December 22; the whole operation was expected to be completed by April 1805.

This vast project, the sum of four considerable separate operations, was capable of producing an admittedly secondary but by no means negligible result in combining the Toulon, Rochefort and Ferrol detachments, as a preliminary to a final concentration—that is, if everything went according to plan. But to open way for the invasion of England was clearly quite another matter. In fact, it could hardly be supposed that the English would be so simple as to fall into the trap by deliberately chasing after the squadrons making their feint towards the West Indies and so leave the Channel approaches wide open to Ganteaume.

Perhaps Napoleon was once more trying to confuse the enemy; perhaps he just wanted to gain a little breathing-space and improve his strategic position whilst awaiting developments he could not foresee. Or perhaps all he wanted was to save face, being well aware that his grand design could never be realised because of the inferiority of his fleet, and that in any case the psychological moment had come and gone. One thing is certain: not even the first step had been taken to carry out his instructions for the Brest squadron, spread far and wide in the evident desire to attract the enemy's attention. Even in the case of the Toulon and Rochefort squadrons there was much delay.

On September 27, 1804 Napoleon wrote to Berthier: "Cousin, I have decided upon the Irish expedition, and in this connection you will hold discussions with Marshal Augereau. There are facilities at Brest for embarking 18,000 men. General Marmont, for his part, is ready with 25,000, and these he will attempt to disembark in Ireland, placing himself under the orders of Marshal Augereau. Meanwhile, the Boulogne main force will embark, and every effort will be made to land it in Kent. . . ."

On September 29 he made clear to Decrès his views on the landing in Ireland of Augereau and Marmont's forces, observing: "One or other of these operations must succeed, and then, whether I have 30,000 or 40,000 men in Ireland, or whether I am in both Ireland and England, we shall have won the war."

On the same day he wrote again to Berthier, about the command of the troops for the Toulon squadron, to which. as we have seen, General Lauriston had been appointed:

"I wish General Lauriston's appointment to remain unpublished as long as possible; he will report there as if for normal duty."

Then he sent word to Decrès: "You may call into consultation the captain at Boulogne who has a good knowledge of the sea off Guiana. But tell him nothing. At the last minute he will proceed to Toulon, report to General de Villeneuve, and then do everything to make known the fact that he has embarked."

*

If it had been a game of poker, the Emperor's play could not have been more subtle. But the game was only beginning, and it was not long before unforeseen developments were to alter its course.

Thus on October 5, 1804 an English squadron off Cadiz wantonly intercepted four Spanish frigates on their way back from the Americas with twelve thousand million silver piastres on board. For some time England had been taxing the nominally neutral Spanish court with favouring France, and an incident was brewing. The commander of the small Spanish division refused to be interrogated, and the English opened fire. After a few minutes, one of the frigates blew up, and the other three had to surrender, as they were too lightly armed to resist.

This characteristic act of aggression aroused the wrath of Spain; its immediate effect was to draw her closer to France. Two months later, on December 4, 1804 Spain declared war on England.

Meanwhile at Toulon, on October 26, Admiral Villeneuve had taken the place of Latouche-Tréville in command of the squadron, and hoisted his flag in the *Bucentaure*. The very next day he wrote to Decrès:

"I cannot but tell you, Sir, how satisfied I am with all I have seen of the squadron."

This was an encouraging tone. In fact, Villeneuve had entered upon his task with no less enthusiasm than enterprise. From the beginning of November he began arranging for the embarkation of the troops, with their munitions and supplies, so as to be ready to put to sea at the first signal. But it was not until December 19 that a special courier brought him the Emperor's final orders. Once again events had failed to keep abreast of Napoleon's plans. It may be recalled that during his stay at Mainz he had decided that the Mediterranean squadron must set sail by mid-October at latest. But his approaching coronation upset everything. Admirals Bruix and Ganteaume, who had travelled specially from Boulogne and Brest, were conspicuous at the ceremony in Notre Dame on December 2. Unless they were there by the Emperor's special intention in order to mislead the spies, their presence indicated more clearly than pages of reports that the invasion of England was far from imminent.

When the coronation illuminations were extinguished, Napoleon found himself once again, as the year 1805 opened, a prey to hesitation and doubt.

The war had lasted eighteen months. To gain the necessary strength to deal her enemy a decisive blow, France had increased her forces to a level never reached before. The situation on the Continent, which she had found highly alarming in October, had now clearly eased. England had failed to draw Russia into the war; Prussia's attitude had at one time been threatening, but she had now hastily withdrawn into her shell; whilst Austria, who had recently been crouched for a spring, was now at pains to declare her peaceful intentions.

The Emperor was not deceived. He fully realised that the easing of tension in his rear was only provisional, and that if a blow were not soon struck at England's heart, "St George's Cavalry" would in the end engage the armies of Russia, Prussia and Austria in an attack on France. So he must act, and act quickly, since Spain was now on the side of France, and had brought her a valuable accession of strength. But what action should he take?

War with England, as Napoleon knew from experience, was different from other wars. It was an endurance test in which the sea, ubiquitous and beyond human control, was the crucial factor—it determined the present and moulded the future. Although his father had actually wanted Napoleon to be a sailor and although he was, of course, an islander like his foes, the sea had no place in Napoleon's make-up. It escaped his genius, it tried his patience, and it bedevilled his normally clear vision. He turned to the sea at the wrong moment, and besides, he had not the means of putting himself on an equal footing with England, even with luck on his side. No doubt the invasion fleet was an immense achievement, but its very nature precluded comparison with the French Grand Fleet as it had been known in the time of Tourville and Colbert. In those days, indeed, it would have been an epic struggle!

Once again, then, action was necessary; first, because of the pressure of the political situation, and secondly because after months of hope and tension, a sense of discouragement was beginning to take hold of the minds of ordinary people.

Major A. Thomazi states that the morale of the Grand Army was weakening. Out of 130,000 men there were 4,000 deserters and 10,000 sick. Forfait the engineer was complaining, "It seems clear to me that the army no longer believes in the invasion: I hear the subject discussed daily in terms that make me despair."

And the Naval Prefect of the 1st District, for his part, went so far as to propose that most of the invasion fleet vessels should be disarmed: "Since the political veil that covers a mighty operation has slipped aside to reveal an obvious postponement, of which, indeed, everybody is aware, there can be nothing wrong in taking such steps as prudent economy prescribes."

There was no further question of the landing in Ireland. The Brest squadron had not budged. On the other hand Missiessy at Rochefort and Villeneuve at Toulon were all ready to put to sea.

The instructions given at Mainz concerning Missiessy had been only slightly modified. Villeneuve's orders, on the contrary—which as we have seen he had received at Toulon on

December 19—had been considerably altered. All idea of operations in Senegal and St Helena had now been abandoned. Villeneuve was appointed commander-in-chief of naval forces for the Americas. He was instructed to make straight for Cayenne from Toulon, take on reinforcements there, and proceed to attack Surinam and Demerara. At Martinique he was to join up with Missiessy, who would meanwhile have captured Dominica and St Lucia, to raid the British West Indies and carry supplies to San Domingo. Finally they were to return to Rochefort via Ferrol in order to lift the blockade of Gourdon. Naturally the whole plan was timed, minuted and laid down in every detail by the Emperor with an equal mixture of care and misgiving regarding those who were to carry it out.

So, then, the game was on. But Napoleon still hesitated. He was sorely troubled. So much so, in fact, that on January 2, 1805 he attempted to open peace negotiations by addressing a final and pathetic communication direct to "My brother the King of England":

"My dear Brother,
"Since I was called to the throne of France by Providence and by the suffrage of the Senate, the people, and the army, my foremost and most earnest desire has been for peace. France and England are squandering their prosperity. Their struggle may continue for centuries. But are their governments discharging their most sacred duty? Is not their conscience-troubled by such a useless effusion of blood with no real end in view? I count it no dishonour to be taking the first step in this matter. I fancy I have shown the world that I am nowise daunted by the hazards of war; indeed, war holds no terrors for me. Peace is the dearest wish of my heart, but war has never diminished my reputation. I charge Your Majesty not to reject the happy opportunity of yourself conferring peace upon the world. Let not that sweet satisfaction be left to your children!"

Enlarging the scope of the discussion, the Emperor appealed to the conscience of his illustrious correspondent across the Channel:

"For, all things considered," he continued, "there has never been a fairer juncture or a more auspicious moment for stilling all the angry passions and listening only to the voice of humanity and reason. If the moment passes, how can this war reach an end, when all my efforts have failed to bring it to a conclusion?"

Then, hoping to carry conviction by an appeal to reason, he added:

"In the last ten years Your Majesty has won more territory and wealth than all Europe contains. Your kingdom is on a peak of prosperity. What advantage can it hope to gain from war? To form some coalition of the continental powers? But the Continent will remain undisturbed; the only result of such a coalition would be to increase the pre-eminence and the glory of France. To revive internal conflicts? But times have changed. To ruin our finances? But a financial system founded on a basis of sound agriculture can never be ruined. To relieve France of her colonies! But for France colonies are a secondary factor: and in any case has not Your Majesty already more colonies than you can maintain?"

He concluded: "If Your Majesty will but consider the matter personally, you will see that the war is purposeless, and can lead to no definite result. And it is a miserable prospect for two peoples to fight merely for the sake of fighting. The world is big enough for both our peoples to live in. Reason commands the means of reconciliation, given good will on both sides. In any case I have discharged a sacred duty, and one very dear to my heart.

"I trust that Your Majesty will credit the sincerity of the sentiments I have expressed, and of my desire to prove them in action."

This final appeal was carried by an *enseigne de vaisseau* on board a brig belonging to the English cruiser squadron on watch off Boulogne. It arrived at the end of a war of nerves, dull, yet painful, and of many months' duration, in the course of which both nations, defying each other across the Channel, had reached the summit of their powers, the one offensive and the other defensive. It could therefore no longer carry any weight.

It was indeed too late to turn back the course of history. On January 8, 1805 an agreement was signed by Admiral Decrès on the one hand and Admiral Gravina on the other to regulate naval co-operation between France and Spain. By the terms of the agreement France undertook to maintain at sea 47 of the line, and to expedite the construction of a further 16; Spain, on her side, undertook to arm 32 ships of the line and frigates by March 30. Thus in the spring Napoleon would have available some 70 of the line instead of 45. Admittedly this fell far short of the English fleet of 150 of the line—both in numbers and quality (for many exaggerated ideas of the condition of the Spanish fleet were current). But a fleet of such size, properly trained and under vigorous command, throwing all into the balance, could still force an opening in the Straits of Dover, and, given control of the sea for a few hours, could ensure a successful landing. This fleet, however, was very far from being ready for action; meanwhile the forces available must not be squandered on operations of secondary importance, for these, besides having no bearing on the main object in view, might cause serious trouble—as indeed occurred in the case of the Rochefort squadron.

On January 11 Missiessy took advantage of the bad weather that kept the watching English cruisers out of sight, and set sail from the island of Aix for the West Indies with five ships of the line and five frigates. He made all speed to the Bay of Biscay, and thus opened the campaign—a campaign that was ultimately to spell the doom of the French navy.

Three days later the Cabinet in London replied to

Napoleon's message to the King of England with a temporising statement of a not unthreatening nature:

"His Majesty considers it impossible to give any definite reply to the overtures which have been received until he has had time to communicate with the Continental Powers to whom His Majesty is attached in close relationship by alliances, especially with the Emperor of Russia who has given the strongest proofs of the wise and noble feelings which actuate him and of the interest that he takes in the safety and independence of Europe."

At last, on January 18, Villeneuve in his turn put to sea from Toulon, with the same destination as Missiessy—the West Indies.

VII

A MESSAGE GOES ASTRAY

VILLENEUVE was ready to put to sea at the end of December, but had to wait another three weeks for a favourable wind before he could start out on his mission.

His squadron comprised 11 ships of the line, seven frigates and two light craft. On board were 6,500 soldiers under the command of General Lauriston.

At dawn on January 18 a brisk north-westerly breeze sprang up, and the admiral immediately gave the order to move. One hour later the French squadron was on its way, much to the surprise of two English frigates that Nelson had stationed out to sea. . . .

Now, in the red glow of the sunset, the twenty vessels headed south. All day the English frigates had kept them under observation, and it was only as evening came on that the latter made a half turn and sailed eastwards, on their way to warn their Commander-in-Chief.

On December 27 Villeneuve had made an announcement in order to allay the anxiety of both troops and crews, who had no notion of the enterprise on which they were launched: "There is no cause for alarm if we sight an English squadron; their ships are worn out after two years' cruising duty."

But the men had not been greatly reassured: nor, for that matter, had Villeneuve himself. In the quiet of his cabin he wrote repeatedly to Decrès:

December 31. "The departure of my squadron is known all over the Mediterranean. Nelson knows it too. It will not be easy to slip away from him."

January 4. "Admiral Nelson certainly knows what is known all over the Mediterranean—that we have set out, and that there are landing forces on board. As it is so much to his interest to catch up with us, we must suppose that all our escape routes are carefully watched. It will be all the more difficult for me to succeed in this enterprise, because I have reason to believe that the sailing of the ships in the squadron will be very uneven."

January 7. "It will be hard for me to reach Gibraltar unimpeded. I only hope I may come through with flags flying."

But alas! The flags were destined to droop long before the squadron sighted the Pillars of Hercules.

*

Meanwhile Nelson lay at anchor with 11 ships of the line off the island of Maddalena at the northern tip of Sardinia. At three o'clock in the afternoon of January 19 his frigates from Toulon appeared on the horizon.

These two frigates had run before a following wind with unusual speed and suddenly appeared out of the blue with a signal at the mast-head: "The enemy fleet has put to sea."

For months Nelson had longed to see that signal, and now he lost no time. The commanders of the frigates were immediately called on board, and declared that when last seen the French were heading south. From this Nelson deduced that without a doubt Villeneuve was making for Egypt. He must therefore sail into the Tyrrhenian Sea without delay and try to bar his route. By 4.30 the whole squadron was under sail and had entered the narrow channel between Maddalena and the north-easterly point of Sardinia. An hour later it was coming out into the open sea.

Night was falling. The wind had freshened considerably during the afternoon, and there were signs of an approaching storm that would severely test ships and men alike. One hundred and fifty miles away Villeneuve was also beginning to experience it. His ships that had been sailing in good order the previous day, were now in confusion. The *Indomptable* had lost two topmasts, and together with three frigates had become separated from the main body; the *Annibal* had broken her foreyard and was drifting alongside the *Neptune* which had lost her mainmast. Other ships, rolling from side to side, seemed exhausted and incapable of keeping in line.

The confidence of the French sailors and their commander sank as the sky lowered.

On January 20 the hurricane that had travelled from the Gulf of Lions across Sardinia reached the Tyrrhenian Sea.

Thanks to Nelson's precautions, the English fleet was lying to, and safely weathered the storm. But the French fleet became even more disordered. The soldiers screamed with fright. The sailors, instead of calming them down, yielded to their own lack of experience, and talked of nothing but returning to port. Villeneuve himself, dogged by the fear of seeing Nelson fall on his rear to crown his misfortunes, did not know which way to turn. He "meditated" in his cabin, glued to his armchair. Should he ride out the storm, or should he put about and return to Toulon?

A conversation with Lauriston precipitated a decision, and towards five o'clock in the afternoon the fleet turned back for France once more. It regained Toulon the following day, more worn out than if it had sailed three times round the world. One ship of the line, the *Indomptable*, that had run for shelter to Corsica, and three frigates were missing.

Nelson, being Nelson, held on: he held on to the end. The storm did not die down before January 26. It was then that he learnt that the *Indomptable*, much battered, had entered the harbour of Ajaccio on the 21st. He paid no attention to this, but set a fresh course to Palermo, which he reached on the 28th. When he was assured that nobody there had word of Villeneuve he shrugged his shoulders: "Most certainly," said he, "he must have done as I did, so—unless he has gone to the bottom—he is in Egypt." Without disembarking, therefore, he made straight for Alexandria, arriving on February 8, feverish, and almost ashamed of having lost track of his antagonist. It was not until February 14 that he learnt the truth, and groaned with frustration. He wrote to the Admiralty: "I consulted no man, therefore the whole blame of ignorance in forming my judgment must rest with me."

But he quickly corrected himself, adding: "At this moment of sorrow, I still feel I have acted right."

*

It was thus that a plan that had cost the Emperor more than three months' work was demolished in less than three days.

There can be little doubt that the success or failure of the Toulon squadron's mission had little bearing on the success of the invasion of England. Unfortunately, however, Villeneuve's fiasco not only left Missiessy's squadron "up in the air", but was to cause widespread repercussions. Even before it put to sea, the French Mediterranean fleet had no very brilliant record; now it had lost the little reputation that remained to it, and, worse still, its admiral had turned out a complete failure.

Villeneuve had scarcely anchored before he was sending to Decrès a catalogue of his misfortunes: "I have bad news for you of the squadron and of its return to harbour here. . . ."

For form's sake he still spoke of his good fortune as the "lucky" man, satisfied that he had escaped the worst—Nelson to wit ("fortune did not abandon me at this juncture"), then added with a deep sigh: "The Toulon squadron made an excellent showing in the roadstead, the crews well equipped and carrying out their exercises efficiently. But as soon as the storm caught up with us, things became very different. . . ."

The only proposal he made in the end was to resign his post:

"I beg you to recall that I never sought command of this squadron, and furthermore, that my aim was a career of usefulness, rather than of glory. . . .

"I have no hesitation in telling you that the reward of my profession is nothing but shame and embarrassment. Those who think differently are in my opinion presumptuous, blind and incapable of rational thought, ignorant alike of our own situation and of the enemy's.

"I should be extremely pleased if the Emperor would appoint a successor to me in this Command, whether the intention is to remain in port, or to put to sea again. My only wish is to see my conduct of the affair justified. At all costs I would avoid becoming a byword in Europe after a succession of fresh disasters."

Decrès sent a stern reply. He considered, not unreasonably, that "the dismasting and separation from the main body of the line of battleship *Indomptable* was a contingency that might have been foreseen, and repairs could surely have been carried out at the appointed rendezvous".[1]

But he took care not to inform the Emperor of Villeneuve's desire to be relieved of his command.

In fact all indications are that Napoleon was given an incomplete report; he merely shrugged his shoulders, expressing once more his distrust of naval officers incapable of giving effect to his plans. What could he do with admirals whose only thought was to return to harbour in their dismay at the first taste of bad weather? On February 5 he wrote to Lauriston: "Your admiral showed a lack of decision. A few smashed topmasts, and a certain amount of confusion during a storm, are nothing out of the ordinary. A couple of fine days would have cheered up the squadron again and put everything to rights. The most serious defect of our navy is that the men in command are new to all the vicissitudes of command."

His words were justified and profoundly true. They were to be echoed by the English, though they had not heard them; for, in justification of his long and fruitless chase after the French squadron, Nelson wrote: "I considered the character of

[1] The *Indomptable* had taken shelter at Ajaccio, and returned to Toulon on February 17. The three frigates that had also become separated from the main body rejoined on February 10, March 4 and March 18 respectively. Two of them had succeeded in sinking two English sloops escorting a convoy off Cartagena, one mounted with 32 carronades and the other with 10.

Bonaparte; and that the orders given by him, on the banks of the Seine, would not take into consideration winds or weather, nor indeed could the accident of even three or four ships alter, in my opinion, a destination of importance."

He added, with a certain pride:

"These gentlemen [the French sailors] are not accustomed to a Gulf of Lions gale, which we have buffeted for twenty-one months and not carried away a spar."

Nevertheless, the fact that Napoleon was not violently agitated by Villeneuve's set-back, and had not immediately punished him severely, was a clear proof that the Emperor now attached no more than a relative importance to the abortive scheme.

The reason was simply that ever since he had given Villeneuve his final orders (December 19), and especially since the treaty with Spain (January 8), Napoleon had been unceasingly hatching fresh schemes. So it was that on January 16, five days after Missiessy had sailed and two days before Villeneuve's false start, he had bluntly told Decrès that he intended to undermine English power in India by dispatching thither a strong detachment of several dozen French and Spanish ships with an army of 30,000 to 35,000 men on board.

For several reasons, among them the departure of the Rochefort and Toulon squadrons, this surprising scheme was not followed up. But the fact that it was in the Emperor's mind shows clearly that on the eve of embarking on a course of action—or rather, at the very moment when his latest orders were beginning to be put into execution—he was in a state of strange indecision as to the direction in which to strike, whether in the West Indies, in India, in Ireland, or at Boulogne. The map of the world swam before his eyes and he found himself unable to decide on any one area and stick to it.

All in all, it was no great embarrassment that Villeneuve's expedition had misfired; on the other hand, it was very annoying that Missiessy, whose mission had succeeded, was now lingering at Martinique, awaiting the Toulon squadron, thus putting France in danger of being deprived of the valuable assistance of his 10 warships for a considerable period. Immediate steps were taken to give him the alarm.

On February 1, less than four days after Villeneuve's first dispatch arrived in Paris, a brig sailed from Lorient to meet Missiessy in the West Indies. She carried a message from Decrès announcing Villeneuve's set-back and cancelling the combined operation previously arranged.

For another whole month the Emperor hesitated between two extreme courses: whether to continue his recent diversionary tactics by striking at England through her overseas possessions—India especially—or whether to return to the strategic offensive of the previous year by launching a direct attack on the very soil of "Albion", using the High Seas Fleet to open a passage for the invasion fleet of Boulogne.

At length the diplomatic situation on the Continent eased considerably, and he gained an unexpected breathing-space; at the same time the Spanish fleet, then being armed, was represented to him once more as a powerful trump card. He therefore decided on the more dangerous alternative, which would, if successful, be the only means of putting a speedy end to the war—overpowering England on her own soil.

How achieve this object?

If the gallant Missiessy had not taken his "untimely" departure, Napoleon could have resumed, with slight variations, the plan he had lately entrusted to Latouche-Tréville. But apart from the fact that he now had no great confidence in the abilities of Villeneuve, the Rochefort squadron, the pick of the fleet for quality and training, was now in the West Indies. He was thus induced to widen considerably the scope of his scheme of May 25, 1804 and to make Missiessy at Martinique the point of concentration.

And so on March 2, 1805 the following combined movements were ordered:

1. Villeneuve, with 11 ships of the line, six frigates and two

brigs, will set sail from Toulon at the first opportunity, making for Fort-de-France, Martinique. On his way he will pick up at Cadiz the *Aigle* and any of the Spanish ships that might be ready to put to sea. He will join Missiessy at Martinique and wait there 40 days for Ganteaume's Brest squadron. If there is no sign of the latter at the end of this period, he will proceed to San Domingo, disembark 1,300 troops, and cruise to the Canaries to await Ganteaume for another 20 days; then if he had still not arrived, Villeneuve will return to Cadiz where he will receive fresh instructions.

2. Ganteaume will also set sail from Brest at the first opportunity, with 21 ships of the line, six frigates and two transports. He will make for Ferrol and try to relieve Gourdon, with his five warships, and such Spanish warships as are ready, engaging and, if possible, destroying, the English blockading squadron of seven or eight ships. This done, he will sail to Martinique to join up with Villeneuve and Missiessy who will place themselves under his command. He will then have not less than 40 ships of the line under him. With these he will return to Europe, arriving off Ushant and attacking any English ships that may attempt to bar his passage: he will then make directly for Boulogne, where the Emperor will be awaiting him. If he has found it impossible to join up with Villeneuve, the accession of Missiessy's force will be sufficient to prevent any modification of Ganteaume's mission, but if that fails him, he is to return to Ferrol, release from blockade all available forces, and then sail up to Boulogne. In any event, he is to arrive at Boulogne between June 10 and July 10.

It will be noted that this time it was to Ganteaume and *not to Villeneuve* that Napoleon had entrusted the leading rôle. But he was careful not to speak openly to the admiral of the real object of the expedition. He still wished to keep his true intentions secret to the very last, and while actually putting the finishing touches to his plan he had caused a rumour to be spread of an expedition to India, and, to cause even more confusion, he loudly announced his intention of visiting Italy in the near future. But Ganteaume was no fool. As for Villeneuve, he was busy restoring order in his squadron, and all he knew was contained in a note written by the Emperor himself: "The fate of our naval forces is closely linked with the fate of the world."[1] General Lauriston, commanding the troops on board, and so under Villeneuve's orders, was the only man who enjoyed the Emperor's confidence. Furthermore Napoleon, having explained his plans ("say nothing to anybody, whoever it may be"), ordered him to keep an eye on the admiral, and not to let him give way to his natural indolence. It was clear that His Majesty had no further confidence in the abilities of "lucky Villeneuve".

There remained Missiessy.

It may be recalled that on February 1 a brig had sailed from Lorient to apprise the commander of the Rochefort squadron of the changes that had taken place in the Emperor's plan following Villeneuve's abortive expedition. But three weeks later the new scheme suddenly made him the focus of the concentration, and on February 27 therefore, a fresh courier was sent to him urgently asking him to await the arrival of the forces of Villeneuve and Ganteaume in the West Indies, until the end of June.

Napoleon was reckoning, with the success of his combined operation in view, that this new order would reach Missiessy about the end of March or the beginning of April—before he left Martinique to return to France. Counting on his admirals' habitual leisurely movements, and the delays that usually characterised their operations, he seemed in fact to be running no risk. Unfortunately, however, in this instance Missiessy was well up to schedule. For this reason, and because he had completed his mission with remarkable speed, he was never to receive the all-important counter-order upon which all the

[1] On receipt of this letter, Villeneuve wrote to Decrès (March 7, 1805): "I suspect that Martinique is not my real destination." Then again, on March 23: "You settle my doubts on the second meeting place. . . . I have let it be thought here that I am bound for India, as you suggested."

hopes of his sovereign depended. A brief chronology of his operations will be sufficient to make the facts clear:

January 11. Missiessy sails from Rochefort for Martinique where he is to join up with Villeneuve.

February 1. A brig is dispatched by Decrès from Lorient to Martinique to inform Missiessy of Villeneuve's failure, and to cancel the intended rendezvous.

February 20. Missiessy arrives at Fort-de-France with his five ships of the line and five frigates in perfect trim. He had made an uneventful crossing apart from thirteen days' delay through contrary winds in the Bay of Biscay.

February 27. Decrès dispatches a second brig to Martinique ordering Missiessy to remain in the roadstead at Fort-de-France until the end of June, awaiting the arrival of the Toulon and Brest squadrons, this combination being part of a new plan.

March 12. Missiessy returns to Fort-de-France after sailing to Dominica to land General Lagrange's troops and support their assault. As he awaits the rendezvous with Villeneuve, the only arrival is the brig that sailed from Lorient on February 1 with the first message of Decrès: "Rendezvous cancelled."

March 22. Missiessy feels sure that the Emperor wishes him to return to France. In spite of the protests of the Governor-General of Martinique (Admiral Villaret-Joyeuse) he is unwilling to remain any longer in the Caribbean, and sets sail for Rochefort via San Domingo, where he has to land reinforcements.

March 28. Having provided 500 men, together with supplies and munitions, for the San Domingo garrison, which was then occupied with a Negro revolt, Missiessy sets his course for France.

March 30. Decrès' second message reaches Martinique, but too late. Missiessy has left.

May 20. Missiessy finally reaches Rochefort after an exhausting crossing, having been delayed by contrary winds and long periods of calm. His efficiency and perseverance have been to no purpose.

That is all. It has been said of this incident that it was "the first grain of sand to get into the wheels of the vast machine that the Emperor's genius had set once more in motion".[1] But before Napoleon learnt of it—and his wrath may be judged by Missiessy's three years' subsequent disgrace—he was confounded by another blow, a grim omen at the start of what he hoped would be a decisive operation. For on March 18, 1805, there died the great Admiral Bruix, commander of the invasion fleet at Boulogne.

[1] René Jouan, *Histoire de la Marine française*, Vol. II, p. 139.

VIII

THE CHASE TO THE WEST INDIES

To Europe, in her state of feverish tension, the spring of 1805 seemed pregnant with drama.

In Paris Napoleon issued his final orders. He worked incessantly with Decrès at his side—the only Minister who enjoyed his confidence. He pored over maps covered with dates, figures and arrows, always awaiting the arrival of dispatches from Boulogne and Brest, and personally directing the departure of couriers for Toulon and Spain.

At Madrid, Manuel Godoy, "the Prince of Peace", was perpetually receiving acrimonious notes from the Emperor. He was also lending an ear to Admiral Gravina, and forcing himself to believe that the Spanish fleet, despite its present sorry state, would revive the glories of Lepanto and avenge the wrongs of the Invincible Armada. Supplies, men and money were, of course, lacking. Nevertheless Gravina was completely under the spell of Napoleon, and swore he would follow the French fleet whatever happened. Godoy was careful not to discourage him, for he knew that a single rebuff would jeopardise his astonishing good luck.

In London the mood was tense. Pitt was organising the country's defence and preparing to strike back. Under parliamentary pressure he had just given supreme powers to an admiral of 80, Sir Charles Middleton, later Lord Barham. Sir Charles had hardly ever held command at sea, but he knew the workings of the British Navy better than anybody else, and for more than a quarter of a century had been looked upon as "the life and soul of the Admiralty and the mainspring of the Service". The old admiral awaited news of Napoleon's intentions from the numerous English agents in France. Indeed, a report dated March 1 was already on its way from a mysterious "friend" within the very walls of the Tuileries, asserting that "if the Toulon squadron can get out of port, it will join up with Gravina's force, and both will then sail for the West Indies to ravage Jamaica". This was at any rate half of Napoleon's plan.

For the rest, Sir Charles Middleton had to rely on his own intuition. Nor was he lacking in this, any more than he lacked the wherewithal both to act and to gather information. Throughout western Europe there was not a single key point that was not closely watched by a British squadron.

Thus to the north Admiral Keith, with 11 ships of the line and 150 miscellaneous vessels, was in control of the sector bounded by northern Holland and the Channel Isles. His special assignment was the six Dutch line of battleships at the Texel and the invasion fleet at Boulogne, the latter now commanded by Rear-Admiral Lacrosse, who had taken the place of Bruix. Admiral Cornwallis lay off Brest with a squadron of 18-25 ships of the line, and never let Ganteaume's 21 warships out of sight. Admiral Cochrane, with six ships of the line, was on the track of Missiessy who had left Rochefort for the West Indies. Admiral Calder, with 10 ships of the line under his command was off Ferrol blockading Gourdon's five French ships and 10 Spanish vessels in process of arming. Admiral Orde was cruising off Cadiz, with six ships of the line against seven of the allies (one of them being the French ship *Aigle*) that were ready to put to sea. Lastly, in the Mediterranean was Nelson, with 13 ships to contain the Spanish squadron of five ships at Cartagena and, above all, Villeneuve's 11 at Toulon. He had a roving commission based on Maddalena, between Sardinia and Corsica.

Such was the vast deployment maintained by the British Admiralty, as it groped after Napoleon's real intentions. In addition, several cruisers were permanently stationed at the

POSITIONS OF THE TWO FLEETS IN MARCH 1805
The figures refer to the number of ships

approaches to the Irish Sea, nine or ten ships of the line were standing by at Portsmouth, ready to set sail immediately, more than 700 little ships organised in flotillas, surrounded the English coast, and British naval units were off Africa and India, and in the Pacific. The French, then, had small chances of success in breaking through this wooden wall, as the Emperor had commanded, in order to regroup somewhere or other, and thence launch their direct assault on "perfidious" Albion.

*

By March 24, 1805 Ganteaume had completed the victualling of his ships; his crews were at full strength, and his troops on board. He signalled Napoleon from Brest:

"My naval force is ready, and can put to sea to-morrow evening. But there are 15 English line of battleships in the Iroise, and I cannot get out without risking an engagement. There can be no doubt of the result. I await Your Majesty's orders."

Napoleon replied at once:

"In the circumstances a naval victory will be fruitless. Your only object must be the fulfilment of your mission. You must slip out without an engagement. The man who is to join up with you has started already."

Being thus obliged to open up his own route to the West Indies by stealth rather than by force, all Ganteaume had to do was to await a favourable opportunity. He thought he had one on the 27th as there was a mist, and he gave orders to move. But he had hardly reached the outer anchorage when the mist lifted to reveal a mass of sails on the horizon. The look-outs counted 10-12-15 then 18 English line of battleships. It was thus impossible to sail out unnoticed, let alone slip by without an engagement. In any case, in the hope that the wind might after all scatter the enemy, Ganteaume dropped anchor under cover of the forts. For a day and a night he remained there, but after that the wind freshened, making the anchorage dangerous, and in the end he had to give up. Beaten without even being once shot at, the squadron turned its back on the sea and re-entered port.

One more set-back.

Meanwhile at Toulon, at much the same time, Villeneuve was preparing to try his luck for the second time. After a stiff easterly gale, a light breeze sprang up from the west, favouring his departure.

On the morning of the 30th, he wrote to Decrès: "My dear General, I am on the point of departure: may it be God's will that I continue to enjoy fortune's favours, for I think I shall need them badly. Whatever the outcome may be, I entrust to your long-standing friendship all that I hold dear. I have been unable to approve a number of your decisions concerning me, but this I attribute to the difficult position in which you are placed. I hope the future may have something better in store for me. And so I take my leave, assuring you of my sincere attachment."

At four o'clock in the afternoon the squadron began to move. One by one, in single line ahead, and led by the *Bucentaure*, the 11 heavy ships emerged from the roadstead to round Cape Sicié on their way to Gibraltar. Six frigates and two brigs led the way. It was cold, for the sun was already setting behind the pine-clad hills surrounding the city.

Of course, two of Nelson's frigates were prowling out at sea, and noted every detail of what they saw.

So began a game of hare-and-hounds, unprecedented in naval history, between Villeneuve and the victor of Aboukir.

When Villeneuve set out on March 30, 1805, the situation was not dissimilar to that of January 18. Once again two English frigates observed the departure of the squadron, and once again Villeneuve was completely ignorant of Nelson's exact position. And so the Toulon squadron was on the open sea, already swallowed up in the darkness. But the next morning the two English frigates, which had never lost contact, disengaged one after the other and hastened to inform their commander.

The agony of Villeneuve, now on his southerly course, and expecting Nelson to appear at any moment out of the blue, only lasted twenty-four hours in all. In fact, on April 1 a merchantman informed him that the English admiral was at Palmas, in south-western Sardinia, some 280 miles away. Evidently Nelson was clinging to his idea of a roving commission to watch the *route to Egypt*. Villeneuve heaved a sigh of relief. Seizing his chance, he immediately made course for Spain, so as to pass between the Spanish coast and the Balearic Isles on his way to Gibraltar. The distance separating the two fleets was thus increased from 280 to more than 320 miles.

Forty-eight hours later, on the morning of April 3, the two frigates found Nelson in the Gulf of Palmas, and informed him of the situation. As this was to the effect that Villeneuve had been making southwards on leaving Toulon, Nelson concluded that the French fleet was on its way to Egypt and would inevitably pass south of Sardinia. He therefore decided immediately to spread out his frigates between Sardinia and Tunis, while he himself awaited the enemy's approach at the entrance of the Sicilian channel.

Time passed, assisting one side and discomfiting the other. While Villeneuve was leisurely coasting along eastern Spain, Nelson was sailing up and down the Sicilian channel in a fury, but all to no purpose.

On the 7th the French squadron appeared off Cartagena to pick up a detachment of five line of battleships under Admiral Salcedo. But Salcedo claimed that he had received no instructions from his government, and refused to move. The enraged Villeneuve continued on his way, while Nelson, now 600 miles away, turned his back on him and made for Palermo in the hope of picking up some intelligence.

It was then that things began to move fast.

On the morning of the 9th the French squadron entered the Straits of Gibraltar, was fired on by the batteries on the Rock, but suffered no damage. In the afternoon the frigates signalled that they had sighted 11 ships of which six were of the line. This was Admiral Orde's squadron. He evidently had some misgivings at the prospect of taking on a fleet that he estimated at "20 or 24 sail", and immediately sheered off. As darkness fell, Villeneuve anchored off Cadiz. Six Spanish ships of the line and a frigate under the orders of Admiral Gravina together with a French line of battleship—the *Aigle*—and two brigs were waiting for him there, ready for sea. The commander-in-chief wished to lose no time in getting away from what he considered to be a dangerous locality, and hurried on the preparations for departure. The Spaniards did their best, but it seems they were not quick enough, for at two in the morning Villeneuve put to sea again, leaving them to sort themselves out and follow him as best they might.

At dawn on the 10th the whole allied fleet began the long Atlantic crossing. Only one Spanish warship, that of Admiral Gravina himself, had succeeded in joining up with the main body. The rest of them were far behind and might have been caught by Orde who was known to be in the area. But the latter was busy sending messages to all his fellow admirals to warn them of what he had seen—to Nelson in the Mediterranean, to Calder off Ferrol, and to Gardner (who had replaced Cornwallis, fallen sick) off Brest.

"I believe they (the Allies) are headed westward," Orde wrote to Gardner, adding that he was on his way to join him, so as to be ready for any eventuality. (Orde succeeded in joining up with Gardner off Ushant on April 30.) At the same time he dispatched a cruiser to Cape St Vincent to maintain contact with the enemy.

Thus, as Villeneuve began the second phase of his mission, Orde was effecting a concentration with Gardner, and eventually with Calder, that would prove an effective barrier if at any given moment the Franco-Spanish fleet turned north, that is, towards Brest and the Channel.

As for Nelson, on this same April 10, he had just put in to Palermo in low spirits. "All my frigates are out cruising," said he, "and I know nothing." He then received intelligence that a convoy from Portsmouth, with 10,000 English troops on board, was on its way to the Mediterranean. This information proved false, for the convoy did not leave England till the 17th, but Nelson believed that it contained the key to his problem. "Then I must suppose that the French are sailing westward," he cried. With no further delay, therefore, he decided to retrace his steps and sail westwards himself, intending to go as far as Toulon, to see if by any chance Villeneuve had returned to harbour there.

But Nelson's luck was out. From April 11-15, a relentless head-wind kept him penned in the Sicilian channel without being able to advance a single mile.

In the meantime, Villeneuve, his mind at last made easy, was sailing towards the West Indies. He had won the first lap. During this time Napoleon had stopped at Lyons on his way to Italy, and was constructing a fresh plan—yes, another plan! The continued failure of the Brest squadron to put to sea, despite his repeated exhortations, had shaken his confidence in Ganteaume. The latter could not be held responsible for the fact that he had been becalmed for some time, but the Emperor was not going to put up with an indefinite delay and thus risk the failure of his schemes. He had been impressed by Villeneuve's neat get-away, and he now decided to entrust him once more with the leading rôle. Of course the arrangements he had made on March 2 were changed from top to bottom.

"Our intention is to put you in command of the entire navy," he wrote to Villeneuve on April 14.

As a first step, Rear-Admiral Magon, taking two line of battleships lying inactive at Rochefort, was to join Villeneuve at Martinique without delay. If, 35 days after the arrival of Magon at Fort-de-France, Villeneuve still had no news of Ganteaume, he was to return to Ferrol, relieve the 15 blockaded Franco-Spanish ships that were ready to put to sea, sail up to Brest with them, where Ganteaume would join him, and then, with a force of more than 50 ships of the line, enter the Channel and join the Emperor at Boulogne.

Not content with this herculean task, which involved seizing naval supremacy by force, Napoleon gave Villeneuve a second commission. While awaiting the arrival of Ganteaume in the West Indies he was to *shed lustre on his expedition* by the conquest of St Lucia, or, failing that, some other island. The unfortunate Villeneuve, who had started out without any clear idea of Napoleon's ultimate objective, and whom nobody had told that he was to be engaged in a colonial war on arrival at Martinique, most certainly had no expectation of such great honour and such great responsibility.

Let us now return to Nelson, whom we left in the Mediterranean struggling against a westerly wind. On April 16, when he had got no farther than the south of Sardinia, the captain of a merchantman told him that the French fleet had been sighted south-west of Cartagena on the 7th. At once his spirits rose. "I am going to ascertain," he told the commander of one of his frigates, "that the French Fleet is not in Toulon, and then to proceed to the Westward, and this is all I can tell at present.... I shall send you information, when I am sure where French fleet is gone, or that I am likely to leave the Mediterranean after them."

Three days later, when the wind finally changed, events took a dramatic turn: the commander of a ship from Gibraltar asserted that the French fleet had cleared the straits on the 9th, ten days earlier. Ten days! "I am heading west," cried Nelson immediately. But he was not entirely convinced, and it was not easy to alter ideas that had once taken root in his mind: he was therefore careful to maintain a screen of frigates between the Sardinian and Tunisian coasts, so as to "intercept any expedition the enemy may send to Sardinia, to Sicily, or to Egypt". Egypt again!

Next day, the 20th, the wind once more checked the English squadron. Since the previous day Nelson had made no more than twenty miles, and he was again in despair. "My good fortune seems flown away. I cannot get a fair wind, or even a side wind. Dead foul!—Dead foul!" But his mind still reasoned with fearful clarity:

"The Enemy's Fleet having so very long ago passed the Straits and formed a junction with some Spanish ships from Cadiz," he wrote, "I think it my duty, which must be satisfactory to their Lordships, to know exactly my intentions. I have detached the *Amazon* [a frigate] to Lisbon for information, and I am proceeding off Cape St Vincent as expeditiously as possible; and I hope the *Amazon* will join me there, or that I shall obtain some positive information of the destination of the Enemy. The circumstances of their having taken the Spanish Ships which were for sea, from Cadiz, satisfies my mind that they are not bound to the West Indies (nor probably the Brazils); but intend forming a junction with the Squadron at Ferrol, and pushing direct for Ireland or Brest, as I believe the French have troops on board; therefore, if I receive no intelligence to do away my present belief, I shall proceed from Cape St Vincent, and take my position fifty leagues West from Scilly, approaching that Island slowly, that I may not miss any vessels sent in search of the Squadron with orders. My reason for this position is, that it is equally easy to get to either the Fleet off Brest, or go to Ireland . . . I shall bring with me eleven as fine ships of war, as ably commanded, and in as perfect order, and in health, as ever went to sea."

From this time and until May 5 (when Nelson arrived at Tetuan, still held back by contrary winds) there was a sort of interlude. Both parties spent it in a state of feverish suspense, awaiting detailed information of their own and each other's movements.

On the French side Decrès received at Paris the fresh orders Napoleon had drafted at Lyons. These he forwarded to Villeneuve via Rochefort, for they were to go by the hand of Admiral Magon, starting for the West Indies. He added a resounding postscript:

"The fate of the world hangs on your reaching Boulogne

successfully. Happy indeed is the admiral with whose name such a memorable event will be gloriously associated!"

Presumably the Minister was under the impression that all he had to do now was to let matters take their course. He was wrong. Napoleon had arrived in Italy on the 20th and had just heard how Villeneuve had given Nelson the slip: he was wild with enthusiasm, and as a natural consequence was once more engaged in altering his plans! He was convinced that Nelson would remain for some time a prey to his besetting sin—the Egyptian delusion—for the French press were under orders to print accounts of Villeneuve on the way to Alexandria. He therefore sent word to Decrès on April 23 that the time thus gained must be put to profitable use: in Europe, the Spanish squadron at Cartagena must reinforce Cadiz, and in the West Indies Villeneuve must operate on a vastly extended scale.

"He must seize St Vincent, Antigua and Grenada. Why should we not take the Barbados? I leave to your discretion the issue of orders for the recapture of Tobago and Trinidad."

Decrès received the imperial missive in Paris on April 29, and immediately hastened to convey fresh instructions to Villeneuve. These are not notable for their clarity, and may be divided under six heads.

1. "Nelson is pursuing you to Egypt." (This is a ridiculous and groundless assertion, which we know to be inaccurate, for Nelson had been sailing for Cape St Vincent since April 20.)

2. "His Majesty has sent Admiral Magon to you . . ." (As Decrès was writing this, Magon was still at Rochefort.)

3. "All the instructions you have received hitherto agree on the point that your sojourn in the Windward Islands must be signalised by the capture of English possessions." (Nothing could be falser, and Decrès admitted this later when he wrote in his own hand on the draft of his letter, "I note that this phrase has been wrongly incorporated into my letter!")

4. "His Majesty considers it quite possible for you to eject

the English from all their colonies in the Windward Islands with the troops under your command."

5. "All these projects must be subordinated to the successful carrying out of the main operation, by which His Majesty's arms must be crowned with victory." (What exactly does this mean?)

6. "If Ganteaume puts to sea, he will send his fastest ship ahead to warn you of his arrival, and thus enable you to concentrate your whole force during the ten days following the arrival of this ship."

Such were Villeneuve's final instructions in the West Indies before his return to Europe. The orders of April 17 were entrusted to Admiral Magon, who sailed from Rochefort for Fort-de-France with his two ships on May 1; those of the 29th, together with a copy of those sent by Magon, were to be carried by the frigate *Didon*, which left Lorient on May 3. Meanwhile Ganteaume, at Brest, was still waiting for a favourable wind.

Now for the English side. The Admiralty was deeply worried. What had happened to Villeneuve after he left Cadiz and joined up with Gravina's Spanish ships? Had he sailed westwards, to the West Indies in fact? Or had he turned north to release the forces blockaded at Ferrol, to rejoin Ganteaume at the approaches to Brest, and then to sail up the Channel with him? Nobody knew, for the cruiser sent by Orde to Cape St Vincent had lost contact.

Nevertheless, little by little, the idea of a Franco-Spanish enterprise in the West Indies began to gain ground among the Lords of the Admiralty. Was this due to native intuition, or on the authority of spies in Paris? On April 23 an agent operating in the French capital wrote, "The Brest squadron is making preparations for departure; there are 18,000 men on board, and the admiral's treasure-chest contains 900,000 francs". "Nobody knows," he added, "the exact destination of the Toulon squadron that got away from Cadiz: but the general opinion afterwards was that it was bound for the West Indies."

This letter was received on London on the 27th; but as early as the 25th the Admiralty took the prudent course of requesting the senior officer at Gibraltar to divert a couple of warships to the Barbados "if Lord Nelson is not on the enemy's heels". Forty-eight hours later came the Paris agent's message, and the Admiralty instructed Admiral Collingwood, who was at Cawsand (near Plymouth) with nine ships of the line, and Admiral Orde to join forces at Madeira and hasten in pursuit of the enemy. Curiously enough on April 30 Admiral Gardner, stationed on Ushant, saw fit "to put off Admiral Collingwood's departure until fresh orders had been received and until fresh information on the enemy's movements was to hand".

Frankly, the English no longer knew which way to turn. But for all the agonising delay, the solution was not far off. For Nelson, having at last ridden out the adverse winds, was once more on the scene, and on May 5 he anchored in the bay of Tetuan. The voyage from Sardinia had taken him a fortnight. He immediately demanded news of Villeneuve, but nobody could tell him anything. He was furious.

"I believe my ill luck is to go on for a longer time, and I now much fear that Sir John Orde has not sent his eight Small Ships to watch the Enemy's Fleet . . . to give me information that I might know how to direct my proceedings; for I cannot very properly run to the West Indies, without something beyond mere surmise; and if I defer my departure, Jamaica may be lost."

Nelson's fears were only too well grounded. Not only had the look-out ships posted by Orde at Cape St Vincent on April 11 failed to maintain contact, but the officer commanding them had just announced with a straight face, and against all probability, that "On April 22 Villeneuve was still at Cadiz"! In fact the mystery, instead of clearing, was deepening.

Still at Tetuan on May 6, and then at Gibraltar on the 7th and 8th, where he had put in to revictual his ships, Nelson gathered only slight and negative information, to wit, that there was no news of Villeneuve at Lisbon on April 28. But on May 10 everything changed. Lying off Cape St Vincent Nelson received intelligence that a convoy of English troops (this was the famous convoy of which he had heard before) was on its way to the Mediterranean, and placed itself under his protection. Immediately afterwards one of his frigates brought him a report from an American merchant ship that had left Cadiz on May 2. This gave a clear account of the arrival of Villeneuve off that port, and of his joining with Gravina. Two alternative destinations were suggested for the combined naval force: Ireland or the West Indies—Jamaica in particular. Finally, on the evening of the same day, as he cast anchor for the night at Lagos (east of Cape St Vincent), Nelson received on board the *Victory* an English officer in the Portuguese service, Vice-Admiral Campbell, *who was able to give him a formal assurance that Villeneuve had sailed for the West Indies.*

This time Nelson's troubles were over. More good news followed: on the morning of the 11th, the convoy arrived at Lagos on its way to the Mediterranean, reporting that they had seen nothing of the enemy en route. So now everything was plain.

"My lot is cast," cried Nelson, "I am going to the West Indies, where, although I am late, yet chance may have given them a bad passage, and me a good one!"

Leaving behind one line of battle ship to look after the convoy, he sailed at seven o'clock in the evening and started for the west with a fine following wind—at last the wind was on his side!

It was none too soon, for in London public opinion was beginning to accuse him of laziness, while the Admiralty, repeating the order of April 27 that Gardner had held up, had just requested Collingwood to prepare himself to sail for the West Indies.[1] None too soon indeed, for within forty-eight

---

[1] Collingwood received his final orders on May 17. He was already on his way to Lisbon with nine ships when the Admiralty learned on June 5 of Nelson's decision to run for the West Indies—a decision of which they heartily approved.

hours, on the other side of the Atlantic, Villeneuve's look-out men gave a joyous hail as they saw a dark mass rising out of the horizon, "Land ahead!"

*

It was in fact on May 14, 1805 that Villeneuve anchored in the roadstead of Fort-de-France. He had had a satisfactory crossing, though the slow sailing of some of the French ships had held him up.

Three of the Spanish warships that had made a late start from Cadiz had arrived a little before him, but one was still missing. It turned up in the end during the 16th, and so for the first time the Fleet was at full strength, with a total of 29 sail, composed of 18 ships of the line, seven frigates, and four corvettes or brigs. Apart from the crews, there were 5,088 effective troops on board.

In accordance with the Emperor's orders of March 2—the only ones he had so far received—all Villeneuve had to do was to wait 40 days, for Ganteaume to arrive, that is, until June 23.

He had no idea of attacking any of the English islands. However on May 21 he conceived the idea of attacking Dominica, in order to demonstrate his initiative. With this end in view he sent Lauriston with two frigates to bring reinforcements from Guadeloupe. But he never followed up the idea. It seemed that Dominica was "immune to all attack". Furthermore, at just about the same time, "indirect" reports came in of a "strong squadron" in the neighbourhood of Puerto Rico and San Domingo. What could this mean? Villeneuve had no idea. It was, in fact, an English detachment of six warships under Admiral Cochrane on its way to Jamaica; it had sailed from Europe in March to look for Missiessy. But in his dilemma, Villeneuve thought it best to give up any idea of large-scale operations in which the support of his warships would be required.

Another week went by—the second since the arrival of Villeneuve's force. There was still no news of either Ganteaume

or of the enemy. Lauriston returned from Guadeloupe on the
25th: he had nothing to report. This lack of news and conse-
quent inactivity began to pall. On the 27th Villeneuve gave
orders for two frigates to cruise to windward of the English
islands, and in a letter written the same day, explained this
decision to Decrès at great length.

"My object in detaching these frigates is to obtain news and
intelligence of what is going on, not only in these waters,
but in Europe, from any vessels that may come from there.
For no ships come here, and *I have not the least idea of what is
happening*. In actual fact, and in view of the importance of the
steps the Government has taken, I do not consider myself
authorised to detach ships from my force. But I hope that
whatever happens you will not blame me for detaching these
frigates to damage the enemy's commerce, to take advantage
of their stay in these waters, and to procure supplies for the
squadron and for the colony by taking whatever prizes they
can."

Such a letter demonstrates far better than pages of explanation what a gulf lay not only between a Villeneuve and a
Nelson, but between the French and English conception of
how an order should be carried out in this year of 1805. The
English admirals never shrank from responsibility (as when
Nelson cried "I am off to the West Indies!"), but the Emperor's
admirals were always terrified of being condemned for the
most trifling actions. If three frigates were detached on a fifty-
mile reconnaissance, a letter had to go off to the Minister
immediately, which he would receive a month later and lay
before his master. For Napoleon was the supreme arbiter, and
reserved once and for all the right of personally ordering the
movements of all units of the fleet, even if they were ten
thousand miles away. He would comment, protest, possibly
approve, and finally send off via Decrès a reply, an order or
counter-order, a reprimand or commendation, that never
reached its destination at the right time.

After the frigates had left, Villeneuve decided, for want of anything better, to take possession of an English observation post, the little island of Diamant off the south-west tip of Martinique. This was an operation well within his capacity, certainly advantageous, and apparently very simple, for the garrison numbered no more than 130 men in all. It was launched on the 30th with two ships of the line, one frigate and 200 soldiers. The remainder of the force looked on with envy as their comrades started out towards the islet—these were the men who were to have the chance of "stretching their legs". But their interest was soon diverted by a very different spectacle, the arrival at anchor of a frigate from France. It was the *Didon*.

It was then that Villeneuve read the orders of April 17 and 29, dictated by the Emperor to Decrès. It will not be out of place at this point to recall the gist of them:

April 17. I am sending you Admiral Magon. If a month after his arrival you have received no news, return to Boulogne via Ferrol and Brest. You will have turned your thirty days of waiting to advantage by taking St Lucia or some other English island if that fails.

April 29. Nelson is looking for you in Egypt. You have time at your disposal. Since your stay in the West Indies should be signalised by the capture of some English possessions, take St Vincent, Antigua, Granada and perhaps Barbados too. And why not Tobago and Trinidad? When you have accomplished this—and it is quite feasible—you will return to Ferrol, etc. . . .

To round off this resumé we may append the last-minute postscript of Decrès: "The Emperor's intentions remain the same (*sic*)."

Villeneuve could not be called an excitable man; at the same time he was not devoid of intelligence, and was also essentially modest. He neither felt intoxicated with the honour conferred on him ("Happy indeed is the admiral . . ." etc.), nor did he lose control of his temper; the business of the English islands was hypocrisy pure and simple. On the contrary, he took his time in considering and weighing up every item in the new orders. This occupied him for a day and a half, and it was not until June 1 that he acknowledged their receipt. He then wrote two letters to Decrès. These deserve to be quoted at length *not only* as a valid protest and defence, but because the hard truths they contain sharply underline the incompetence of the central authority.

First letter (Fort-de-France, June 1, 1805):

"The frigate *Didon* arrived the day before yesterday. She brought me your dispatch of April 29, to which was attached a copy of that of the 17th and of my new instructions. The delay in the arrival of Admiral Ganteaume is indeed driving me to despair, but it was nevertheless with the greatest astonishment that I read the paragraph of your letter of the 17th where you say: 'All instructions you have so far received, Sir, are at one on the point that your stay in the Windward Islands should be signalised by the conquest of English possessions, or at the least, by expeditions calculated to destroy the prosperity of the enemy's colonies.'[1] *Where, pray, was I to find orders to launch expeditions against the enemy's possessions in any former dispatch? My orders were to renew my water supply as soon as possible after arrival at Martinique, and to maintain my force under sail against the first sign of Admiral Ganteaume's arrival, for he was to sail straight on and not even drop anchor;* to draw on the colony's stores for my supplies during my stay at Martinique; I was finally informed that the fate of the world hung upon the carrying out of these measures, and upon the fate of the naval force. General Lauriston, for his part, had orders to disembark the greater part of his troops, guns and supplies on arrival at Martinique.

"Very well, sir: all these orders have been carried out.

"However, as I see you will condemn in advance the inactivity to which I was condemned by my instructions alone, I may say that from the day of my arrival I was anxious to take

[1] It may be recalled that Decrès subsequently wrote on the draft of this letter "I noted that this phrase has been wrongly incorporated into my letter" (See p. 117.)

action. I will prove it by the attached letter that I wrote to General Ernouf on May 21.[1] My object in so doing is not to justify my inactivity, but to make it clear to you that I found it intolerable.

"However that may be, as soon as the Diamant affair is finished, we shall set out to attack either Antigua or Barbados. Preparations have been made for embarking guns and troops."

Second letter (Fort-de-France, June 1, 1805):

"I have informed you how vexatious it was that my former instructions gave me no authority to act from the moment of my arrival. To-day, things are very different: the enemy is on his guard, having been warned of my leaving Gibraltar by the frigate *Mercury* which was dispatched by Admiral Orde and arrived on May 2. She dropped anchor here thirteen days ahead of me. Consequently they have had more than a month to prepare for our visit. Nevertheless we shall take steps to carry out the Emperor's orders.

"His Majesty intended that I should wait another thirty-five days in the colonies after the arrival of General Magon; but, my lord, I beg you to note that the state of my rations simply will not allow me to wait for such an extended period; the fact is, that I started from Toulon with six months' rations for about 11,500 men, who composed the crews of my squadron; but troops on board have increased that number to something like 15,000, so that my six months' rations are good for no more than four and a half months. With all his good will and zeal, the Governor of Martinique will have the greatest difficulty in collecting for me the equivalent of one month's rations for the whole squadron, and even so he will be acting beyond his powers. So you see I have rations for five months and a half from my departure from Toulon. I cannot undertake the

---

[1] Villeneuve had indeed written to General Ernouf, Captain-General of Guadeloupe, to inform him of Lauriston's arrival and of his intention to attack Dominica. His purpose, he said, was "to signalise our appearance in these waters by some dramatic incident". He added, "I fancy that such a course would be in full accord with the Emperor's views".

operations in my orders unless I leave here with at least two
and a half months' rations; and if you consider the squadron's
slow rate of sailing and the calms that occur at this time of
year, rations for three months would not be excessive.

"I left Toulon on March 30, that is, two months and three
days ago. Therefore, as of to-day, I can count on only three
months and twelve days' rations. Even that estimate does not
take account of what has to be thrown away every day owing
to the rations becoming stale—and we are about to undertake
an operation! My only reply to you must be that, in the circumstances, I shall be forced to leave the West Indies immediately after this, due to shortage of rations; and, in this event,
I shall return directly to Ferrol, according to my instructions. . . .

"The Spanish squadron is no better off in this respect, and
since my arrival at Martinique Admiral Gravina has reduced
his crews' rations by a quarter, which he pays them in ready
money."

Even so, the will of the Emperor had to be done, and
Villeneuve chose to proceed to the attack of Barbados, to the
south-east of Martinique.

The garrison of Diamant island capitulated on June 2. Forty-
eight hours later, when the whole army was ready to put to
sea—the expedition was to start the following day—Magon
arrived from Rochefort in the very nick of time, to join up
with his two ships of the line.

That was on June 4.

By a prank of fate it was on the very same day that Nelson
himself, arriving also in the very nick of time, dropped anchor
at Barbados. This extraordinary chase had begun three months
before in the middle of the Mediterranean; after leading the
two adversaries to the opposite extremity of the ocean, it was
now to bring them back to Europe. The second lap was about
to begin.

IX

NELSON IN THE LEAD

LET US pause a moment to take stock.

On June 4, 1805 in London, that ancient worthy Sir Charles Middleton, First Lord of the Admiralty, emerged from a prolonged agony of suspense. He had just received in one delivery three letters written by Nelson at the beginning of the previous month between Gibraltar and Cape St Vincent. In these letters the Commander-in-Chief of the Mediterranean squadron announced that he was once again on the track of Villeneuve, and had received trustworthy information that the latter was making for the West Indies. He was starting off in pursuit immediately. This good news put an end to a host of uncertainties; and Nelson's successful initiative was indeed praiseworthy. Furthermore, there was now no need to send Collingwood to India. He would replace the indolent Orde at the approaches to Cadiz, where he would be prepared to bar access to the Mediterranean, or in case of need cover Calder's flank before Ferrol.

On the same June 4, 1805 at Milan, although the constitutional establishment of the Kingdom of Italy, and the disturbed state of Continental diplomacy (the third coalition had been in existence since April 11) were pressing on Napoleon, he nevertheless gave his undivided attention to a long report Decrès had sent him on the position at sea.

The picture he painted of Nelson was by no means awe-inspiring: "He is as much braggart as fool, but he has one outstanding quality, namely, that among his captains he claims to be no more than brave and lucky. The result is that he will accept advice, and when he is in a difficult position, although he is nominally in command, the actual direction of affairs is in other hands." But the Minister was not particularly optimistic. He was convinced that the English admiral was on the track of Villeneuve, and believed that "fifteen days from now the God of Battles will have given his decision". If Villeneuve survived this encounter, there would inevitably be another battle "off Brest, west of Ushant and of the Chaussée de Sein [an island five miles off Raz Point, Brittany]", in which Ganteaume would find it very difficult to play a useful part. Lastly, he feared that Villeneuve would have with him no more than 49 ships of the line before Brest, to face 44 or even 50 English ships of unquestionable efficiency; and 19 of these 49 would be Spanish "on their first trip out of harbour, commanded by captains of little experience and poorly armed. . . ."

Napoleon was, up to a point, aware of all this. He knew, if he wanted results, that a battle off Brest was unavoidable, and he also knew that the Spanish warships were not the equals of the French, let alone the English men-of-war. But in his eyes what counted was an eager fighting spirit and the will to victory. Indeed, had he not foreseen everything? The very month before had he not literally predigested Villeneuve's task for him, sending him a new plan, of wider range, more flexible and more complete than any that had gone before?

Yes, indeed, *a new plan*! For on April 30, that is, twenty-four hours after Decrès had sent off to Villeneuve the instructions the latter was preparing to carry out on this June 4, Napoleon was informed of Missiessy's impending arrival, and realised that once again he must revise his calculations.

Two considerations had struck him most forcibly:

1. If he insisted that Villeneuve remain at Martinique for an additional 35 days after Magon's arrival to wait for Ganteaume or for fresh dispatches, as indicated in his former instructions, he ran the risk of the admiral returning with his rations completely exhausted.

2. If Ganteaume left Brest after May 20, there was every chance that he would find nobody left at the rendezvous in the West Indies.

This was why the Emperor first gave orders to Ganteaume that, if he had not put to sea by midnight on May 20, he was to wait for the blockade to be lifted, and then instructed Villeneuve to set sail as soon as possible—by June 20 at latest. He reckoned that as soon as he was back in Europe the admiral would rally to his flag the squadron of Gourdon at Ferrol and such Spanish warships as were ready to put to sea, and would then be able, if he considered it advisable, to sail up to the island of Aix and join up with Missiessy's squadron, whose return was now only a question of days. Villeneuve would then have two alternative courses: either to raise the blockade of Ganteaume so as to enter the Straits of Dover with him—but in this case, if there were to be a battle, it would have to take place nearer Brest, so that Ganteaume could join in without delay; or to slip past Cornwallis at Ushant and reach the Texel and Boulogne after making a circuit of Ireland. "The principal aim of the whole operation," Napoleon had laid down, "is to achieve a few days' supremacy off Boulogne." However, as every eventuality, even the worst, had to be taken into consideration, he had foreseen the possibility of a set-back. If, "following developments in America or during his voyage" Villeneuve found himself unable to fulfil his mission, he was to proceed to Cadiz, where he would receive fresh orders.

Such were the new instructions that Decrès transmitted to Villeneuve by the frigate *Topaze*, which sailed from Nantes for the West Indies on May 15. But even these were not the very last. On the morning of May 21 news reached Paris that Ganteaume, as might have been anticipated, had been unable to get away from Brest within the prescribed period. Decrès had therefore immediately dispatched a further message to Villeneuve by the brig *Nearque* and the frigate *Le Président*, sailing from Lorient, to tell him not to count on the Brest squadron, and to hasten his return. Two days later, the Minister was informed that Missiessy had anchored at Rochefort on May 20. He had lost no time in ordering the latter to sea again with his five ships of the line to join Villeneuve: if he

failed to find him, he was to put himself under the orders of
the Captain-General of Guadeloupe for an attack on Dominica.
Finally he sent a fourth message to Villeneuve by the frigate
Département-des-Landes, sailing from Rochefort, to confirm his
dispatch of May 21, and to inform him of the return of Missiessy.

*

No doubt Decrès felt that Napoleon would confirm his
decisions. As a matter of fact the Emperor heard of Missiessy's
return to the fold on May 27 when he was at Milan; he feigned
surprise, and at first burst into violent language, approving the
steps taken by Decrès. Forty-eight hours later, however, he
concluded that no further useful purpose would be served by
sending the Rochfort squadron back to the West Indies. He
therefore asked the Minister to cancel his order, and to consider the possibility of sending Missiessy on a cruise of deprada-
tion along the coasts of Ireland, after which he was to await
Villeneuve's return off Ferrol, and eventually join up with him.

So, the Emperor's sole pre-occupation on June 4, 1805 was to
put Missiessy's ships to the best possible use. He considered that
he had taken all other possible precautions. Four light vessels
were speeding towards Villeneuve with detailed instructions
in which every contingency, even the most adverse, had been
taken into consideration.

Unfortunately, as the incident of Missiessy had clearly
demonstrated, the cleverest machinery sometimes goes wrong
when the mechanic expects to control it from a distance. What
nobody had foreseen was that the four courier vessels would
never make contact with Villeneuve. When they reached Martinique, the frigate *Topaze* on June 19 and the three others
between July 1 and 4, the Admiral was already on his way to
Europe. He had anticipated the Emperor's plan without having
any clear knowledge of it!

Let us now return to the West Indies and regain touch with
the actual events.

On June 4, 1805 Villeneuve had succeeded in embarking the

800 men he had borrowed from the Captain-General of Martinique, and was ready to leave the anchorage of Fort-de-France on his way to conquer Barbados via Guadeloupe. Counting Magon's two vessels, the combined force amounted to 32 sail, of which 20 were ships of the line—14 French and six Spanish.

At the same moment Nelson had just anchored at Barbados, congratulating himself on having made an exceptionally fast crossing of the Atlantic. His squadron had at times made nine knots, and covered an average of 135 miles every twenty-four hours. But he was impatient for news of his opponent.

Where was Villeneuve, and what was he doing? Admiral Cochrane[1] hastened to meet Nelson with two of his line of battleships (the rest remained at Jamaica) but could tell him nothing. Fortunately, however, a letter came from the officer commanding the troops on St Lucia, stating that the enemy, "28 sail strong", had passed by on the evening of May 28 making "towards Barbados or Trinidad".

Were there, then, 28 French sail off St Lucia on May 28 when, actually, on that day only three of Villeneuve's frigates were at sea? The commanding officer at St Lucia had seen more than double. But Nelson nevertheless informed the Admiralty: "Let neither the army nor the navy be in doubt: the enemy is about to attack Tobago or Trinidad." Accordingly, that was the direction in which he sought for information. By nightfall 2,000 soldiers from Barbados had embarked on his ships of the line. A few hours were enough for him to take breath—he did not even find time to step ashore and stretch his legs. It was indeed true, as he had admitted on his way to Madeira, that the party he was engaged upon "was no picnic".

*

It is now June 5.

At 5 o'clock in the morning Villeneuve's combined force

---

[1] It will be remembered that Cochrane had left Europe to follow Missiessy.

left the anchorage of Fort-de-France for Guadeloupe. There he was to take on board 700 soldiers which he claimed he needed to attack the islands. Lauriston had been sent ahead to muster them.

Four hours later Nelson set sail from Barbados, making for Tobago, and having taken under his command Cochrane's two ships.

And so the two fleets drew apart, as once before they had done in the Mediterranean; but this time it was on the high seas and in a north-south line.

Villeneuve arrived at the anchorage of Basse-Terre, on Guadeloupe, at 3 o'clock in the afternoon of June 6, after passing under the lee of Dominica. Here he quickly took on board his 700 soldiers—thus raising his total effective strength to 8,600—and immediately started off again in a northerly direction, towards Antigua.

For twenty-four hours Nelson had been expecting the Franco-Spanish fleet to appear at any moment on the horizon. Now, on the same afternoon of June 6 at 5.30, within sight of Tobago, he encountered a schooner, which gave him the news that the French were at Trinidad! He speeded back thither, arrived the following afternoon, but found nothing. To be sure, at that moment Villeneuve was cruising near the northern extremity of the chain of islands, between Barbuda and Antigua, busily chasing a convoy of fifteen grain ships. This occupied him part of the night of June 7-8, and he secured 14 prizes, but the most valuable result was the information that Nelson had recently arrived at Barbados with "twelve or fourteen ships of the line and a number of frigates".

This game of blind-man's buff certainly produced a crop of miracles. Hardly had Villeneuve been warned of the presence of his adversary than the latter in his turn received information of the Franco-Spanish fleet's position, On June 8, Nelson was informed that Napoleon's forces had taken the islet of Diamant, which was true, and that they had just been reinforced by 14 ships of the line from Ferrol, which was not true.

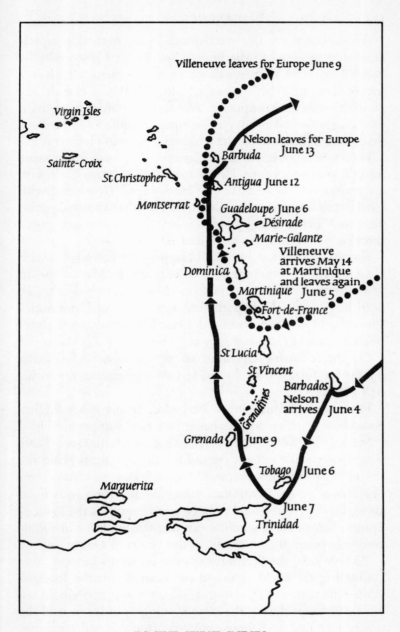

Villeneuve leaves for Europe June 9

Nelson leaves for Europe
June 13

Virgin Isles

Sainte-Croix

St Christopher

Barbuda

Antigua June 12

Montserrat

Guadeloupe June 6
Désirade

Marie-Galante

Villeneuve
arrives May 14
at Martinique
and leaves again
June 5

Dominica

Martinique

Fort-de-France

St Lucia

St Vincent

Grenadines

Barbados
Nelson
arrives
June 4

Grenada   June 9

Tobago   June 6

Marguerita

June 7

Trinidad

IN THE WEST INDIES

Nelson was not in the least daunted by the numerical superiority thus imputed to the Franco-Spanish fleet. Naturally he decided to head northwards to look for them. "However strong they may be," he said, "they shall not launch any major assaults with impunity. My force is compact; theirs is unmanageable, and although a very pretty fiddle I don't believe that either Villeneuve or Gravina know how to play upon it."

Nelson was not mistaken. Villeneuve had plunged once more into the gravest anxiety. He pictured Nelson at his heels with a squadron of "12 to 14 line of battleships". Combined with Cochrane's force these would equal the total Franco-Spanish fleet, in Villeneuve's opinion—if they did not, in fact, prove superior owing to their three-deckers.

Should he continue his island campaign in accordance with the Emperor's orders? Or should he return to Martinique, to wait the prescribed 35 days from Magon's arrival—that is, until July 9—for the hypothetical appearance of Ganteaume? There can be no doubt that the decision had already been made: *he must return to Europe as soon as possible*.

On the following day after asking the advice of Gravina purely for form's sake, he made two announcements to his staff officers:

First, he would not attack Barbados, or any other English possessions, such enterprises being henceforth impracticable.

Second, he would not be returning to Martinique. There were two equally cogent reasons for this: he must avoid the risk of an engagement that might leave his force with no means of refitting; also, if Ganteaume succeeded in getting away from Brest, his departure could only be good news for the Franco-Spanish forces, for it would mean that the English had simultaneously raised the blockade on the Straits of Dover.

To conclude, the fleet must at once return to Europe.

One frigate would escort to the nearest port the fourteen grain-ships captured off Antigua, whilst four others would sail for Guadeloupe during the same evening in order to land the troops that had been borrowed from the colonial garrisons.

These frigates were to rejoin the main body in the Azores when their tasks were accomplished. There was not much time, and Villeneuve was anxious to get away from these waters where he always felt uneasy for fear of Nelson's sudden appearance at any moment. He was going against the Emperor's orders—those that had reached him—but paradoxically enough, in complete accordance with those of May 15 and 21, of which he knew nothing, and which were being conveyed to him across the Atlantic by couriers whom he would never see.

In actual fact Nelson had to feel his way the whole time. He had just arrived at Grenada, out of breath. The inhabitants told him that the Franco-Spanish force had passed south of Guadeloupe on June 6, headed northwards. "Capital!" he replied. "So we shall see whether they propose to attack Antigua or St Christopher, or to return to Europe. I shall act on my own judgment, for I have been too often led astray by false intelligence."

With these words he set sail once more, in a fever of excitement, a hunter on the track of his quarry.

On June 10, as the Franco-Spanish ships were already sailing for Europe, the English squadron narrowly missed the frigates Villeneuve had detached to return the colonial troops to Guadeloupe. Two days later, on the evening of the 12th, they anchored at Antigua, completely at a loss. The admiral questioned the inhabitants, who gave him the following information: on the 8th Villeneuve had been off Antigua on his way from Guadeloupe; on the 11th (the previous day) his frigates had disembarked troops at Guadeloupe—Was this a blind, announcing a change of plan? Closeted in his cabin, with a portrait of Emma before him, Nelson weighed these contradictory ideas against one another. Suddenly his fist struck the table:

"I am starting for Europe!"

Without a moment's delay he sent orders to the brig *Curieux* to sail on ahead to England to herald his arrival.

This was a brilliant decision. On the very next day the

squadron was under way, making for the Old World; its congested load of troops had disembarked during the night.

Nelson was certainly not yet in a position to discern Villeneuve's purpose—that is, Napoleon's. Before starting off, he had written, "I think the whole or part of the Spaniards will go to the Havanna, and the rest of the fleet to Cadiz and Toulon, and upon this opinion I am going to the Streights Mouth, for they will be thinking they can go to Egypt in comfort."

Still the Egyptian bee in his bonnet!

However, before long the idea that Villeneuve might be heading for Ferrol began to establish itself in his mind. He spent the first six days of the voyage ruminating on it, in an attempt to distinguish possibilities from probabilities. All of a sudden, on the 19th, he shook off his indecision and sent a frigate to Admiral Calder, blockading Ferrol. At the same time he sent out a general alert to "all His Majesty's ships cruising in the West Indies and not proceeding on any more important service".

"I believe that the enemy's fleet is on its way back to Europe, but am uncertain whether its destination is Ferrol or Cadiz. I earnestly beg you will proceed to Ferrol with this warning for the admiral commanding the cruiser squadron off that port, so that he may be on his guard against an enemy attack in overwhelming force."

It seemed another whim of fate that on this same June 19 the brig *Curieux*, on her way to Plymouth, sighted the Franco-Spanish fleet 900 miles from Antigua. Its course was obviously not for the Mediterranean, but for western Europe—Ferrol for certain. To turn back to inform Nelson would have wasted precious time, and the captain of the *Curieux* quite correctly preferred to keep on his course, with increased speed if he could, and so get the Admiralty moving at the earliest possible moment.

*

Everything was now a matter of timing.

In the vast Atlantic, the two fleets were pitching and rolling as they lumbered on towards their new destinations. Meanwhile, Pitt in London and Napoleon in Italy, neither of whom had had any news of them for several weeks, were reckoning and weighing up their chances.

The Emperor wrote to Decrès on June 6: "I do not expect Villeneuve to reach Ferrol before July 20-29, Brest before July 29-August 8, and Boulogne before August 8-18."

Three days later he had laid down in detail a plan of action for the Rochefort squadron. It would sail due west, and from July 4-9 would cruise off the Irish coast; it would then return southwards and await Villeneuve 40 leagues west of Ferrol from July 29—August 3. If by the latter date no news of the Franco-Spanish force had been received, the squadron would proceed to the open sea on the route to Brest, and wait there till August 13; at the end of that period it would anchor at Vigo.

In common with all the Emperor's speculative schemes, this schedule was too precise, and not without its flaws. Nobody had any certain knowledge of Villeneuve's actual sailing, and he was the pivot of the whole plan; moreover, it is clear that the Rochefort squadron could not leave its base unless the English allowed it to do so; and finally, at the last minute Missiessy, smarting under the reprimand he had received for the too efficient discharge of his duty in the West Indies, had asked to be relieved of his command on grounds of health. On the proposal of Decrès he had been replaced by Captain Allemand, who took over on June 26.[1]

Meanwhile Villeneuve kept on his course and was approaching his destination. On July 1 he was off the Azores, where he was rejoined by the frigates he had left behind in the West Indies. All in all, he had not done too badly, for Nelson was

[1] Zacharie Allemand was born at Port-Louis (Brittany) on May 1, 1762. He was the son of a lieutenant in the navy, and began his career as a master's mate at the age of 12. In particular he had served under Suffren and Latouche Tréville. He was a hard, quick-tempered man, but of high moral character, and a first-rate seaman.

still 175 miles behind him. Unfortunately on the 4th the wind began to drop, and a squall approached from the north-east, forcing the fleet to beat against it. Not even Nelson was exempt from the vagaries of the weather—he was becalmed and for a whole week could scarcely make any progress—but for Villeneuve this was a disastrous blow, *for he thereby lost all chance of reaching Ferrol before the English were warned.*

In fact it was on the evening of July 7 that Nelson's assiduous courier, the *Curieux*, sped like an arrow into Plymouth harbour; she had run before the wind the whole way. Thirty hours later the First Lord of the Admiralty was roused from his bed by the news that Villeneuve was making for Ferrol. The First Lord may have been 80 years old, but that same afternoon he sent messages to the blockading squadrons before Rochefort (Admiral Stirling) and Ferrol (Admiral Calder) to combine their forces without delay, and proceed 100 miles due west of Cape Finisterre.

So the English forces of interception were set in motion, and combined to remarkable effect, as may be seen from the following summary:

July 11. Cornwallis was warned off Ushant.

July 12. Napoleon had returned quietly to Fontainebleau from Turin on the previous evening, and had not yet read Villeneuve's report of his arrival at Fort-de-France, which Decrès had received forty-eight hours earlier. Stirling, on the contrary, at his post before Rochefort, was duly informed, set sail, and proceeded to Ferrol with his five ships in accordance with the First Lord's instructions.

July 15. Stirling and Calder joined up off Ferrol with a total of 15 ships of the line, and immediately made for the spot assigned them for the interception of the Franco-Spanish fleet, that is to say, 100 miles west of Cape Finisterre.

July 16—nine days after the arrival of the *Curieux* at Plymouth—the English defence machine was finally in place and set for action.

With the 18 line of battleships of Cornwallis before Brest,

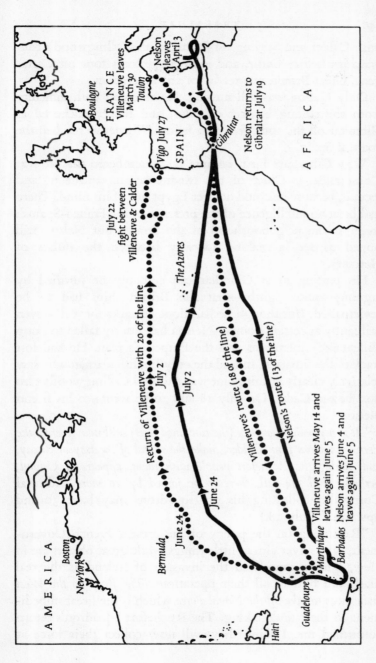

THE CHASE TO THE WEST INDIES AND THE RETURN TO EUROPE

with Calder and Stirling off Ferrol, with Collingwood's four warships before Cadiz, and with Bickerton's four off Cartagena, Great Britain was ready for any emergency.

Only Nelson was still missing. He emerged with difficulty from the stifling blanket of calm, and finally anchored at Gibraltar on the 19th, five days before Villeneuve reached the coast of Spain.

Why Gibraltar? First, because he remembered that he was Commander-in-Chief of the Mediterranean squadron; and second, because he could not get Egypt out of his mind. There had been no intelligence of the presence of the Franco-Spanish force in the neighbourhood of the Straits, but Nelson still hoped to see it making its way between the Pillars of Hercules.

His putting in at Gibraltar can certainly be justified by arguing—quite rightly—that the British ships had to be revictualled. But though he had done remarkably well—even brilliantly at certain points—Nelson had utterly failed to grasp Villeneuve's intentions and the Emperor's plan. He had lost track of the situation. Indeed the only English seaman who saw relatively clearly at this point was Admiral Collingwood at his post before Cadiz. On July 18 and 19 he wrote to his friend Nelson:

"*It is my belief that they (the combined fleet) will now liberate the Ferrol squadron from Calder, make the round of the Bay of Biscay, and, taking the Rochefort people with them, appear off Ushant, perhaps, with 34 sail, there to be joined by 20 more.* Admiral Cornwallis collecting his out squadrons may have 30 and upwards." (July 18.)

"Reasoning on the policy of the present French Government, who never aim at little things while great objects are in view, I have considered the invasion of Ireland as the real mark and butt of all their operations. *The flight to the West Indies was to take off the Naval Force* which is the great impediment to their undertaking. The Rochefort Squadron's return confirmed me. I think they will now collect their force at

Ferrol, which Calder tells me are in motion—pick up those Rochefort, who, I am told, are equally ready, and will make them above 30 sail; and then, without going near Ushant, or the Channel Fleet, proceed to Ireland. Detachments must go from the Channel Fleet to succour Ireland, when the Brest Fleet—twenty-one, I believe, of them, will sail, either to another part of Ireland, or up the Channel—a sort of force that has not been seen in those seas, perhaps, ever." (July 19.)

Nelson would certainly not fail to be impressed by the implacable logic of Collingwood's reasoning. But let us look at the position from the French side.

We have seen that the Emperor returned suddenly from Turin and on July 12 began to go through the latest reports of Villeneuve to reach Paris. Since then he had been informed of Nelson's arrival in the West Indies about June 20, but this information was false, for he had made landfall on June 4. Napoleon was therefore disposed to think that this would induce Villeneuve to put to sea with all speed and make for Ferrol, in accordance with the instructions of April 17 brought him by Rear-Admiral Magon, or, failing him, by the frigate *Didon*. But in that case, it was more than probable that the admiral could not be aware of the orders of May 15. Therefore it seemed advisable to repeat the gist of them to him. Accordingly, on July 16 Napoleon dispatched a letter to Villeneuve at Ferrol giving expression to this thought: after joining up with Gourdon, who was at Ferrol with five ships of the line, he must "gain command of the Straits of Dover, by combining either the Rochefort and Brest squadrons under your command, or the Brest squadron only, or the Rochefort squadron only, and, with this joint force round Ireland and Scotland in order to join up with the Texel squadron."

This was an echo of the orders of May 15, with the proviso that, *in case of unforeseen contingencies*, Villeneuve *could at all events make for Cadiz*, after releasing from blockade the ships at Ferrol and Rochefort. On this particular point Decrès added a word:

"The Emperor has foreseen the possibility, which may proceed from circumstances beyond our reckoning, of your being unable to put his plans into execution—those plans that may have such an effect on the fate of the world. In these circumstances only, the Emperor desires to concentrate a strong force at Cadiz."

The question of Villeneuve being thus settled, Napoleon cancelled his orders of June 9 to the Rochefort squadron, considering that it was now too late for the latter to sail to Ireland. He thought the squadron would serve a more useful purpose by remaining in port and thereby pinning down an English force of at least equal strength. Unfortunately Captain Allemand, in command, was on the very point of sailing, for since July 13 he had been free of the presence of Stirling who had gone to join Calder. He actually sailed on the following morning. Opening the secret packet containing the Emperor's instructions, he was amazed to find that his first assignment was to cruise off the Irish coast from July 4-9. Clearly it was rather too late to do this. On the other hand, it was too soon to enter upon the second part of this programme: "Wait for Villeneuve 40 leagues west of Ferrol from July 29 to August 3." So Allemand, having some twelve days to kill before he was due at this rendezvous, had no alternative but to plunge westwards, in order to spin out his time as far as possible from the coast.

And so once again—as before under Missiessy—we have the crack Rochefort squadron left "up in the air". It was on July 19 that Napoleon and Decrès learned of its departure. The next day Decrès hastened to warn Villeneuve in a letter addressed to Ferrol. But although he informed him of the two proposed positions of Allemand, from July 29 to August 3, and then from August 3-13 "well out to sea on the route to Brest",[1] he omitted to pass on the equally important information that after the 13th he was to anchor at Vigo! Napoleon for his part was highly excited by reports from Brest that the

[1] See p. 137.

English blockading squadron appeared for some days to have been relaxing its vigilance. Could this mean that Villeneuve would soon be on the scene? He turned to Ganteaume:

"When you receive this letter, I shall be already at Boulogne in person. All troops will be embarked, and the invasion fleet will be drawn up outside the anchorage. Thus, given control of the sea for three days, and with reasonable weather, *I have no doubt whatever of our success*. If the enemy has left his position in front of you, it means that he thinks our offensive will come from Villeneuve. Confound his calculations by seizing the initiative yourself!" Thus, though he had always enjoined on Ganteaume that he must get out of harbour without an engagement, Napoleon now suggested that he should attempt it by force, provided the enemy's strength did not exceed 16. He would be certain of victory, and would enter the Straits of Dover to ensure *"the final eclipse of England"*.

But alas! Though Cornwallis had indeed given the impression of momentarily relaxing his grip, he was soon back at his post with 20 line of battleships. So Ganteaume failed to break out, and it was once again on Villeneuve's shoulders alone that the task of altering the course of England's destiny devolved.

It was now July 22. One hundred and fifty miles from Ferrol the Franco-Spanish fleet, completely demoralised after three weeks' battling against contrary winds, was advancing in three close-packed columns through a morning mist. It was nearly noon. Suddenly a streak of sky became visible. The curtain of mist lifted. A line of grey shapes loomed on the horizon.

"Ten sail ahead!"

It was Calder.

*

It was indeed Calder and Stirling but, luckily for Villeneuve, not Nelson.

The two fleets were now groping in the mist which had reformed. The English had 15 ships of the line, including four three-deckers, and the Franco-Spanish fleet numbered 20, though the six Spaniards were worth no more than three. They approached one another, and twice more, though only for a moment, the mist lifted, allowing them to recognise their antagonists. Calder took the opportunity of manœuvring to attack the enemy centre, missed it, and found himself level with the head of the rear-guard. Villeneuve was already going about, apprehensive of being surrounded. Calder did the same, to bring him back to the centre, and a few minutes later went about again, to such effect that in the middle of the afternoon the two fleets found themselves on parallel courses and within easy range of each other's guns. Gravina, leading the Franco-Spanish fleet, then opened fire, and for the rest of the day the sea was lit up by flashes of red, soon absorbed in the mist. Both sides were firing at discretion at ill-defined silhouettes, so that Villeneuve, lost in the middle of his line, could no longer tell whether the English were on his port or starboard.

At six o'clock, when the light broke through, the French saw one of the Spanish ships drifting towards the English line. Then the mist came down again, and the strange battle ended as it had begun. It became known as the "Fifteen-Twenty".

The night was uneventful; dawn broke, pale and grey. Villeneuve mustered his force and called for a casualty return. There were 41 killed and 158 wounded—few enough, considering the number of shots exchanged. And although many of the ships were damaged and some masts had been broken, this was nothing very serious. Much more significant was the fact that two of the Spanish warships were missing, the *Ferme* and the *San-Rafael*. They had fallen disabled into the hands of the English.

The whole Franco-Spanish fleet could see these two warships, sisters in captivity, being towed by Calder's squadron along the horizon. A brisk pursuit, carried through with dash and confidence, could have rescued them. *The allied fleet were already masters of the field*, and could thus have scored a decisive success. *Calder was obviously anxious to escape*, having suffered casualties of 82 killed and 179 wounded, and with one battle-ship drifting out of control. But, just as Calder was no Nelson, so Villeneuve was simply himself—a leader incapable of taking a bold action that was not prescribed by the book of rules, and, above all, incapable of moulding his subordinates to his will or of firing their enthusiasm. And so the action turned out to be a short one. After wasting the whole morning in re-forming

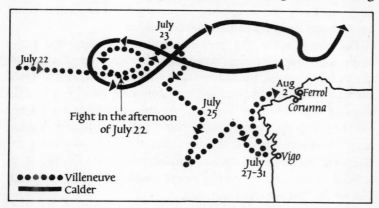

THE BATTLE OF JULY 22, 1805—KNOWN AS THE
BATTLE OF THE "FIFTEEN-TWENTY"

his fleet in battle-line, Villeneauve took until half-past one in the afternoon to decide to order a general pursuit; he had gone on board a frigate so as to take more effective control. At three o'clock the whole force was at last in line ahead, moving in to the attack. But at a quarter past three the wind dropped, and as Calder was still too far off, according to Villeneuve, to be overtaken before dark, the latter postponed the pursuit to the following day.

Next day the wind veered to the north-west, favouring the English, who were still determined to get away with their precious prizes. Villeneuve therefore called off the whole plan of pursuit, and at nine o'clock his force resumed its course to Ferrol, just as if nothing had happened.

But Villeneuve was not yet at the end of his tribulations, for in the evening the weather broke up. One of the Spanish ships had its tiller smashed and was driven to leeward, whilst others had their sails carried away. Soon the disorder was such that Villeneuve "in constant apprehension of seeing a ship dismasted", began to think that it would be really dangerous to attempt to double Cape Finisterre, though his force was within five or six hours' sailing of Ferrol. He decided to anchor at Vigo. Early the following afternoon he changed his mind once more, and steered a course for Cadiz.

For three hours the fleet ran towards Cadiz, under the impression that its ordeal was over. However, all of a sudden the wind dropped, the sea became a lake of lead, and a storm broke. Symbolically enough the foremast of the admiral's flagship was struck by lighting. At the same time a contrary wind sprang up, barring their route southwards and dashing their short-lived hopes. Again defeated by the elements, the fleet had to reset its course northwards, towards Ferrol. It looked as though it would never reach the port to which Napoleon had directed it.

The lack of water and rations, and of all facilities for tending casualties, whether sick or wounded, made for a critical situation. The wind was continually changing. During the afternoon of the 26th it suddenly veered from south to west, then to north-west and north. From then on, Villeneuve hesitated no longer, and at six o'clock on the evening of the 27th, the harassed fleet, after interminable tacking, anchored in Vigo Bay.

It was fifty-two days since they had started from the West Indies.

X
THE END OF THE INVASION

No HARM whatever was done by Villeneuve's putting in at Vigo rather than Ferrol. To make this point clear, it is only necessary to look at the general situation on the day after his arrival there, that is to say July 28, 1805.

On the English side, the dispositions adopted after the return of the *Curieux* had altered little. Cornwallis was before Brest with his 20 ships of the line; Collingwood and Bickerton, with four ships each before Cadiz and Cartagena respectively, had not moved. Calder alone was not in position. Returning from the "Battle of Fifteen-Twenty" with fourteen ships (he had sent the worst damaged one into Plymouth), he approached Ferrol in order to find out whether Villeneuve had put in there. On the 26th he notified Cornwallis that in the event of the Franco-Spanish fleet being in harbour there, he would rejoin him, after reconnoitring Rochefort on his way. Lastly, Nelson reappeared on the scene off Cape St Vincent, heading northwards. Whilst at Ceuta on the 24th he had received a letter from Collingwood informing him of the encounter of the *Curieux* with Villeneuve on June 19. He then realised that the French admiral's real destination was not after all the Mediterranean, as he had so long imagined. He decided to act and informed Collingwood, Calder and Cornwallis: "The squadron is certainly somewhere in the Bay of Biscay. I am sailing north with 11 line of battleships." It is a remarkable fact, which emphasises the independence of action allowed to the English admirals, that soon after Calder's report on the action of July 22 was received, the Admiralty wrote to Nelson in precisely the same sense.

"We beg your Lordship to lose no time in taking your

squadron to Ushant, and to put yourself under the orders of Admiral Cornwallis."

On the French side confusion still reigned. Towards the 25th the Emperor finally learned from English sources the date of Villeneuve's departure from the West Indies. He immediately became afraid that the admiral might not have received his April orders conveyed by Magon and the *Didon*, and would thus have carried out those issued in March. Since these had instructed him to cruise for 20 days in the Canaries on his way back from the West Indies and then to proceed to Cadiz, he sent him a letter addressed to this port, telling him to join up immediately with the forces at Ferrol, Brest and Boulogne in succession.

"If for a period of three days only you can make me master of the Straits of Dover, with God's help I shall put a period to England's fortunes and to her very existence."

At the same time he sent a letter to Vigo warning Allemand that he must join up with Villeneuve at Cadiz if he had heard nothing of him by August 3. But in this case the Emperor had confused his dates, for according to his previous instructions it was on the 13th, not the 3rd, that Allemand was due at Vigo. On the 3rd he would still have 10 days more to pass at sea. Consequently—once again—he had acted to no purpose.

Napoleon finally learned on the 27th that the English squadron at Ferrol had raised the blockade; as we have seen, it had gone out to meet Villeneuve. He therefore asked Gourdon, in command of the five French ships at Ferrol, to ascertain Allemand's position and make contact with him, cautioning him at the same time against joining the force at Cadiz *before August 8*. This was only on the assumption that he was without news of Villeneuve, and that the English squadron had not returned.

Thus in the space of twenty-four hours Napoleon had issued three sets of orders. The first, addressed to Villeneuve, did not reach him until August 22, and so was useless; the second, to Allemand, was based on an error of dates, and was thus invalid; while the third, to Gourdon, could only have the effect of completely paralysing a man who was already prone to hesitation, and averse to taking the initiative. So all this feverish activity had only a negative result. Furthermore, whatever Napoleon might do, the final decision was no longer in his hands.

On the Franco-Spanish side there were 22 ships at Brest, 14 at Ferrol (including nine Spanish), and five cruising off it (Allemand's division), 18 at Vigo (Villeneuve), and 12 Spanish ships at Cadiz and Cartagena. Thus on the front between Ushant and the entrance to the Mediterranean the allies deployed 71 ships of the line; the English had no more than 54.

The allies' chances were consequently unaffected, and as Édouard Desbrière has written in his study of Trafalgar, it only needed a lucky concentration at a given spot, and a victory—even a partial one—to upset the balance and deprive England of her mastery of the sea. But, once again, this was not in the hands of the Emperor. It was the sole concern of his admirals, and, among them, of Villeneuve in particular, who held the central position, and could concentrate the forces of Ferrol, Rochefort, Cadiz and perhaps even Cartagena under his flag.

But what in fact was Villeneuve doing on July 28, 1805? He was hunched over his writing-desk groaning as he penned a long report to Decrès, telling him all his troubles:

"If, as I had every right to hope, I had made a fast crossing from Martinique to Ferrol, I should have come upon Admiral Calder with his six ships of the line, or nine at the most, I should have beaten him, and having combined our squadrons, having still a month and a half's rations and water left, I should have joined up with the Brest squadron, and cleared the way for the great expedition; I should have been the greatest man in France! All that should have happened, and not necessarily with a fast-sailing squadron, but even with ships of quite ordinary quality. But the wind was against me for nineteen days. Two north-easterly squalls did us some damage, because we have bad masts, bad sails, bad rigging, bad officers and bad seamen. Our crews fall sick. The enemy had wind of us and called up reinforcements. He actually dared to attack us, though his strength was inferior. Our captains had little battle experience and knew little of squadron manœuvres, and in the mist the only rule they obeyed was to follow the man in front. *We are the laughing-stock of Europe.*"

Villeneuve went on to explain how the "compelling and irresistible force of circumstances" had forced him to enter Vigo.

"The captain of the *Achille* wrote that he had had 200 men on the sick list, and that he had had to demolish all the bulkheads and galleries in the orlop-deck to make room for them; and that he only had enough water for five days. General Magon, on the *Algésiras*, informed me that he was in the same state. The *Indomptable*, the *Intrépide* and the *Aigle* each had over 110 men on the sick list; in fact all the battleships had between 60 and 120, with no kind of relief to give them. I was forced to a decision, and since there was no port but Vigo within my reach where I could set matters right, I was compelled to put in there."

The admiral concluded: "As soon as I have taken on some water, and got the worst cases of sickness ashore, I shall set sail. I am informing Gourdon. *But if the wind is contrary for a course to Ferrol, I shall make for Cadiz.* I have not sufficient rations for a whole month. To conclude, our position is extremely vexing. I may add that the complaints from which the men are suffering are not in the least dangerous—scurvy and dysentery, with one or two cases of fever. Proper treatment and medical supplies could bring the majority back on to our effective strength."

So on July 28 Villeneuve, though he had found no imperial instructions awaiting him at Vigo, apparently decided to carry on with his assignment. But he was already thinking of retracing his steps to Cadiz, in case of adverse winds, and said so again in a fresh letter to Decrès written forty-eight hours later.

This was not the tone of a man who was likely to achieve success.

*

One thousand two hundred sick and wounded and three ships that were considered in no condition to proceed further, were left behind, the latter being the French vessel *Atlas* and the Spaniards *España* and *America*. The remainder of the Franco-Spanish force, now reduced to 13 French and two Spanish ships of the line, sailed out of Vigo on July 31 on its way to Ferrol.

With his thoughts on Calder, Villeneuve had written the previous day: "It seems to me that it will be difficult to make this voyage without fighting." But even as he sailed, Calder, back at his post off Ferrol on the 29th, decided to move up to Ushant and send Stirling to reconnoitre Rochefort. This was an error; it was mitigated by his maintaining a small observation force (one battleship and three frigates) west of Cape Finisterre, but it allowed Villeneuve to complete his passage undisturbed.

On the morning of August 2 his fleet sailed into the bay of Corunna. The Spanish warships were already entering the narrows leading to Ferrol, when a dinghy put out from the land with a courier on board carrying the Emperor's order of July 16. This order expressly forbade Villeneuve's force to anchor at Ferrol. He therefore allowed the Spanish ships to carry on, whilst his own hugged the wind and anchored in the bay. Once this had been done he was free to open his correspondence—the first he had received for two months. It included:

1. The Emperor's instructions of July 16—quite new to Villeneuve, as Decrès said in his covering note. By these he was ordered to "make himself master of the Straits of Dover for four or five days", but was allowed a wide choice of means in doing so. He could either operate with the Rochefort and Brest squadrons combined, or with either separately, in

making for the Texel via Ireland and Scotland. In case unforeseen circumstances prevented these combinations—*and in that case only*—he was to fall back on Cadiz with a view to a more decisive concentration.

2. The dispatch of July 20 from Decrès containing information of Allemand's departure from Rochefort and of his positions until August 13 off Ferrol and on the route from Ferrol to Brest, but, as he we have seen, omitting to say that he would be at Vigo after August 13.

Whether the contents of these messages were good or bad, debatable or not, at least they called for a quick, spirited decision. But the affair of July 22 had deprived Villeneuve of what little remained to him of confidence in either his force or himself. His optimism was not likely to be restored by being forced to anchor in the Corunna roadstead, where it was particularly difficult to carry out the repair and revictualling of the ships.

Of all Napoleon's orders, the only point that stuck in his mind coincided exactly with his own ideas—the possibility of falling back on Cadiz. His letters to Decrès of July 28 and 30 show that he had already thought of Cadiz twice before.

However as he had to reply, and, above all, to act, Villeneuve betook himself to Ferrol to confer with Gravina, and reached the following decision, which he communicated to Decrès on August 3 : *He would move off as soon as possible and attempt either to enter Brest, or else to give the enemy the slip, and enter the Channel, sailing close under the Lizard: finally, if these courses of action turned out to be "impracticable", he would set his course for Cadiz.*

He thus declined to take the northern route by Ireland and Scotland, which was in any case much too long for insufficiently provisioned and badly equipped ships. But on the other hand he had no intention of doing without the co-operation of Allemand and his squadron. So on the 4th he ordered the frigate *Didon* to proceed to the second prescribed position of rendezvous (Latitude 45° 56′ N, longitude 9° 30′ W, from

August 3-13) to fetch in the squadron. But it seemed that the Rochefort squadron was always fated to be a source of disappointment. Allemand had been at his first rendezvous position at the proper time, and was perfectly aware of the movements of Calder. But not knowing Napoleon's real intentions, he had unfortunately made no attempt to approach Ferrol to see what was happening there. Furthermore, by an unexpected misfortune, the *Didon* never reached him. She only left Corunna on the 6th, but on the 10th, after a heroic resistance celebrated in French naval history, she was captured by an English frigate, and with her perished all prospects of the junction between Villeneuve and Allemand.

With its entry into the Bay of Corunna, the Franco-Spanish fleet had come to the parting of the ways. From now on, as we have seen, everything depended upon Villeneuve's energy and the manner in which he would translate his intentions into action. He knew better than anyone what was at stake. He must have been aware of the excited anticipation across the Gulf of Gascony, where, once the news of his return to Europe had spread, the whole French people was waiting to see him sail up the Channel with flags flying. The Emperor was already at Boulogne to lead his prodigious army that burned to repeat the triumph of Caesar and bring "perfidious Albion" beneath the standards of his legions.

Once again, however, the man on whose feeble shoulders this mighty destiny rested, was very far from sharing in the general exaltation. He spent the whole day dismally in his cabin on board the *Bucentaure* composing a catalogue of his disappointments.

In a letter informing Decrès of his intentions, he wrote: "I shall not attempt, my lord, to describe my position: it is terrible! Ever since His Majesty honoured me with so much of his confidence, placing under me his whole navy and that of his allies, I have found myself hampered by the most deadly adverse circumstances. Everything—even Heaven—is against me."

Doubtless he had no intention of shirking his duty. He had always obeyed, and he would therefore continue to obey, though quite convinced that the tasks laid upon him were beyond human capacity, and that everything he did was destined to failure, ridicule or disaster.

On August 6 he once more confided in Decrès: "I shall not hide from you, my lord, that the task I have to fulfil appears to me to be very difficult. . . . We are bad at manœuvring; our warships are clumsy; our cordage and rigging are of poor quality and in bad condition. But I recognise the impossibility of remaining here any longer; every day makes our position worse. *I am therefore resigned to what I have to do, for I am committed.* I beg you, my lord, to bring my unfortunate situation to His Majesty's notice, and implore him, whatever happens, to bear in mind only my devotion, the formidable task with which I am faced, and the effects of ill luck."

We can read between the lines of this all too clearly.

What is more, zero hour was at hand and the game was beginning in earnest.

*

On August 3, 1805 Napoleon arrived at Boulogne, accompanied by Marshal Barthier, Minister of War. Decrès followed a few days later.

All was ready for the invasion.

Rear-Admiral Lacrosse, Bruix's cousin and successor, had found the invasion fleet still half disarmed at the beginning of the year, but by sheer drive during the preceding four months had brought its strength beyond what it had been the year before. If we include the detachments stationed at Ostend, Dunkirk, Calais, Étaples, Wimereux, Ambleteuse and Boulogne, it had now reached the fantastic total of 2,343 vessels, capable of·transporting 167,590 men and 9,149 horses. At Boulogne alone there were 1,153 craft, 694 of them armed, comprising gun-sloops and gun-boats.

As for the army, it only awaited the signal. It was 129,000

strong, of which 90,000 were on the spot, and divided into five army corps. The advance guard was at Wimereux under command of Marshal Lannes, General Oudinot and General Gazen; the right wing was at Ambleteuse under Marshal Davout and Generals Bisson and Friand; the centre was stationed on Boulogne under Marshal Soult and Generals Vandamme, Suchet, Legrand and Saint-Hilaire; the left wing at Étaples was commanded by Marshal Ney and Generals Dupont, Loison and Malher; and lastly the reserve, under command of Prince Louis, was split up between Calais, Dunkirk and Ostend.

Never before had any nation assembled such a force for an expedition beyond its own coasts. This concentration, covering 75 miles of coast-line, with its fleet of small boats specially designed and constructed for a unique operation, with its army of 100,000 men specially trained and rightly considered the finest troops in the world, represented such a mighty achievement that even the most sceptical could not withhold their admiration and enthusiasm.

"The surprising thing about it," Maret has written, "is the great silence everywhere; not a man is in sight, but at a single drum-beat, 100,000 will spring to action."

The feverish suspense of the encampment was thus depicted by the Secretary of State: "As the sun rises each morning every eye is turned to the white cliffs of the English coast, and every one is venting threats against the English and imprecations against the sea. Calculations, conjectures and suppositions all point to an early embarkation."

Of this early embarkation Napoleon himself seemed to be in no doubt. The day after his arrival he reviewed the infantry, lined up over nine miles of shore, and boldly announced that, since he had been in command, "he had never seen such a splendid sight".

"The English have no idea what is hanging over their heads," he wrote to Decrès that very evening. "If we can control the Straits for twelve hours, it is all up with England."

But as he stood facing the island surrounded by its girdle of mist, so near and yet so far, and although he tried to close his mind to all thoughts but those of the invasion, he could not help being aware of a rumbling in the East, growing steadily in volume—the alliance of England, Russia and Austria that was forming in his rear.

The Czar Alexander said of Napoleon, "The man is insatiable. There is no end to his ambition. He is the scourge of the world. He wants war; he shall have it, and the sooner the better."

After long hesitations Austria was now arming to her full capacity. She had been deeply hurt and irritated with Napoleon for setting up the Kingdom of Italy, and was anxious to take advantage of the fact that he was far from her frontiers and fully occupied with the anxieties of the war at sea. She was encouraged and reassured by the presence of the Grand Army at Boulogne and Ostend. "Bonaparte cannot get here before our allies join us," they were saying in Vienna. Meanwhile attempts were being made to drag Prussia into the adventure, troops were moving towards the frontiers, and the Austrian and Russian generals were planning their campaign.

Perhaps the Emperor thought he had enough time to invade and crush England before the Continental coalition opened hostilities. This was certainly so when he arrived at Boulogne and during the subsequent 10 days, that is to say, until he received definite information of Austria's attitude. (She joined the Anglo-Russian pact of St Petersburg on August 9.) His state of mind during those ten days, his agitation, and his anguished suspense, were beyond imagining. He was torn between the worries of diplomacy, which threatened to upset all his plans, and those of the naval situation, which he could not fully grasp, and which forced him to be continually on watch for the hypothetical arrival of Villeneuve or Ganteaume. He rushed from charts of the Atlantic and the Channel to maps of Germany, dreading to be taken by surprise on one front or the other. He was more painfully racked, and yet his mind was clearer than it had ever been, or ever would be.

On August 5 he learned that Nelson had returned to Europe and was in the Mediterranean. Then, one after the other, came reports of his reappearance on the high seas on the 7th, and on the 8th he heard of the battle of July 22 and of Villeneuve's arrival at Vigo.

At the same time that Allemand was beginning his spell at the second point of rendezvous, and that the frigate *Didon*, dispatched by Villeneuve, was on her way to meet him, the Franco-Spanish fleet had completed revictualling with rations and water for 45 days, and was preparing to leave Corunna and Ferrol.

Villeneuve was exasperated by the presence of General Lauriston, who was continually criticising and denouncing his weakness and sloth in messages to the Emperor. His only supporter was Gravina, but even he, for all his gallantry, was beginning to feel that things might turn out badly. Villeneuve was still trying to decide which direction he should take, Brest or Cadiz.

He became aware—we are not sure how—that Captain Allemand would touch at Vigo on August 13. He therefore sent to him there the following letter, which confirms his intentions as communicated to Decrès the day after his arrival at Corunna:

"To Captain Allemand, in the anchorage at Vigo.

"I dispatched to you, my dear Captain, the frigate *Didon* to inform you of the arrival at Ferrol of the combined fleet which you have been ordered to lead. I hereby inform you that I am about to leave for the destination it has pleased His Majesty to prescribe for all his combined forces now concentrated here. I must therefore advise you of the route I am to take, though it is possible that circumstances may cause me to alter it.

"If we are unable to join up before Ferrol, and if you are informed that the combined force has left there, you will proceed towards Brest with the idea of landing at Penmarch. In the event of my encountering difficulties in taking the same route, *my ultimate destination will be Cadiz harbour*, and you must likewise join me there, taking care to avoid Cape St Vincent on your way, for an enemy cruiser is probably stationed there. When you reach Cadiz, you will receive fresh instructions cancelling, by His Majesty's order, all those you may have previously received."

On August 10, after a two days' struggle against contrary winds, the whole force was back in the bay of Arès at the approach to Corunna, except for three Spanish ships that had found themselves unable to get out of harbour at Ferrol.

"I am on my way," wrote Villeneuve to Decrès, "and I shall shape my course either for Brest or for Cadiz, according to circumstances."

It was none too soon, for Napoleon, his nerves still further strained by reports of the battle off Ferrol was worrying Decrès, and he in his turn was at this moment writing to Villeneuve:

"The Emperor commands me to convey to you his hopes that you will have persevered in your assignment, for if three hours' bad weather and an engagement with 14 ships of the line should cause His Majesty's grand plans to miscarry—those plans of which he has confidentially informed you—the resulting humiliation to His Majesty's navy will be intolerable."

But Villeneuve had not yet reached the limit of his misfortunes. On the 11th an east wind dashed all hopes of getting out of harbour; the 12th was a dead calm. To crown his ill luck, 200 sick men had to be disembarked from the two French ships *Achille* and *Algésiras*, and in order to replace them a frigate had to be almost entirely stripped of its complement. Immediately the admiral plunged into complete pessimism:

"All is completely changed," he wrote to Decrès. "Our forces which should amount to 34 line of battleships will muster at most 28 or 29. The enemy, however, have effected a more formidable concentration than ever before, *and scarcely allow me any choice but to make for Cadiz.*" (August 11.)

It seems that we have here a final resolve—a last acknowledgment of helplessness. But meanwhile Lauriston was informing the Emperor "We are starting for Brest". On this same August 11 at Boulogne, Napoleon was in a rage after reading a dispatch to the effect that the Franco-Spanish force had entered the bay of Corunna and anchored there.

By two o'clock on the afternoon of August 13 the three Spanish ships left behind at Ferrol had succeeded in rejoining the main body, and Villeneuve finally set sail, heading westwards. Under his command were 29 ships of the line (18 French), six frigates (five French) and four corvettes (three French). Rear-Admiral Gourdon had fallen sick and handed over his command to Rear-Admiral Dumanoir.

The huge squadron moved out to sea at great speed, driven by a fresh north-easterly wind. M. Ailhaud, a French agent at Corunna, watched it go, and the same evening sent the great news off to France: "Admiral Villeneuve has left Ferrol, on a westerly course."

*

By a curious chance as the Franco-Spanish fleet was beginning to leave the Spanish coastline behind it, Napoleon at Boulogne was dictating two letters that give us the measure of his anxiety. They show, above all, that he was ready to make a *frontal attack*, but threatened with an attack *in the rear*, he had no intention of leaving the initiative in the hands of his foes.

The first letter was to Villeneuve, whom Decrès had been asked to upbraid the very same day ("Convey my displeasure to the admiral for his wasting of such precious time"). To him the Emperor declared:

"I was pleased to note that during the engagement of July 22 a number of my ships behaved with the gallantry I should have expected of them. I appreciate your skilful manœuvre at the beginning of the battle, which upset the enemy's plans. I could have wished that you had employed your numerous frigates to assist the Spanish men-of-war, for they were the first to engage and would naturally need it most.

"But I am emphatically of the opinion that the victory was ours, since you succeeded in entering Corunna harbour. *I trust that this dispatch will not find you there still,* and that you will have driven back the English cruisers in order to effect your junction with Captain Allemand, sweeping away everything in your path, and entering the Channel, where we are anxiously awaiting you. If you have not done this yet, do it now. Advance boldly against the enemy.

"The English are not so strong as you suppose. They are everywhere in a state of apprehension. *If you show yourself here within three days—even for only twenty-four hours—your mission will be accomplished.* Send a special courier to Admiral Ganteaume to inform him when you are leaving. Finally, bear in mind that no squadron has ever run a few risks in a greater cause, nor could French soldiers and sailors shed their blood to achieve a mightier or more noble result. We are all ready to die cheerfully for this great objective of furthering the invasion of England—the nation that has been oppressing France for six centuries."

His second letter was addressed to Talleyrand:

"I have made my decision. I wish to attack Austria and be in Vienna before next November. Alternatively I wish (and this is the word I want) that there should be no more than one Austrian regiment in the Tyrol. I want the Austrian household troops to betake themselves to Bohemia or Hungary and leave me in peace to carry on my war with England."

So on August 13, while making his preparations for the invasion of England, Napoleon issued a warning to Europe in general and Austria in particular: "I need time to succeed in the enterprise I have undertaken, and which I intend to carry through to its conclusion. But if you will not immediately guarantee the safety of my rear, then beware! The army that to-day treads the sands of Boulogne and the shingle of Wimereux, may well fall upon you like a thunderbolt."

However, once more, it was upon the admirals' movements that all depended, and more especially upon those of Villeneuve. He had finally gone to sea again, as the Emperor wished, and he was now on his way to Brest in a disturbed state of mind. At dusk on the 13th, as the combined force was heading westwards, two unidentified warships and some frigates were sighted to windward in the distance. Villeneuve changed his course to north-north-east, and then, during the night, to north-west. About noon next day his look-out once more picked out suspicious sails on the horizon—14 at first, then 8, which vanished as suddenly as they had appeared while the whole fleet watched them.

What did all this mean?

In Villeneuve's mind there was not a shadow of doubt, obsessed as he was with the idea of the English always at his heels. These unknown ships could only be those of Nelson or Calder, waiting on the high seas to bar his progress, and repeat the performance of July 22. It might perhaps have been as well to make sure. But Villeneuve's force, it seemed, was no more anxious than "the presumed enemy" to do so. Although Villeneuve was right in assuming that the ships sighted on the 13th were indeed English (they were the cruisers detached by Calder for observation when he left Ferrol and they went off at once to warn Cornwallis that the Franco-Spanish fleet was out[1]) those sighted on the 14th were neither Nelson's nor Calder's. On the 14th Calder was off Ushant, and had been there since the day before, having joined Cornwallis. Nelson, for his part, was, as we have seen, on his way from the Mediterranean also to join Cornwallis, and was at this time fifteen leagues from Ushant, having been delayed by contrary winds during the initial stages of his passage. Actually, the ships sighted on the 14th were not English at all; *they were Captain Allemand's squadron* on its way back to Vigo. He had ceased cruising at the second point of rendezvous on the 11th and not,

[1] Cornwallis received this information on August 19.

as ordered, on the 13th, believing that Calder was on the prowl in the vicinity on his way north.

So it was that, while the Franco-Spanish fleet had been looking for the Rochefort squadron since August 4, the two forces just passed one another by. Each took the other for an enemy detachment, hesitated to sail closer, and thus they failed to recognise each other.

On the morning of the 15th the north-west wind freshened; the combined force had to run west-north-west, and one of the Spanish warships lost her topmast. In the afternoon three further unidentified ships were sighted—a man-of-war and two frigates—one towing the other. Before long, however, a passing merchantman supplied the information that they were part of an English squadron of 25 sail.

Of course this information was false. The man-of-war sighted was the *Dragon* of Calder's cruising detachment at Cape Finisterre, flanked by the frigate *Phoenix* towing the *Didon* which she had encountered and defeated on August 10. But even if the information had been true, one would have thought that it was hardly sufficient to alarm an admiral with 29 ships of the line under him. But coming as it did when the "climate" was threatening after the mysterious sightings of the 13th and 14th, it drove the unfortunate Villeneuve to take an irrevocable step: as night fell a signal was run up at the mast-head of the *Bucentaure* ordering the whole fleet to go about and set course southward, for Cadiz.

That was the end of the invasion of England!

With a single gesture, Villeneuve had succeeded in bringing Napoleon's plans to the ground, in nullifying for ever the combined efforts of tens of thousands of his countrymen, and in demonstrating the pitiful incompetence of the French navy and its leaders. This was a moral catastrophe of major proportions presaging the final débâcle; it came just at the time when the English navy was showing the full extent of its terrible effectiveness.

On August 15, Nelson, after Calder, joined Cornwallis at

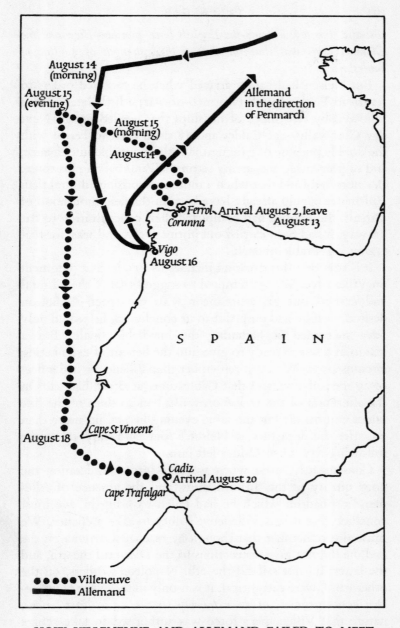

August 14
(morning)

August 15
(evening)

Allemand
in the direction
of Penmarch

August 15
(morning)

August 14

Ferrol Arrival August 2, leave
August 13
Corunna

Vigo
August 16

S P A I N

Cape St Vincent

August 18

Cadiz
Arrival August 20

Cape Trafalgar

●●●●● Villeneuve
━━━━ Allemand

HOW VILLENEUVE AND ALLEMAND FAILED TO MEET

Ushant. *For a few hours the English force guarding Brest and the Channel ports was thus raised to a total strength of 40 line of battleships.*

But Nelson had barely arrived when he received orders to return to England with two men-of-war; a little later he was followed by two more of his ships that needed repair. Next day Cornwallis sent Calder and 18 ships back to Ferrol with the double purpose of gaining the earliest possible intelligence, and of preventing the enemy setting sail and barring his route. We need only add that when a more enterprising admiral than Villeneuve would already have been in the neighbourhood of Ushant, the English had completed their concentration to bar his way. It had been carried out instinctively, and was, for that reason, admirable in itself.

It is true that this situation inclines us to a lenient judgment on Villeneuve. We are tempted to suggest that if the admiral had carried out his assignment with the speed Napoleon desired, or if he had pushed it to its conclusion, he would only have succeeded in hastening the inevitable finale. But a historian is not so ready to give him the benefit of extenuating circumstances. We must remember that Villeneuve had a fleet of 29 men-of-war, and that Ganteaume, at Brest, had 21. On the afternoon of the 15th Cornwallis had 40 ships of the line under command; but the same evening he had no more than 36, after the departure of Nelson's four, and only 18 on the following day when Calder left him.

Consequently, even when we take into consideration the poor quality of the Spanish ships, and the absence of Allemand's squadron which he had failed to bring in, we must conclude that it was Villeneuve's duty to take a chance. We must also remember that though he reached Corunna on the 2nd, he did not give instructions to the *Didon* till the 4th, and the latter did not sail till the 6th. Napoleon's orders, on the other hand, were categorical. It was only in the event of *unforeseen* contingencies, of an *extremely serious*, or at least *serious*, nature that Villeneuve's force was authorised to take refuge

Cornwallis
Nelson
Calder   40 of the line
                              Brest
        Ushant   Ganteaume
                       21 of the line
                                           F
45°39′N   R
13°31′W ·   45°56′N   A
         ·9°30′W   N
    ◄——————   C
   Allemand 5 of the line   E

Villeneuve
& Gravina
29 of the line
                        Ferrol
                        Corunna

                     Vigo

              S P A I N

                                    Cartagena
         6 of the line   Bickerton
         Cadiz   4 of the line
                              6 of the line

              Gibraltar

Collingwood
4 of the line

                    ☐ French and Spanish ships

                    ■ English ships

THE TWO FLEETS ON AUGUST 15, 1805

at Cadiz. But since the affair of July 22, and his experiences at Vigo and Corunna, these contingencies existed only in Villeneuve's imagination. He was obsessed by a painful inferiority complex, and a report of English ships in the vicinity, whether five or 50, immediately made him lose his head.

On his arrival at Cadiz Villeneuve felt obliged to write a circumstantial report to Decrès to justify his decision. The essential passage runs as follows:

"I found the wind at sea set in from the north-east, and for the whole of the 14th and 15th I beat up to windward in a west-north-westerly direction. There was no sign of change in the weather. I could feel no confidence in the state of my fleet's armament, in their sailing ability, or their co-ordination of manœuvre. In addition, the enemy was concentrating his forces and had full knowledge of all my movements after I had reached the Spanish coast. All these circumstances have combined to crush my hopes of achieving the great task to which my force has been assigned. If I had continued to struggle against head-winds, I should have suffered irreparable damage and my units would have become separated. The Spanish man-of-war *San-Francisco-de-Asis* has already lost her main top mast. I am convinced that there has been a radical change in the situation since His Imperial and Royal Majesty issued his orders. No doubt his object in sending the greater part of his naval forces to the colonies was to divide those of the enemy. The attention of the English was to be diverted to their distant possessions, so that our own navy could spring a surprise and deal them a mortal blow by returning suddenly to Europe and combining in a united force. I am further convinced that this plan has failed, as it has been disclosed to the enemy by the passage of time, and by the calculations the movements of our ships have enabled him to make; further, that the enemy is in any case now in a position to defeat it, for the concentration of his forces is at this moment more formidable than ever before—superior even to our combined squadrons of Brest and Ferrol. I am therefore unable to envisage any possibility of success in the present circumstances, and consequently, in accordance with Your Excellency's dispatch of July 16, I made the decision at nightfall on August 15, the third day after my departure, to make course for Cadiz, being at that time in a position 80 leagues west-north-west of Cape Finisterre."

Thus one paragraph put paid to all the hopes that Napoleon, unaware of the true situation, still cherished.

XI

NAPOLEON'S INQUEST

ON AUGUST 16, while Villeneuve's fleet was on its way to Cadiz, Commodore Allemand put in to Vigo and found Villeneuve's letter of the 8th, informing him of his intention to proceed to Brest, and ordering him to a rendezvous at Penmarch. Without delay, he set sail once more to carry out the orders of his superior officer. So the general post continued, but this time the players had altered their courses, Villeneuve being on the high seas headed southwards, and Allemand coasting northwards. Thus both lost their last chance of combining.

At Ushant three days later one of the English frigates from the cruiser detachment at Cape Finisterre brought Cornwallis news of Villeneuve's departure from Ferrol. Cornwallis sent her straight off to Calder (who had left Ushant on the 16th, as we have seen) with orders "to pursue the enemy, rather than proceed to Ferrol, and to attack him". It was now the 19th. On the previous day Collingwood. closing the blockade of Cadiz, got wind of Villeneuve. This shows that whether north or south, the English had not relaxed a jot of their vigilance.

At dawn on the 20th Villeneuve's fleet was in sight of the approaches to Cadiz, as also were Collingwood's four ships. Villeneuve gave immediate chase but his men entirely failed to catch the four ships up. From what we can gather, they were tough watch-dogs, and not to be shaken off easily. When evening came, in spite of all that had been done to scatter them, they were still there to observe the 39 Franco-Spanish men-of-war entering the bay of Cadiz—a prison from which they were not to emerge until they sailed out to meet their doom.

By a moving coincidence, on that same day Napoleon was at Boulogne—in an optimistic mood.

He wrote to Decrès: "I have no idea what the issue of all this will be, but you can see that, in spite of so many false moves and adverse circumstances, the plan is so sound at bottom that the advantage is still on our side."

On the same day also, at Brest, Ganteaume received a dispatch from the Emperor: "Are you anchored at Bertheaume? I trust you appreciate the importance of this juncture, and that you know what I expect of you." He therefore decided to proceed next day to anchorage at the prescribed spot, that is to say at the seaward end of the narrows, not far from Camaret.

But the time was near which would sweep away every illusion.

On August 22 Collingwood received a reinforcement of seven ships of the line, bringing the strength of his blockading force at Cadiz up to 11; three had come from Tangier, and the other four were the blockading squadron from Cartagena. At the same time, within the anchorage, Villeneuve was writing a private letter to Decrès. This was a continuation of the report from which the essential passage has already been quoted, and confirms his complete lack of confidence in the enterprise: "I cannot deceive myself. Whatever decision the Emperor comes to, nothing can lift me from the pit of misfortune into which I have fallen. But ever since my departure from Toulon I have been prepared for this, and I was never able to foresee any good coming of the operations I was to undertake." At Brest, meanwhile, Cornwallis had given chase to Ganteaume forcing him to the humiliating course of abandoning the Bay of Bertheaume; he had to re-enter the narrows and return to his normal anchorage in the small roadstead. At the same time a courier from Ferrol brought the Emperor at Boulogne news of the sailing of the Franco-Spanish fleet.

Never had Napoleon received such joyous news! M. Ailhaud the French agent who, as we have seen, was a witness of the fleet's sailing, stated that on emerging from Ferrol the fleet had headed west. Clearly no conclusion could be drawn from such a vague statement. But in a private letter to the Emperor, General Lauriston was more precise: "We are starting for Brest!" And already Napoleon, who could remember nothing but that one magnificent phrase, gave himself up to a mood of exaltation.

He summoned General Duroc and ordered him to start immediately for Berlin.

"You must persuade Prussia to sign a treaty of alliance with me. I will let her have Hanover, but only on condition that she accepts my offer at once. A fortnight hence, and the offer will no longer be the same. But at present I must be covered on the Atlantic side when the time comes to embark!"

He then dictated two messages addressed to Ganteaume and Villeneuve. To Ganteaume:

"I have already told you by telegraph that I desire you will not be the cause of Villeneuve losing a single day. In order to make the most of my superior force of 50 ships of the line, you will therefore put to sea immediately to carry out your destined task, and proceed to the Channel with all your forces. At such a critical juncture I am relying on your ability, your strength and your character. Start now, and sail here. We shall avenge the wrongs and humiliations of ten centuries. Never have my soldiers and sailors risked their lives in such a magnificent cause!"

To Villeneuve:

"I hope you have reached Brest. *Start now—there is not a moment to lose. Sail up the Channel with my squadrons united. England is ours! We are all ready: embarkation is complete. Show yourself for twenty-four hours and our business is done!*"

Hardly had the special courier left Boulogne carrying these two hopeful messages, than Decrès was announced. He, too, had received news from Ferrol, including in particular Villeneuve's letters of August 10, 11 and 13. Their tone, which seemed to indicate an early arrival of the Franco-Spanish fleet at Cadiz rather than at Brest, had filled him with consternation. As much from honesty as from prudence, he was determined to put the Emperor on his guard against the enthusiasm that was in danger of soon giving place to terrible disillusionment. He had guessed rightly. At the mention of Cadiz Napoleon exploded.

Thiers who, as Bainville recounts, "collected many oral traditions and had access to many documents", has given a perfect picture of the scene:

"Your precious Villeneuve," said the Emperor to Decrès, "is not even fit to command a frigate! What can you call a man who loses his head and throws his plans overboard just because a few seamen fall sick on two of his ships, or the end of a bowsprit is broken, or a few sails are torn, or there is a rumour that Nelson and Calder have joined forces? But if Nelson had joined Calder, they would be at the very entrance of Ferrol harbour, ready to catch the French as they came out, and not on the high seas. All this is as clear as crystal to anyone not blinded by fear!"

Thiers adds, "Napoleon further called Villeneuve a coward, and even a traitor, and immediately had orders issued to bring him back to the Channel from Cadiz by force, if indeed he was there, and in the event of his having sailed for Brest, to give Ganteaume command of the two combined squadrons."

Decrès withdrew with bitter feelings. An hour later a note from the Emperor was brought to his quarters:

"If Villeneuve is at Cadiz, I desire that he proceed to the Channel taking along the six line of battleships that are there already, with two months' rations on board. If he can possibly bring the Cartagena squadron as well, let him do so!"

Decrès replied the same evening, warming to the defence of his subordinate with a degree of courage he had never before shown.

"On my knees, I implore Your Majesty not to include Spanish ships in the operations undertaken by your own naval squadrons. Your Majesty has gained nothing by it, and you now intend to enlarge this association by taking over the

Spanish vessels at Cadiz and Cartagena. You wish to entrust to such a heterogeneous fleet a task whose inherent difficulty is only increased by the diverse components of the force, the inexperience of its leaders and their unfamiliarity with the exercise of command on active service—Your Majesty knows this is well as I do, and it is pointless to go over it again.

"In these circumstances, and seeing that Your Majesty has no regard for my experience or my common sense, I can think of no more painful condition than my own. . . .

"If Villeneuve's fleet is at Cadiz, I implore Your Majesty to consider this circumstance as a mere set-back which will preserve it for other operations. I implore you on no account to make the fleet come from Cadiz into the Channel, because at the present moment that would bring nothing but misfortune on the great enterprise. Above all, I implore you not to order it to make such a voyage with no more than two months' rations, for I believe M. d'Estaing took 70 or 80 days (it may have been more) to reach Brest from Cadiz.

"It is my misfortune to have a knowledge of naval matters, for this knowledge neither commands Your Majesty's confidence, nor does it achieve any results in Your Majesty's plans. Truly, Sire, my position is becoming too painful to bear. I doubt if any man could bear it. For the conduct of the war at sea, I beg you, form a Naval Council, an Admiralty, whatever Your Majesty pleases. For my part, I feel that far from gaining strength, I am growing weaker every day."

Napoleon received this letter in his large Boulogne residence, the Castle of Pont-de-Briques, and although it was late, replied with a short note:

"Pray send me in the course of tomorrow a memorandum on the question: In the present circumstances, and assuming that Villeneuve remains at Cadiz, what should be done?

"Rise to this occasion—the mighty confrontation of France and England; write me no more letters like the one you have just written—all that is meaningless. *My one and only aim is success.*"

A night that began in such an atmosphere must of necessity have been a short one for both men concerned. The discussion was resumed the following morning (August 23) with an exchange of dispatches at a distance of no more than a mile and a half, in an attempt to determine the course Villeneuve had finally taken after sailing westwards out of Ferrol. This was based on the meagre particulars furnished by M. Ailhaud. By five o'clock in the afternoon Decrès had re-read Villeneuve's latest dispatches, and turned M. Ailhaud's report inside out; he then addressed the following vital message to the Emperor:

"Seeing that it is my duty not to leave Your Majesty in the least doubt as to my feelings, even when they run completely counter to your own arrangements, I have the honour to inform you that, having given the fullest consideration to the route taken, and to Admiral Villeneuve's last letter, *it seems to me that there can be little doubt he was making for Cadiz.*"

Napoleon made up his mind with extraordinary speed. Whether Villeneuve had actually gone to Brest or to Cadiz, would soon be definitely known. Meanwhile the wisest course was to be prepared to face two alternative possibilities: the immediate invasion of England if the admiral entered the Channel, or war with Austria if he had gone south to Cadiz. Therefore, without making any alteration in the shore dispositions for the invasion of "Albion", preparations would have to be put in hand for the campaign against Austria. Within the hour he advised Talleyrand:

"My decision is made. My fleets passed out of sight off Cape Ortegal on August 14. If they appear in the Channel, there is still time; we shall embark, and the invasion will take place; in London I shall be able to cut the knot of all their alliances. If, on the other hand, my admirals show themselves lacking in character, or if their manœuvres are at fault, I shall strike my camp on the coast. I shall march into Germany with two hundred thousand men, and I shall not stop until I have reached the gates of Vienna, seized from Austria Venice and any other possessions she retains in Italy, and chased the Bourbons out of

Naples. I shall not let the Austrians and Russians join forces; I shall strike them before they can do so. Once I have brought peace to Europe, I shall return to the shores of the ocean and recommence my labours for peace on the sea."

Then came a cataclysm of orders: to Marshal Bernadotte, commanding in Hanover, to get the artillery and heavy stores of his army corps moving within ten or fifteen days towards the road-heads leading into central Germany, and to see that the significance of these movements was not generally understood: to General Marmont at the Texel to bring his baggage trains and supplies to such a state of preparedness that they could move off within three days: to Prince Eugène, Viceroy of Italy, to concentrate the troops now deployed between Genoa and Bologna, and bring them to the line of the Adige. . . .

In the evening Napoleon came back to the war at sea, as he digested the long report Decrès had sent him in reply to his question of the day before: "if the combined fleet remains at Cadiz, what must be done?" So far as we can judge, the Minister was embarrassed. He was allergic to forceful measures and enterprises on the grand scale. All he could recommend was a sort of piratical warfare with the fastest sailing ships of the French fleet acting as privateers against English commerce. The invasion fleet would be reduced to the role of a bogey intended to mislead the enemy or keep his attention permanently distracted. "*That*," said he, "*would be a war after my own heart!* We should drive the enemy to despair; we should do him unimaginable harm; we should put him in a state of deadly anxiety; we should raise up commanders of squadrons from among whom, perhaps, admirals might arise: our seamen would acquire the dash that comes from experience and success." Nevertheless, in the event of the Emperor persisting in the projected invasion, the best plan would be to take the 20 fastest sailing ships of the squadron now concentrated at Cadiz, send them out in the spring with rations for six months, to sail to Boulogne via the north of Ireland, combining at the Texel with the seven ships of the line of the Batavian squadron.

In fact, Decrès' proposals amounted to precisely nothing. To terrorise England by commerce-raiding was a folly France had already tried under the Pontchartrain Ministry in the time of Louis XIV. He had been unable to bring the English to terms. As to the postponement of the main issue for six months, unless the invasion fleet had the means of facing an attack by a considerable English concentration, that would merely lead to a futile repetition of the current campaign—and with Villeneuve in command into the bargain!

The Emperor saw through it. No doubt he was anxious to shine at sea as well as on land, and he scrawled on the back of his minister's report: "Form 7 cruiser squadrons: find out. . . ." But he had already made up his mind: he had no further expectations of his navy. It had been nothing but a liability all along, and now even the man at the head of it, speaking from his heart in a moment of crisis, was seriously suggesting the limitation of its activities to minor operations which could not in any case, on any reasonable view, bring England to her knees.

The next forty-eight hours were the last reprieve granted to the grand plan, and were tinged with pathos. Napoleon clung to his dream, still refusing to believe that Villeneuve would never come. He went from his quarters to the beach, scanned the sea, snatched at the most trivial report from the innumerable officers posted all along the coast to watch the horizon, while a thousand possibilities ran through his head. Perhaps Villeneuve's fleet had made a wide détour out at sea, to deceive the enemy: perhaps it was becalmed; perhaps it had taken the route round Ireland so as to enter the Channel from the north. On August 25, when he had already roughly drafted various orders for striking camp, he questioned Decrès. The latter replied:

"In my view the chances of Villeneuve rounding Ireland are *25 to one against*.

"The chances of his coming to Brest are more difficult to calculate, but considering the data in his letters, the passage of time, and the prevailing winds, I should put them at four to one against."

That was the end.

And so, without even waiting for definite information whether Villeneuve was at Cadiz or not, but going purely by instinct Napoleon launched his campaign against Austria.[1] He wrote to Talleyrand:

"From now on, I am redirecting my fire. They [the Austrians] have no idea how quickly I shall make my 200,000 men spin round!"

Shaking with rage he then summoned Daru, one of his chief secretaries. "Do you know where Villeneuve is?" he asked. "Do you know? At Cadiz!"

He then unleashed the anger that he had kept too long under control, and for five full minutes a furious stream of words poured from him. He accused the seamen of sabotaging his plans, he complained of everything and everybody, pacing up and down the room, his eyes flashing and his features hard and set. Suddenly he halted: "Sit down and write!" Then, at a single stretch, with no detail omitted, and with a mathematical precision that held Daru spell-bound, he dictated the plan of his campaign of 1805—the campaign of Ulm and of Austerlitz. This lasted several hours—sufficient time to take the regiments of the Grand Army one by one, to bring them out of their quarters at a precise moment, to wheel them about, and to fit them into an immense torrent of men moving at top speed towards the Austrian frontier. Daru was stupefied—"struck dumb with admiration". He had reason to be, for, as Madelin says, never had this man appeared "to such a degree a master of events". He had practically "laid down exactly

[1] It has often been said that it was on August 25 that Napoleon heard of the arrival of Villeneuve at Cadiz on the evening of the 20th. Nothing could be more inaccurate. It was not till September 1 that the news reached Boulogne. This would be quite normal, as the post journey between Cadiz and Boulogne took a minimum of 9 or 10 days.

when the first shot would be fired, and the day he would enter Vienna".

By the evening of the 26th everything was ready, and the signal to "turn right about" could be given. But in a forlorn hope of seeing Villeneuve sail in, Napoleon decided to give himself another twenty-four hours' respite. He spent the whole of the 27th in gazing out to sea for the last time, staring at the ocean that was always eluding him, that he would never understand, and upon which he could never make himself understood. At last, when the sun set behind his enemies' island home, and its rays had still not picked out the long awaited sails of Villeneuve, he gave up. At nightfall, while couriers were galloping off with his orders to Bernadotte and Marmont, the hundred thousand men in the encampment received orders to make up their kit ready to march at dawn the next day.

"My brave lads of the Boulogne camp!

"You are not going to England after all. English gold has seduced the Austrian Emperor, who has just declared war on France. His army has broken over the line it should have respected. They have invaded Bavaria. My men, fresh glories await you beyond the Rhine. Let us hasten to conquer the enemy—they are beaten already!"

The army was moving eastwards on August 29, when news came from London of the junction of Cornwallis and Nelson on the 15th, of the return of Nelson to England, and of Calder's sailing southward with his 20 men-of-war. This last item made the Emperor start.

"What a chance Villeneuve has missed!" he cried. "If he had approached Brest from the open sea he could have played ducks and drakes with Calder's squadron and then fallen on Cornwallis, or alternatively beaten the 20 English men-of-war with his own 30 and so given us a decisive superiority!"

No doubt he was right. . . . But it was futile to waste time in regrets, for everything now pointed to the fact that Villeneuve had not taken the route for Brest.

On August 30 he decreed the demobilisation of the invasion fleet. On September 1, just as the Emperor was packing his bags for Paris, a courier from Spain brought him news no longer of the least importance, that the Franco-Spanish fleet had entered Cadiz harbour in the evening of August 20.

*

It was only twenty-four hours later, on the way from Boulogne to Paris, that Napoleon was able to understand exactly what had happened. For he then received at once from Vigo a copy of Villeneuve's instructions to Allemand, and from Cadiz the admiral's report of August 22 explaining his change of direction, as well as a letter from Lauriston dated the 21st.

We already know the contents of Villeneuve's dispatch to Allemand ("Proceed to Penmarch . . .") and of his notorious report ("Having encountered at sea . . ."), but Lauriston's letter is something new—Lauriston,[1] the man Napoleon trusted, and Villeneuve's bitterest enemy; it is a terrible indictment:

"On sailing from Ferrol after our dispatches had been sent off," Lauriston explained, "the admiral said to me 'Our final destination is Cadiz, and I have so informed the Minister.' I replied that no doubt he was carrying out Your Majesty's orders."

After a circumstantial account of the passage to Cadiz and of the fleet's arrival there, he proceeded:

"Sire, I am no more than a passenger, but I have the honour to be Your Majesty's aide-de-camp. I am thoroughly humiliated to find myself a witness of so many shameful proceedings, yet unable to do anything to vindicate the honour of Your Majesty's arms. We are shuffling along like a lot of merchantmen, terrified of being attacked by four or five men-of-war. One man only is the cause of all this. . . .

[1] General Lauriston joined Louis XVIII in 1815. As a Peer of France he voted for the death penalty at the trial of Marshal Ney. He was himself made a marshal in 1823.

"The captains have no more the heart to do their best. They take no notice of signals, which remain at the mast-head for two or three hours together. Discipline has gone to pieces. *This squadron needs a man—and an admiral at that—who is full of confidence and enthusiasm for our cause.* The utmost steadfastness is required at this stage. Sire, I am not disgusted at this humiliating campaign—I am ready to make a fresh start in the most miserable conditions of service, but at least let it be with a real man, and let me be spared the shame of witnessing the humiliation of our navy in which serve so many splendid men at whose side any undertaking would be possible."

This time Napoleon saw red. The moment he arrived at Malmaison he wrote two letters to Decrès, couched in terms of unprecedented violence. His rage made him almost incoherent, and each phrase was like a whiplash:

"Admiral Villeneuve has gone too far. When he left Vigo (?) he ordered Captain Allemand to proceed to Brest, and at the same time wrote to you that he himself intended to sail for Cadiz. That is treason, pure and simple! Here is Allemand's squadron placed in an impossible position, wandering about the ocean for months on end. Words fail me! Draft me a report on the whole expedition. *Villeneuve is a wretch who must be hounded out of the service.* He has neither enthusiasm nor courage and would throw everything away so long as he could save his own skin. He puts in jeopardy a squadron as important as that of Captain Allemand, just as he lost the unfortunate *Didon* by his own errors and slackness. After this, I am forced to acknowledge Missiessy as a hero!"

Never before had he spoken of a general officer in such terms. It was in vain that Decrès attempted to intervene—

"I am in despair about the affair of Villeneuve, and I am looking at it in its proper perspective. In my view the reason was that he lost his head, not that he was a coward." (September 6.)

—and he had his knuckles rapped for it. Napoleon replied: "I will spare you my comments on the letter you sent me. You should never have entertained the possibility of Villeneuve's coming to Brest! He wrote to you 'I am going to Cadiz'. He deceived Lauriston, who wrote to me on August 14, 'We are at last going to Brest', but his letter from Cadiz says that the admiral's first word to him as he set sail was 'We are definitely making for Cadiz, and I have so informed the Minister!' Until you can find something more plausible to say I beg you not to mention such a humiliating business in my hearing, nor to remind me of such a cowardly wretch!"

This quarrel might have been a long one, but to cut it short, and also, we may suppose, to get back into his master's favour, the Minister put forward a secret plan on September 11, which consisted of sending the invasion fleet, *without naval support, but under cover of a winter's night*, to attack the dockyards and naval installations in the Thames. At one stroke Napoleon swept aside this piece of outdated wool-gathering in a memorandum intended to justify his action in the eyes of posterity and to preserve it for history (September 13).

"If only Admiral Villeneuve, instead of putting in at Ferrol, had joined with the Spanish squadron, and made sail for Brest to join up there with Admiral Ganteaume, the army could have made its landing and England would have been finished!"

According to the Emperor the best course at the moment was to resume the invasion project on a revised plan, concentrating an army of 60,000 to 80,000 men at Boulogne that could serve equally well against England or against Germany, and drawing up the invasion craft in line once more. This would give the English the idea that he was only waiting for naval support to make the crossing. England would thus be kept in continuous apprehension, and would be compelled to maintain considerable military and naval forces along her coastline. Once superiority at sea had been achieved (no doubt at the price of a fresh programme of ship-building), the invasion could at last be attempted.

But these were no more than castles in the air. At present

the first priority was the disposal of the fleet shut up in Cadiz harbour.

*

As soon as he arrived, Villeneuve had requested the Spanish arsenal to effect repairs to his damaged squadron, and to supply them with "Rations for fifty to fifty-five days for the crews, and for 17,000 troops in addition." His frigates were short of sail, and the rigging of many of the men-of-war was in a sorry state. At once he came up against serious difficulties, which both embittered his stay, and prolonged it beyond all reason.

For the Cadiz arsenal had sacrificed all its resources in fitting out the Spanish men-of-war, and was completely stripped of supplies. Furthermore, money was short. Apart from the fact that the Spanish treasury was completely empty, nobody in the peninsula felt inclined to allow credit on the security of the French fleet, which represented the only capital available to Villeneuve and the Commissioner-General who represented the Empire in the province of Andalusia.

"The monarchy and people of Spain have no place for France in their hearts," remarked the ambassador de Beurnonville.

This was true enough. Even in the combined force itself, in spite of the efforts of Gravina, relations were strained. The Spanish seamen had not forgiven Villeneuve the loss of their two men-of-war on July 22. Each evening bloody brawls broke out between the French and Spanish in the harbour dives. Knives were drawn and throats cut. It was indeed an uneasy alliance.

To crown all, Villeneuve, whose morale was already at zero, had a sharp attack of bilious colic. Nor was the continual reinforcement of the English cruiser squadron outside the harbour calculated to raise his spirits.

We may recall that when Villeneuve's fleet sailed into Cadiz, Admiral Collingwood had no more than four line of battle-ships under his command. Next day, with reinforcements from

Cartagena and Tangier, he could muster 11 for the first time. At this stage Villeneuve might still have passed word to the six Spanish ships of the line anchored at Cartagena to put to sea, and himself gone out to meet them with 15 of his best ships. The risk would have been worth taking. Not only were the six ships in question of excellent quality, but in combination with them Villeneuve would have outnumbered Collingwood by two to one, and could have inflicted on him a decisive and final defeat.

Such speculations are pointless. Villeneuve was incapable of the initiative, at this point, just as he had previously failed to pursue Calder or to join up with Allemand. Perhaps he imagined that the English Admiralty would still give him time to choose his opportunity. He was able to gauge his error on September 3 when he discovered that not 11, but 30 English ships were blockading Cadiz! For now Collingwood was no longer alone. Calder had at length learned, on August 26, of the arrival of the Franco-Spanish fleet at Cadiz, after a long cruise southwards beset with uncertainty. Hastening to join Collingwood, he arrived less than four days later with his invaluable reinforcement of 18 ships of the line.[1]

Thanks to the superior organisation of its intelligence service, the English fleet was once more ready. As an instance it may be mentioned that Nelson heard of Villeneuve's arrival at Cadiz on September 2—almost at the same time as Napoleon—and Cornwallis received the same news at Ushant on the 5th. The English were indeed ready, but Villeneuve was still waiting for Allemand's squadron which seemed to have vanished without trace. Nobody knew what had happened to it.

Actually, it had sailed from Vigo to Penmarch and was marking time at the rendezvous prescribed by Villeneuve, where it remained till September 6. On that day Allemand received word that the Franco-Spanish fleet had not put in anywhere along the French coast, and accordingly set his

---

[1] Calder reached Cadiz on August 30, but it was not until September 3 that Villeneuve became aware that the blockade had been reinforced.

course southwards, for Cadiz. On the 10th he was off Lisbon, and heard of Villeneuve's arrival in the Spanish port; he was therefore on the right route. But he was brought up short on the following day by the news that an English force estimated at not less than 26 ships was also at Cadiz.

Should he stake all on one throw, at the risk of being caught in the enemy's trap?

Most prudently he decided to sail no closer to Villeneuve, thereby acting in accordance with Napoleon's orders of June 9, instructing him to attack English merchantmen in the event of his being unable to join Villeneuve. Answering to the wind, this fine squadron turned away to starboard, and slowly disappeared into the west, never to reappear in the battle-area. If only it had entered on the cue given by the Imperial stage-manager, it would no doubt have spared the rest of the cast the tragic fiasco that was even now being prepared in the wings.

*

By mid-September Napoleon had become anxious not to allow the fleet to stagnate any longer at Cadiz, and at the same time to replace the defaulting admiral at the earliest possible moment—in this he was, of course, influenced by Lauriston's report. He therefore made two swift decisions:

1. To send Villeneuve to Naples with his troops, so that they might join an invasion force concentrated in Tuscany. The fleet would then return to Toulon.

2. To appoint Vice-Admiral Rosily as commander-in-chief of the combined fleet, having promoted him admiral for this purpose.

It was indeed a strange notion to send the unfortunate Villeneuve into the Mediterranean at a time like this—and for the sake of a very minor assignment. Doubtless one may suppose that the Emperor was determined to see his fleet back at Toulon as soon as possible. It was a safe harbour, and he probably thought that 11 English ships of the line constituted no

sort of obstacle to Villeneuve's sortie from Cadiz. The latter
had written in his last letter to reach Paris, dated September 2,
that he had no more than 11 British ships before him. All
the same he added that news had reached Lisbon of Calder
moving south "with 23 men-of-war", but stated emphatically
that he scarcely believed Calder would join up with Collingwood "at least for some time"!

However, even if Villeneuve, as usual, had no very clear
picture of the situation, Napoleon for his part was well aware
—and had been so since August 29—that Calder had set sail
southwards from Ushant with about 20 ships. "This is a
remarkable blunder by Cornwallis!" he had remarked at the
time. Unless he was as simple-minded as his admiral (and he
certainly was not), he must by now have realised that when
Villeneuve gave orders to move, there would surely be more
than 11 enemy ships ready to fall upon him. It followed, then,
if one gave the matter a little thought, that to force the fleet to
move out from Cadiz in such uncertain circumstances, was
deliberately to risk an engagement with an enemy of almost
equal strength, when, moreover, the issue at stake did not
warrant it.

The Emperor wrote to Villeneuve in precise terms: "Our
intention *is that wherever you find the enemy in inferior strength*,
you will attack him without hesitation, and *make it a decisive
engagement*. You will no doubt realise that the success of these
operations depends to all intents and purposes upon how soon
you can get away from Cadiz. I count on you to leave nothing
undone that may speed your passage, and in the course of this
important expedition, let me impress upon you the importance
of boldness and the utmost energy in action."

Decrès also wrote:

"My dear Admiral, I cannot over-emphasise to you the
importance of seizing the first possible opportunity of sailing
out of Cadiz, and I beg to repeat my heartiest good wishes for
your success."

These letters are dated September 16 and 17. But on the

previous day Napoleon had already fixed on Rosily (who had not held a command at sea for 15 years) as Villeneuve's successor. The instructions issued to the new commander, in case he arrived at Cadiz before the fleet had left, differed in an astonishing degree from those that had been sent to Villeneuve. This is shown in a letter of Decrès dated September 18:

"The Emperor attaches the greatest importance to your carrying out your assignment without delay. But if you find insurmountable obstacles in your way, His Majesty's desire is that you should at the least get the fleet out, or some sections of it, whenever the weather permits."

Thus, while the necessity for *boldness* was impressed on Villeneuve, his successor was simultaneously recommended to act with *prudence*. We may either believe with Jurien de la Gravière that in writing to Villeneuve Napoleon was not afraid of overstatement, his opinion being that "he was one of those men who needed the spur more than the bridle"; or, more simply, we may suppose that he held him in such contempt as to be convinced that he would once more shirk his duty.

It is easy to multiply conjectures still further. But there is no doubt that if the Emperor and Decrès wished to drive Villeneuve to despair, they could hardly have gone about it in a more effective way. *They had left him without news* since September 2, and the wretched man was at his wits' end.

"I await the Emperor's orders with the utmost anxiety. I am counting the hours and minutes, and still they do not come. The judgment you will have to transmit will be for me either a much-needed consolation for having been unable to render more signal services, or else the acme of all my misfortunes, supposing my conduct has not been judged as indulgently as I dared to hope it might be." (To Decrès, from Cadiz, September 6.)

We have already observed that Napoleon appointed Rosily the new commander-in-chief on the 15th, but it was not until the 20th—that is, forty-eight hours after Rosily himself had received his instructions, and news of the promotion had reached the Emperor's representatives in Spain, Beurnonville the ambassador at Madrid and Le Roy the Commissioner-General at Cadiz—that Villeneuve himself was notified in a brief note from Decrès:

"H.M. the Emperor has just appointed Vice-Admiral Rosily to the command of the allied force at Cadiz, and has ordered you to return to Paris to give an account of the operations you have just completed.

"As soon as Vice-Admiral Rosily has handed you this dispatch, you are to hand over to him the command, and he will be received with the rank of admiral."

There followed a paragraph on the handing-over of authority.

Jurien de la Gravière has written, "Decrès had a sincere liking for Villeneuve, and his hand was trembling as he drafted this last order. The five lines announcing to this unhappy man his recall and the Emperor's intentions contained no less than twenty corrections."

We may well believe it, for Decrès' conscience must have troubled him at the thought that Villeneuve might learn of his disgrace from "Quartermaster" Le Roy, who had been told forty-eight hours earlier. And he may perhaps have felt subconsciously that such a blow falling on a desperate but honourable man might have tragic consequences.

*

On the same September 20 a letter from Beurnonville brought official intelligence to Paris that on the 3rd the force before Cadiz consisted of "24 English line of battleships, including seven three-deckers". This preliminary warning was ignored. Everybody was busy with the appointment of Villeneuve's successor, and with the working out of a marvellous plan for cruising squadrons. The most important of these was to be put under the command of Rear-Admiral Willaumez, Ganteaume's adjutant at Brest, and was to operate between the Cape of Good Hope and St Helena. Ganteaume, incidentally, had just asked to be relieved of his duties for reasons of health.

Then, of course, there was the Austrian campaign. On September 23, forty-eight hours after Rosily had taken the road for Cadiz, Napoleon left for Strasbourg, arriving there on the 26th. On the 30th he received a letter from Decrès confirming that, according to the latest reports, dated September 16, Villeneuve could make out all the time "24 or 25 enemy ships of the line" but that he would "seize the earliest opportunity of sailing out with his whole fleet". A dispatch from Lauriston also reached him, dated from Cadiz on September 16, which made this interesting observation on the subject of the British ships:

"Their total number, before both Cadiz and Gibraltar, is 28. . . . Information has been received from Tangier to the effect that Admiral Nelson is expected at any moment to take over command of the squadron, bringing six fresh ships of the line with him."

This report was well-founded, for we shall see that Nelson had indeed left England at the head of a fresh squadron, proceeding towards Cadiz. But whether well-founded or not, it showed an elementary logic. It was a matter of common sense for the English, now that the threat from the Boulogne camp was lifted, to concentrate on keeping the Cadiz fleet in port. This fleet was 11 strong on leaving Toulon, but had now increased to over 30, and, with a measure of good luck and audacity might well reach 40 or 45; this would outnumber by a third the strongest force the English could put against it—at least in Southern Europe. British reaction to a favourable opportunity was well known, and had been seen off Ushant on August 15. The combination of Collingwood and Nelson, following on that of Collingwood and Calder, was no airy hypothesis.

Was there any hope that, at the least, Villeneuve would free himself before it was too late? None. Firstly because he lacked the necessary pluck (but then who had appointed him?): secondly because he was struggling against material difficulties that would make it impossible for him to be ready for several weeks. On September 1, replying to the dispatch announcing the arrival of the fleet at Cadiz, Decrès had immediately written: "Take on board rations for six months." But on September 16 Lauriston, who cannot be suspected of any tender feelings towards the admiral, informed Napoleon: "The provision of four months' rations for the fleet is no more than half completed. Lack of credit is the most serious factor holding up supplies."

How was it that Napoleon, faced with such a clear and well-defined situation, did not cancel his orders of September 16 and 17? How was it that, while there was still time, he did not issue instructions to Villeneuve similar to those already entrusted to Rosily? Finally, why did he not even reply—*for he did not*—to the letter from Decrès that reached him at Strasbourg?

We shall never know.

Possibly it will be repeated that Napoleon was "warped" by land-warfare, and understood nothing of war at sea. For him a line of battleships was never anything but just a line of battleships, though it might be a two- or three-decker, it might be armed with 80 or 100 guns, or it might be manned by 500 seasoned seamen or 500 raw pressed men. This would explain why he refused to disturb himself over the fate of this fleet, 33 strong, which he had directed to seek out a decisive engagement with an enemy force that could not exceed 28 to 30—a figure which includes Nelson, but takes account of certain inevitable absentees. But Napoleon had long been aware of the true worth of the Spanish ships that made up half the allied fleet. He was certainly aware—he could not but be aware, after reading fifty reports on the subject from Decrès and Villeneuve—that with two or three exceptions these ships were badly rigged, badly armed, manned by crews picked up from the gutter, and commanded by officers who not only did not know their job, but were in addition fiercely hostile to the Empire and to France. Nevertheless he not only made no changes—not so much as a comma—in the orders which made disaster inevitable, but simply did nothing.

From then on, it was simply a matter of letting events take their course.

On October 10 Decrès received three letters from Villeneuve dated September 28, and transmitted the gist of them to the Emperor as he galloped towards Ulm.

The first of these letters said:

"Our crews are 2,207 men short. 649 men are on hospital at Cadiz."

The second:

"If character and daring are all that is required in the Imperial Navy, I think I can assure Your Excellency that our enterprise will be crowned by brilliant success."

The last was the most important of all, and was written at the very last minute, midnight on September 28:

"I have just received a report that the enemy's squadron has recently been joined by three ships of the line, one of them a three-decker, which have arrived from the west. Thus we know for sure that they have 31 ships of the line in this area."

What this meant was that a certain person whom Collingwood and Calder had long been awaiting under the walls of Cadiz, had now at last appeared. He requested that his incognito should be preserved and that no courtesies should be shown to him by which his identity might be disclosed.

This person's name was Horatio Nelson, of course.

XII

"WE ARE 33; THEY ARE 40"

"At half-past ten drove from dear dear Merton to go
to serve my King and Country. May the Great God
whom I adore enable me to fulfil the expectations
of my Country; and if it is His good pleasure that I
should return, my thanks will never cease being
offered up to the Throne of His Mercy. If it is His
good providence to cut short my days upon earth,
I bow with the greatest submission, relying that he
will protect those so dear to me, that I may leave
behind.—His will be done: Amen, Amen, Amen."
(Nelson: Friday night, September 13, 1805.)

It MAY be recalled that when Nelson arrived at Ushant on
August 15 he found an Admiralty instruction ordering him
back to England as soon as possible. Their Lordships were
anxious to hear his own account of the campaign. Four days
later he reached London, appeared before the aristocratic and
hair-splitting pontiffs of the naval hierarchy, and unfolded to
them, at length and with patience, the complete sequence of
his operations between Villeneuve's departure from Europe
and his return. Once this had been done, and their Lordships
satisfied, he had rushed to Merton. Emma awaited him with
Horatia at her side. She had aged, and was tired, for in February
she had given birth to a second daughter who had only survived three weeks. She had grown stouter, and had been
pining in her long solitude. Could she really believe that life
would begin again and go on as before, or that she and Horatio
would at last come to know the lasting happiness they had so
long pursued? She could not, for she knew that his return this
time was no more than a fleeting visit.

The dream crashed in ruins when Captain Blackwood arrived on the morning of September 2 with the announcement of the Franco-Spanish fleet's entry into Cadiz. Nelson considered that his must be the honour of fighting the final decisive battle. He hurried off at once to London to demand that the forces opposing Villeneuve should be placed under his command. Not only had Lord Barham (formerly Sir Charles Middleton) granted his request, but, with an unprecedented gesture, had given the bold petitioner "the right of freely choosing whatever ships he wished to accompany him".

"Horatio, Horatio, why are you so anxious to run into fresh dangers?"

Emma had wept copiously, but on Friday, September 13, the day before his departure, she had regained control of herself, fighting down her grief so as not to dishearten her man, who, once more, was off to fight for his country—his real mistress. Erect and dignified, hiding her tears with a wan smile, she had walked with him to his carriage. As he was getting in, Nelson did no more than pat her shoulder gently: "You are one of God's brave creatures, Emma! If there were more Emmas, there would be more Nelsons!"

And so the carriage rattled off into the night, leaving in the road, that ran by the white house round which they had built so many dreams, a broken-hearted woman.

*

Nelson set sail on the 15th with his own *Victory* and the frigate *Euryalus*.

On the 18th, off the Lizard, he had been joined by the line of battleships *Ajax* and *Thunderer*. Three more, *Royal Sovereign*, *Defiance* and *Agamemnon* were to come in later.

On September 25 he passed Lisbon, well out to sea, sending the frigate ahead to inform Collingwood of his impending arrival, and to request him to waive the regulation courtesies, so that the enemy's attention should not be attracted.

Thus on the morning of September 29, 1805, Villeneuve

and Nelson found themselves face to face once more. But the French admiral, though aware that the British fleet had received reinforcements, still did not know who was confronting him. He did not find out till October 2, and immediately wrote to Decrès:

"The troops are embarked and everybody is aboard. I am only waiting for the right moment to put to sea with the fleet. Admiral Gravina has received two special dispatches from the Spanish ambassador at Lisbon, informing him that Admiral Nelson has arrived in these waters, with four ships of the line, and with large-scale plans of attacking, bombarding and setting on fire the Franco-Spanish fleet, and Cadiz itself. We have reason to believe that the ships that arrived on September 28 are those referred to by the Spanish ambassador."

Of course this letter could not influence the course of events in any way. Napoleon, though warned by Lauriston's report that had reached him at Strasbourg, had not seen fit to go back on his previous orders, and Decrès was certainly not the one to take it on himself to alter them. Even if he had done so, on receipt of the letter just quoted, it would have been too late.

Villeneuve was eager to carry out the Emperor's orders. Thus, on October 7, without considering the enemy's strength or the condition of the majority of his own ships, but anxious to take advantage of an easterly wind which could bring the whole fleet out of harbour, ran up the signal "Prepare to sail", and then suddenly cancelled it. Was this because the wind, though remaining easterly, had begun "to blow stormy", as he wrote to Decrès the next day? Certainly not: it was rather because at the last minute certain considerations had caused him to think better of it.

"I cannot disregard the accounts that reach me from all quarters of the inferiority of our forces in comparison with those of the enemy."[1]

His best officers were, in fact, unanimous. "The English," they said, "have 31 to 33 of the line before Cadiz, including

[1] Letter to Decrès, October 8, 1805.

eight three-deckers. On our side, three of the Spanish ships are only just out of the dockyards, and not yet in a fit state for action. Our effective strength, then, is not 33, but 30 ships. To put to sea in these circumstances, with the certain prospect of an engagement, would be to take a *desperate course*, not only futile in itself, but against the interests of the allied cause!"

Villeneuve was in a state of the greatest uneasiness. Having cancelled the order to sail, he decided to call a conference for the following morning, October 8, on board his flagship, to which he summoned all general officers and the most experienced captains, both French and Spanish. He began by informing them, under pledge of secrecy "that His Imperial Majesty's intention was that the fleet should put to sea at the first favourable opportunity, and that wherever it encountered the enemy in inferior strength, it was to attack without hesitation, in order to force a decisive engagement". He then passed on to them the information he had received regarding the English fleet—at least 31 of the line and possibly as many as 33—and asked each man present to give "his opinion on the situation in which the allied fleet found itself".

All the officers present agreed that in view of the inferiority of their fleet, in comparison with the English, it was "necessary to await the favourable opportunity" mentioned in the Emperor's instructions, and that such an opportunity might arise either if weather conditions drove off the blockading force, or alternatively if the English were compelled to divide their force at a given moment.

The same evening Villeneuve wrote an account to Decrès: "I shall put to sea at the first favourable opportunity: our method of producing such an opportunity might perhaps be to send the Cartagena squadron off on a rather long cruise—as far as Cape Bon, for example—or to send it straight to Toulon, thus compelling the English to divide their forces. But it has occurred to me that such an order could only come from the Emperor himself."

On this same October 8 four of the Spanish warships at

Cartagena put to sea on hearing that a convoy of English troops, consisting of about fifty transports, was about to leave Gibraltar and enter the Mediterranean. For three days they cruised about on the war-path six leagues from land, but when the convoy failed to appear, they returned whence they had come, and no more was said on the subject. Nelson had therefore nothing to fear.

Indeed, since his arrival off Cadiz, he had drawn the net still tighter by organising the blockade on a rational basis. Five frigates were permanently stationed at the harbour mouth, as a first line: the second consisted of three ships of the line three or four leagues out to sea; while the main body, permanently stationed 16 to 18 leagues west of the coast, on the level of Cadiz, was to close in whenever the wind blew from the east, so as not to be carried further out to sea. The trap was well sprung, but to make assurance doubly sure Nelson went on demanding frigates, and yet more frigates. "I have not forgotten Aboukir!" he kept saying. He wanted scouts posted at every cape, on both sides of the Strait, and before Cartagena, so as not to miss a single movement of Villeneuve. He was also apprehensive of being below strength when the moment came, for he had to send his ships of the line six at a time to Gibraltar and Tetuan for revictualling, which reduced his permanent effective force to 23 or 24 ships at the most. Still, all in all, Nelson was not dissatisfied with himself. On October 6 he wrote:

"I verily believe the country will soon be put to some expense for my account, either a monument, or a new pension and honours; for I have not the very smallest doubt but that a very few days, almost hours, will put us in Battle. The success no man can ensure, but the fighting them, if they are to be got at, I pledge myself, and if the force arrives which is intended. I am very, very, very anxious for its arrival, for the thing will be done if a few more days elapse."

On the 9th the *Royal Sovereign*, of 100 guns, arrived from England, and Collingwood, now second-in-command, was able to transfer his flag to her. Four days later the *Agamemnon* and the *Africa*, each of 64 guns, duly joined up, the former having narrowly escaped Captain Allemand who was prowling out to sea off Oporto. To balance this accession, Sir Robert Calder left the fleet on the 13th on his way to London to appear before a court of enquiry on his conduct of the battle of July 22.[1] He sailed in his own ship, a splendid line of battleship of 90 guns, that Nelson, with the most courteous consideration, was determined to let him take. Perhaps this courtesy was a trifle excessive, depriving him as it did of a ship of such quality at such a juncture, but it was a measure of his contempt for the useless hero of the "Fifteen-Twenty"!

"My dear Coll., perhaps, as the weather is fine . . . you will come on board this forenoon. . . . I am glad Sir Robert Calder is gone. . . . I send you my Plan of Attack . . . but it is to place you perfectly at ease respecting my intentions, and to give full scope to your judgment for carrying them into effect. We can, my dear Coll., have no little jealousies. We have only one great object in view, that of annihilating our Enemies, and getting a glorious Peace for our Country. No man has more confidence in another than I have in you; and no man will render your services more justice than your very old friend!"

During this period Villeneuve was constantly on the watch for his "favourable opportunity". It did not come, but meanwhile on October 15 he received a private letter telling him of the journey to Bayonne "of Vice-Admiral Rosily, on a mission to Cadiz". He was delighted. "No news could be more welcome," he wrote to Decrès. "The experience and understanding of Vice-Admiral Rosily will come most opportunely to my assistance, and when he has taken stock, I shall have nothing to fear from his judgment upon circumstances present or past."

[1] Sir Robert Calder had asked the Admiralty's permission on September 30 to defend himself against the attacks that had been made on him. The court of enquiry met on December 23 and 26, and inflicted a "severe reprimand".

Poor innocent Villeneuve, without spite and without malice! As usual, he was the last to be informed, and the last to understand, and remained totally unaware of his own impending tragedy. Rosily had already been forty-eight hours on the road from Madrid to Cadiz. He had reached the Spanish capital on the evening of the 10th, and left again on the 14th, having been delayed by a breakdown of his carriage. He had called upon Beurnonville the ambassador, handing him a letter of introduction together with Decrès' explanations. Like a true diplomat, Beurnonville was careful to take advantage of the situation and displayed an untimely zeal:

"I did not consider it my duty to advise M. Villeneuve of M. Rosily's arrival in Madrid. Since you did not suggest that I should take any steps in the matter in your letter delivered to me by M. Rosily, and since the Vice-Admiral himself admitted to me that he had given his colleague no information regarding the measures taken in respect of his replacement, I thought it prudent to take the same course." (To Decrès, October 20.)

All the same, when he saw Villeneuve's successor take the road for Cadiz, the ambassador could no longer conceal his uneasiness:

"I have every reason to believe that he will reach Cadiz before M. Villeneuve has been informed of the situation."

But it took a traveller of quality ten days to reach the great port from the capital. Admiral Rosily arrived too late.

*

After veering from west to north, the wind changed suddenly to east, and on October 18 the sun rose upon a beautiful sea. Nelson gave a cry of joy when he saw it:

"The Combined Fleets cannot have finer weather to put to sea," he wrote in his diary as soon as he awoke.

The atmosphere was so clear on the horizon that from the opposite side in the Cadiz anchorage, the French and Spaniards could distinctly see the watch-dogs of the English fleet as they cruised indefatigably two miles out to sea. There were five

frigates, one brig and a schooner. It was proposed that
Magon should make a sally with seven of the line on the
ensuing night in an attempt to chase away the intruders and
capture one or two of them. Meanwhile the Franco-Spanish
fleet was leading its normal routine existence, with cleaning
fatigues, training of recruits, and maintenance of warlike
stores. As usual, Villeneuve was writing to Decrès. But it was
no longer the Villeneuve "Coward in spirit", hitherto so
familiar. A rumour that had reached him at dawn from the
mainland had lit a spark of strange resolution in his eyes. His
pen scratched its way along:

"I am informed that Vice-Admiral Rosily has arrived at
Madrid. People are saying that he is coming to take over
command of the fleet. I shall most certainly be charmed to
yield him first place, so long as I am permitted to occupy the
second; so much is due to his length of service and his abilities.
But it would be altogether intolerable for me to lose all hope
of showing myself capable of better things. Be that as it may,
my lord, I am at a loss to explain your silence on the matter of
Vice-Admiral Rosily's mission, unless it were due to the hope
that I might succeed in carrying out the assignment with which
I am charged at this time. Whatever difficulties lie ahead, if
the wind allows me to leave harbour, I shall set sail to-
morrow.

"I beg Your Excellency to accept my respectful com-
pliments."

The signature is violent to brutality. Perhaps he had in mind
a cruel saying of Napoleon's, which the fleet had recently been
gloating over: "The English will look small indeed when
France has two or three admirals willing to lay down their
lives!"

"If the wind allows me to leave harbour, I shall set sail
to-morrow," Villeneuve had written.

The wind was indeed favourable, and appeared likely to
remain so for a day or two longer: therefore it was becoming
unavoidable for him to set sail. But doubtless providence did

not wish the fate of the whole fleet to depend on one man's bitter feelings. No sooner had the admiral sent off his letter to Decrès than the coastguards gave him an unexpected piece of information: an English convoy anchored at Gibraltar had started for the Mediterranean. This convoy, which had already provoked the Spanish ships into leaving Cartagena, the look-out man went on, had put to sea with an escort of four men-of-war; there was another man-of-war in harbour, with its mainmast missing; yet another was making its way into the Strait, apparently with the purpose of revictualling at the arsenal. Thus, at the very moment that the wind was opening a way out of Cadiz harbour for the allied fleet, the English found their strength docked by six ships of the first rank.

This was indeed the "favourable opportunity", the object of so many hopes, and it had occurred as if miraculously to help Villeneuve to defend his outraged dignity and honour.

There was no more need for hesitation.

The admiral had lost the last scruples that might have kept him in harbour; he summoned Gravina and told him his plan. Already the daylight was waning. At sunset the *Bucentaure* signalled the fleet to prepare to set sail, to unmoor, and to hoist in the boats.

The following day, October 19, 1805, at 9.30 in the morning, Nelson was feeling gay, and had just sent a friendly message to Collingwood: "What a beautiful day! Will you be tempted out of your ship? If you will, hoist the assent and *Victory's* pendants." It was at this moment that the English line of battleship *Mars*, stationed five leagues east of the main body, telegraphed to the *Victory* the brief report just received from one of the watching frigates before Cadiz: "The enemy is hoisting anchor!"

*

Two navies, two schools of thought were about to engage, led by two men, each other's opposite in every respect.

Nelson was forty-seven, and the most illustrious member of

the Royal Navy. This was due less to his courage under fire—
many captains in the British fleet were his equals on that score
—than to the breadth and acuteness of his perception, the
soundness and speed of his decisions, his talent for organisation, his gift for training men, his insatiable ambition, his
supreme contempt for any adversary who was accorded the
honour of engaging him—and, lastly, his unlimited love of
fighting and of life itself.

Villeneuve was forty-two. He was one French seaman
among many others, deeply patriotic, a good service-man, a
good fighter, honourable and straight. But he lacked imagination and daring, enthusiasm and will-power. He was incapable
of understanding his men, nor did they understand him. He
was outpaced and overwhelmed by the stormy genius of his
all-powerful master. He was a weakling, a fatalist, diffident
and sceptical, who was energetic only in his despair, and
resolute only in his resignation.

For a long time these two men had been poised to take each
other's measure, while the vicissitudes of warfare had taken
them from the Mediterranean to the West Indies and back
again to the approaches of the Pillars of Hercules.

During his chase to the West Indies, at Merton in August,
and finally on his way to Cadiz, Nelson had been keeping
before him the principles Rodney had laid down at Les Saintes
Islands as well as his own experiences at Cape St Vincent and
Aboukir. With these in mind he had evolved and drafted a
battle plan bearing his own distinguishing mark, "the Nelson
Touch" as he called it. As soon as he arrived at Cadiz he laid
this plan before all the captains who had assembled on the
Victory to greet him. He gave them a methodical explanation
of what he wished to do, and why. This made a profound
impression—"like an electric shock", if we may believe
Nelson himself. "Some shed tears, all approved. It was new—
it was singular—it was simple! It must succeed if ever they will
allow us to get at them." But Nelson was not content
with this. On October 9 he wrote a "Memorandum"

entirely with his left hand, which was later recopied for the requirements of commanding officers. In this he summed up in black and white the essential principles of the "Nelson Touch", that is to say, of the manner in which he proposed to fight the battle in the event of an engagement with Villeneuve.

We cannot here go into the details of a document that is, in any case, somewhat confused, and was far from being susceptible of a literal application. We shall therefore confine ourselves to illustrating its underlying spirit, and tracing its main outline.

With his acute realism—at least in naval matters—Nelson had fully gauged the importance of the battle that was about to take place. To inflict a decisive defeat on Villeneuve would be to make the seas safe round France and Spain for an indefinite period, and enable England to consolidate her naval hegemony, to increase her colonial power, and thus, in the end, to win the war. In a word, it would change the face of the globe. But in order to gain a victory of such importance, the old beaten paths must be left behind; the tactics used must be very different from those that had regulated so many sea-battles during the past two centuries, and had produced, with only one or two exceptions, nothing but disputed or questionable results.

It was almost certain that the timid Villeneuve, his mind occupied more with defensive than offensive ideas, would adopt the classic formation when he met the English fleet. He would string out his fleet to cover several miles, like some nerveless creature, exposed to attack on all sides. Now, Nelson would not attack this fleet by sailing along one of its flanks in single file, and contenting himself with firing broadsides as he went by. *His aim would rather be to dismember it, and then crush it in detail by previously dividing his own force into three groups, sailing in column.* The first, 16 strong, would be under command of Nelson himself; the second, of similar strength, would be led by Collingwood, Nelson's second-in-command; the third and last, of eight warships, would be on call to lend assistance in this direction or that, according to circumstances.

Two alternative situations had to be considered, depending upon whether the Franco-Spaniards were to *windward* or to *leeward*. If the former, Collingwood's column would begin the action by breaking through the enemy line at the twelfth ship, at the head of the reinguard; Nelson's column would then cut through the centre; while the third column, or advanced division, would break in at the head of the line, about the third or fourth ship "so as to be sure of engaging the commander-in-chief, whom every effort must be made to capture". If to *leeward* (as actually happened) Collingwood would once more attack first, but this time in line ahead, so as to surround the last 12 ships of the French line; meanwhile Nelson, with the rest of the fleet, would busy himself with the advance guard and centre, ensuring that no aid was forthcoming for the group his second-in-command was attacking.

This "Memorandum" postulated a strength of 40 on the English side and 46 on the allied, and provided for a threefold division of the British fleet, as we have just seen. However, no more than 60 ships were in action on Trafalgar day, and the English fought in two columns only. But that is of little significance. The most remarkable thing about Nelson's dispositions was not so much their technical mastery, as the spirit behind them.

The essential in Nelson's eyes was to attack with intelligence and to conquer with resolution. The outline he had traced aimed fundamentally at co-ordination of preliminary movements. For the rest, the admiral avoided laying down any definite rule ("Some things must be left to chance—nothing is certain in a naval battle!"), and placed great reliance on the instinct and daring of his subordinates. "The Second-in-Command will, after my intentions are made known to him, have the entire direction of his line to make the attack upon the Enemy, and to follow up the blow until they are captured or destroyed", he had specified. Then, in order that each officer should feel at ease, he had been careful to add this clause to his orders, which obviated in advance all misunderstandings and lapses:

"In case Signals can neither be seen or perfectly understood, no Captain can do very wrong if he places his Ship alongside that of an Enemy."

Villeneuve, for his part, had no illusions. The day after the engagement off Ferrol he had written to Decrès: "Our naval tactics are outdated. All we can do is to form line, and that is what the enemy wants. I have neither the means nor the time, nor the opportunity to inculcate fresh tactics into the captains commanding the men-of-war of the allied navies. Most of them have never given the matter a thought and have no material for comparison in their heads. I believe they will all stick to their posts, but not one is capable of making a bold decision."

His order of battle had been cut and dried for a long time:

If the enemy were to leeward, the fleet would form line of battle, and attack them "all at once", each ship making for her opposite number in the enemy line;

If, on the other hand, the enemy were to windward, and showed signs of attacking, the fleet would await the attack with its line of battle in close formation.

Villeneuve was well aware, knowing Nelson as he did, that he would be offered no choice between these two plans, the one offensive, and the other defensive; he would inevitably be driven back on the second. Furthermore, with a sort of tragic second sight, he had divined the tactics the one-armed admiral would use to defeat him. He had said to his captains:

"The enemy will not be content with forming a line of battle parallel with our own, and then engaging us in an artillery duel in which victory depends less often on skill than on good luck. *He will try to cut off our rear-guard, to break through our line, and to bring up groups of his own ships against any of ours that he may have isolated, and then surround and destroy them.*"

How was this danger to be met? After full consideration,

Villeneuve decided to form an "observer squadron", under command of Gravina. This group would have the task of sailing to windward of the allied line, so that in case of need it could relieve this or that part of the line where the threat was most serious. In making this arrangement, he was giving a small sop to the vanity of his touchy allies. But Villeneuve, who had virtually abandoned his post at Aboukir, felt deeply convinced that this was not the true solution. It lay in the behaviour of the crews, and, even more, in the steadiness of the officers under fire:

"A captain in charge of a ship must consult his own courage and desire for glory far more than the signals run up by the admiral. The latter may well be in the thick of the fight, and enveloped in smoke, and have no chance of signalling.

"*Any captain who is not under fire is not at his post*; if a ship before or behind him is closer to the enemy than he is, he is not at his post. A signal to recall him to his duty would be a blot on his honour."

The tone of these orders was certainly not without its vigour and grandeur. But, in the words of Johannès Tramond: "What could these last minute exhortations avail against ingrained and habitual passivity, which was considered the highest duty, and had become second nature to the French commanders?"

*

It will be remembered that it was at 9.30 that Nelson received the great news: "The enemy is coming out of the anchorage."

Four hours earlier, at dawn on this Saturday, October 19, the *Bucentaure* had given the allied fleet the signal to set sail.

As on the previous day, the weather was magnificent. The sea was fanned by a light breeze from the north-west. The sun was up, dazzling and warm; visibility was perfect. About 7 o'clock the look-out on the English frigate *Euryalus*, which was nearest the land, had been surprised to note that he could even make out the surf breaking on the beach. And suddenly, as

he stared from beside the harbour towards the forest of bare
and dismal masts that showed where the enemy fleet was at
anchor, he had seen a brown flapping patch against the clear
sky, then two, then ten!

"Ahoy! They are hoisting their topsails! My eye! They're
getting under way! Yes—they're getting under way!"

It was now 7.20. A few moments later the *Euryalus*—Captain
Blackwood—(the very same man who had informed Nelson
at Merton of the entry of the Franco-Spaniards into Cadiz),
was covered with many-coloured squares and triangles of
bunting:

"The enemy is coming out of the anchorage!" And so from
ship to ship, from frigate to man-of-war, the news flew over
the ocean until it reached Nelson's *Victory*, fifty miles away.

"The enemy is coming out of the anchorage, sir!"

"At last! Signal the whole squadron: general chase south-
east!"

Before 10 o'clock Nelson was on his way to close the Straits
of Gibraltar. In view of the lightness of the wind, he did not
expect to be in position until the following day. But this did
not worry him, for he knew that Villeneuve would take at
least as long to get clear of Cadiz—a difficult harbour to
negotiate at the best of times. He also knew that he could
rely on his scouts to keep him in continuous touch with the
situation as it developed.

So the signals followed one another.

At 11 o'clock Blackwood telegraphed:

"19 ships under sail. All the rest have got their top
gallant yards up except the Spanish rear-admiral and one ship
of the line."

At noon:

"In spite of the light wind, the enemy is still coming out. All
the rest, but for one ship, are ready, with their yards hoisted."

At 2 o'clock in the afternoon:

"The enemy is still coming out. Seven ships of the line and
two frigates are clear already."

Meanwhile at Ulm, on the road to Vienna, 30,000 Austrians laid down their arms, and gave Napoleon his first imperial victory.

Rear-Admiral Magon had been the first to raise anchor, leading out the nine ships signalled by the *Euryalus*, and compelling that frigate to withdraw out to sea. But a combination of calm and current had kept the rest of the fleet within the anchorage, and in order to avoid movement at night Villeneuve found himself obliged to postpone further operations until the following day.

During the night the wind veered to the south-east, and the sky became overcast. Rain was falling at daybreak. Magon remained close to the coast, with topsails set, and once again drove away the English frigates, even contriving to recapture from them an American brig they had in tow. Meanwhile Villeneuve was hurrying on the process of clearing the ships that still remained within the anchorage.

At 8 o'clock, in a final letter to Decrès, he wrote: "The whole squadron is now under sail except for three men-of-war. Eighteen enemy ships are signalled. Probably the citizens of Cadiz will be able to give you some news of us during the day." With a touch of melancholy he added: "My only motive, my lord, in making this sortie has been a burning desire to carry out His Majesty's wishes and to do my utmost to wipe out the displeasure he feels at the results of my recent operations. If I succeed, I shall find it difficult not to believe that all went as it should, and that everything was working together for the greater good of His Majesty's service."

By 11.30 the whole fleet was clear of the harbour, and moving in a west-north-westerly direction in more or less disordered formation. There was a heavy swell on the sea which boded bad weather. Wisps of mist drifted across the curtain of rain. Visibility was bad, but just sufficient for an occasional glimpse of the English frigates as they ran for the horizon like hounds on a scent.

In the early afternoon Villeneuve gave orders to wear, and form up in three columns heading south-west. This manœuvre caused some confusion, and had not been completed by 6 o'clock, when the *Achille*, one of the advanced guard, signalled 18 sail to west-south-westward. This was Nelson, advancing from the Straits of Gibraltar which he had reached that morning, under the guidance of his screen of scouts. Villeneuve immediately gave the command for the whole fleet to close up. Two hours later, as the danger seemed to him more definite, he signalled the fleet to form line of battle.

Night had already fallen. Guided only by a flare at the mizzen of Gravina's flagship, now leading the line, the fleet began to straggle out in a long and ill-regulated procession. Every ship was jostling to find its proper position in a terrifying bow-to-stern progress. The seamen served their ships in silence, nerves at breaking-point. From time to time the darkness was shattered by eerie blue flashes accompanied by the sound of gunfire—a sure sign that the English had gathered their whole force and were now on the track of their prey, determined not to let it escape them.

About 5 o'clock on the morning of the 21st the few stars that still pierced the inky sky with their points of silver were growing pale, as eastwards, beside Cape Trafalgar, the grey of dawn began to appear. To the British squadron, on a north-north-easterly course, it revealed the unwieldy mass of the Franco-Spanish fleet, standing out against a dismal curtain of mist. They were in some disorder, headed southward, about 10 miles from the English, and 12 from the land. At first, the English did not seem anxious to interfere with them. But at 6.30 Nelson, who had been on the *Victory's* poop since dawn, judged the moment had come to assume battle formation. After signalling "Form two columns in line ahead", he ordered "Set course east-north-east". This done, he went to his cabin, sat down at the narrow table he used as a writing-table, slipped a sheet of writing-paper under his left hand, and wrote this short note:

"My Dearest beloved Emma, the dear friend of my
bosom. . . . May the God of Battles crown my endeavours
with success, at all events I will take care that my name shall
ever be most dear to you and Horatia, both of whom I love
as much as my own life. . . . May Heaven bless you prays
your

'Nelson and Bronte'."

After adding his blessing to Horatia "his adopted daughter",
he sent word to Captain Hardy, commanding the *Victory*,
and Captain Blackwood, commanding the *Euryalus*, to come
and see him. While he waited for them he took a fresh sheet
of paper, and began again to write:

"Codicil to Lord Nelson's Will;
October the twenty-first, one thousand eight hundred and five,
then in sight of the Combined Fleets of France and Spain
distant about ten miles.
"Whereas the eminent services of Emma Hamilton, widow
of the Right Honourable Sir William Hamilton, have been of
the very greatest service to our King and Country, to my
knowledge, without her receiving any reward from either our
King or Country . . . the British Fleet under my command
could never have returned the second time to Egypt, had not
Lady Hamilton's influence with the Queen of Naples caused
letters to be wrote to the Governor of Syracuse, that he was
to encourage the Fleet being supplied with everything, should
they put into any Port in Sicily. We put into Syracuse, and
received every supply, went to Egypt, and destroyed the French
Fleet. Could I have rewarded these services I would not now
call upon my Country; but as that has not been in my power,
I leave Emma Lady Hamilton, therefore, a Legacy to my King
and Country, that they will give her an ample provision to
maintain her rank in life. I also leave to the beneficence of my
Country my adopted daughter Horatia Nelson Thompson;
[name given to the child at birth] and I desire that she will use

in future the name of Nelson only. These are the only favours I ask of my King and Country at this moment when I am going to fight their Battle. May God bless my King and Country, and all those who I hold dear. My relations it is needless to mention: they will of course be amply provided for. . . ."

This time all was in order. Blackwood and Hardy came in.

Nelson indicated the codicil, and simply asked them whether they would be good enough to act as his witnesses.

*

It was now 7 o'clock in the morning.

On board the French frigate, *Hermione*, scouting ahead, three officers with the aid of their telescopes had just finished a count of the compact fleet looming up out of the west.

"How many sail?" asked Captain Mahé.

"33."

"Right: signal '33 sail to windward—26 of the line, 4 frigates and 3 corvettes or sloops'."[1]

At the same time, on board the *Victory*, Blackwood was speaking to Nelson:

"We are 33; they are 40. . . . Considering the conditions on which they offer us battle, it will be a glorious achievement if we take 14 of their men-of-war."

"No!" snapped Nelson, "I shall not be satisfied with less than 20!"

---

[1] There was an error of observation in this signal. If the *Hermione* really sighted 33 sail, there were not 26 men-of-war, but 27, plus four frigates and only two corvettes.

XIII

THE BATTLE

THE POSITIONS on the chess-board were clear:

Eastwards, that is, towards the mainland, some 15 miles off
Cape Trafalgar, the Franco-Spanish fleet was sailing in a
southerly direction towards the Straits of Gibraltar. Their line
was in disorder.

North-westwards, that is on the seaward side, the English
fleet was on an east-north-easterly course. It presented the
appearance of a half-broken line formation, as it was about to
split into two colums.

There was a light west-north-westerly breeze, the sky was
overcast, and there was a heavy swell.

At 6.30, when in sight of the English, Villeneuve had
repeated his order of the previous evening to form line of
battle on the starboard tack, as his fleet was in a state of confusion. Twenty minutes later he had ordered the frigates to
reconnoitre the enemy. Finally at 7.20 in order to introduce
some cohesion into his line as soon as possible, he had fixed
the interval between ships at a cable's-length (about 200 yards).

Now the frigates were beginning to signal details of the
strength and movement of the English squadron. The *Hermione*, after giving their number as 26 (instead of 27), added
that the enemy, "moving in disorderly groups", was making
towards the rear-guard of Villeneuve's fleet. This was an
important piece of information. Villeneuve considered that
Nelson's object in so doing was not only to overwhelm the
allied rear-guard by weight of numbers, but to make it
impossible for the main body to withdraw to Cadiz. On the
other hand, since it was clear that a battle was unavoidable,
it would be preferable to fight near a friendly port rather than

far away. Consequently at 8 o'clock, without waiting any longer for his fleet to form a coherent line, the admiral ran up the signal to go about together, reversing their order and sailing on the port tack. The order was obeyed, and the fleet, which had been sailing southwards towards Gibraltar leaving Cadiz astern, was now taking a northerly course once more, that is, towards Cadiz and away from Gibraltar.

Nelson grimaced when he perceived this manœuvre. He had no fear that Villeneuve would escape him—it was too late for that; but the approaches to Cadiz are particularly difficult, and, as a storm was clearly brewing, he foresaw the terrible plight of ships disabled and out of control after the battle.

Two more hours passed.

Held back by lack of wind, the two fleets pursued their courses with exasperating slowness, the allied fleet pushing on towards Cadiz from the south, while the English sailed out of the west to meet them.

In order to grasp the relative positions of the two opposing forces, we may picture a bow about to discharge two arrows from left to right. The central part of the drawn bowstring represents the English fleet sailing in line ahead, while the two arrows resting against it and slightly separated from one another represent the two columns in process of forming. The upper arrow is Nelson's column, and the lower, Collingwood's. Finally, the bent bow itself exactly portrays the allied fleet.

In normal battle order, Villeneuve's fleet would have formed a single straight line just over four miles long. But as the ships at the head of his line were taking the wind of the others, the former heading northwards whilst the rear of the column was steering north-east, the line had become curved with the concave side towards the enemy. Thus his 33 men-of-war with their black hulls, some of them picked out with a double band of yellow or a wide band of red and yellow, covered a distance of little more than three miles.

At the head of the line was the Spaniard *Neptuno* of 80 guns,

Neptuno
Scipion
Intrepide
Formidable
(Dumanoir)

Africa

Ajax
Agamemnon

Minotaur

Duguay-Trouin
Mont Blanc

Spartiate

Rayo

Conqueror
Britannia
(Northesk)

Leviathan

San Francisco de Asis

Heros

San Agustin

Santissima Trinidad
(Cisneros)

Orion

Neptune

Bucentaure
(Villeneuve)

Temeraire

Victory
(Nelson)

Redoutable

San Justo

Santa Ana (Alava)

Neptune

Royal Sovereign (Collingwood)

San Leandro

Indomptable

Belle Isle

Fougueux

Mars

Pluton

Tonnant

Monarca

Bellerophon

Algesiras (Magon)

Bahama

Prince

Colossus

Aigle

Achilles

Montanes

Defence

Swiftsure

Defiance

Argonaute

Dreadnought

San
Ildefonso

Argonauta

Achille

Revenge

Principe de Asturias
(Gravina)

Berwick

San Juan Nepomuceno

Swiftsure

Poliphemus

Thunderer

	French & Spanish ships
	English ships

This sketch shows the position of the two fleets at the beginning of the
battle. The English fleet is divided into two columns, the northern led by
Nelson, the southern by Collingwood. The latter was the first to make
contact with the enemy, cutting in two the combined Franco-Spanish fleet.

followed by the Frenchmen *Scipion* and *Intrépide* of 74 each, the *Formidable* of 80, the *Duguay-Trouin* and the *Mont-Blanc* of 74; then came the Spaniards *San-Francisco-de-Asis* of 74, and *Rayo* of 100 guns. The *Rayo's* correct position was immediately behind the *Neptuno*, but she was a bad sailor, being fifty-six years old, and had fallen to leeward.

These eight ships formed a sort of advance guard under the orders of Rear-Admiral Dumanoir, commanding the 3rd squadron, and with his flag in the *Formidable*. Then there was a gap. Next came what may be called the main body led by the *Héros*, a French ship of 74 guns, and comprising the 80-gun Spaniard *San-Agustin*, also fallen to leeward on the starboard of the *Héros*; the Spanish giant *Santissima-Trinidad*, the largest warship in the world at that time (4 decks and 130 guns), carrying the flag of Rear-Admiral Cisneros, commanding the 1st squadron; Villeneuve's own *Bucentaure* of 80 guns; the *Redoutable* of 74, the best and possibly the best officered of all the French ships; the 74 gun Spaniard *San-Justo*; the French *Neptune* and the *San-Leandro* of 80 and 74 guns respectively.

Some 500 yards further southward sailed a reserve of five ships. These were the Spanish 110-gun ship *Santa-Ana*, carrying the flag of Vice-Admiral Alava, commanding the 2nd squadron, and near it the *Indomptable* of 74 guns, fallen to leeward, the *Fougueux* and the *Pluton*, both also of 74 guns, and finally the Spaniard *Monarca* of the same armament, now out to the eastward and trying to regain her correct position in the line.

A little further yet to southward came the Frenchman *Algésiras*, flying the flag of Rear-Admiral Magon, commanding the 1st division of the observer squadron, at the head of a group of 74-gun ships: the Spaniard *Bahama*, the Frenchmen *Aigle* and *Swiftsure* (the latter formerly captured from the English), and the Spaniard *Montanes*, drifting to leeward.

Finally seven men-of-war sailing independently brought up the rear of the line: the Frenchman *Argonaute* of 74 guns, the *San-Ildefonso* of 74 flanked by her fellow-Spaniard *Argonauta* of 92, the Frenchman *Achille* of 74, Gravina's flagship the *Principe-de-Asturias* of 118, the Frenchman *Berwick* (also formerly English) and the *San-Juan-Nepomuceno*, these two last both mounting 74 guns.

The allied fleet thus amounted to a total of 33 ships of the line with an aggregate armament of 2,626 guns, plus seven frigates and corvettes carrying 230 guns, making a grand total of 40 ships and 2,856 pieces of ordnance.

Superficially the English fleet, with 33 ships and 2,314 guns (27 of the line with 2,148 guns, plus 6 frigates and corvettes with 166) was decidedly less powerful. In fact, it was far the stronger, for, quite apart from the high standard of its officers and the superior training of its crews, it included seven three-deckers, as against four in the allied fleet (and all Spanish at that), and on the whole the English ships were faster sailing and manœuvred better.

It was, of course, Nelson with his splendid 100-gun *Victory*, who led the northern English column. Behind him came the *Temeraire* and the *Neptune*, both giants of 98 guns, then the *Leviathan* and the *Conqueror* both of 74, then another mighty 100-gunner, the *Britannia*, flying the flag of Rear-Admiral Northesk, the *Agamemnon* and *Ajax* of 64 guns, the *Minotaur*, the *Spartiate* and the *Orion* of 74, and finally the *Africa* of 64 guns, which had fallen to leeward during the night and was now crowding on sail to regain her position.

The southern column was the more important, consisting of 15 ships of the line against the 12 of Nelson's column. It was led by Collingwood's *Royal Sovereign*, a magnificent 100-gunner, that had been recently refitted. In her wake came the *Belleisle* of 74 and the *Tonnant* of 80 guns (both formerly French, and captured at Aboukir), the *Mars*, the *Bellerophon* known to history as the ship on which Napoleon embarked as a prisoner, the *Colossus* and the *Achille*, all four of 74 guns, the *Polyphemus* of 64, the *Revenge*, the *Swiftsure*, the *Defiance*, the *Thunderer*, and the *Defence*, all of 74, and finally the *Dreadnought* and the *Prince*, both giants of 98 guns, but slower than their companions.

Of all these ships Nelson's *Victory*, despite her forty years of good and loyal service (she had been launched in 1765), was undoubtedly the finest type of the "wooden walls" navy of the time, then approaching its peak.

She was 200 feet in length with a displacement of 2,500 tons. Each of her hundred bronze guns weighed over two-and-a-half tons. They varied from 12-pounders to 68-pounders, and could throw a ball of 30 pounds weight to a range of a mile and a half. In fact, however, the effective range did not exceed 550 yards, and even at that distance many shots fell in the sea short of their mark. But those that reached their destination usually caused heavy damage and cruel casualties as they burst and tore their way through. Nelson had said, "It is a hail of cannon-balls that will give England the mastery of the seas". He was right. The English gunners not only maintained a rate of fire two or three times that of their foes, but were splendidly trained, and excellent shots. The French aimed only at the masts and rigging, in the hope (almost always disappointed) of disabling the ship and so making it easy to capture by boarding. But the English aimed straight at the hull, so as to destroy the enemy's guns and, even more, their men. Human lives were their primary target. It was five years before Napoleon's seamen adopted these tactics to their own advantage, and their rule then became the slogan, "Aim low, my friends—the English don't like being killed!"

Meanwhile, on this morning of October 21, 1805, each side was prepared, after its own fashion, to sell its life dearly. From heavy guns to side-arms that would let out a man's blood in an instant—through the whole gamut of pistols, muskets, grenades and carronades (short pieces for firing hollow shot and charges of grape-shot)—every fearsome weapon invented by man was ready in its place.

Ever since dawn the master-gunners had worn a preoccupied air; for the guns were like the liveliest bucking horse; even a cunning system of ropes held them indifferently secure in their wooden carriages mounted on rollers. It was by no means a docile beast. If it became overheated it could equally well rush forwards or backwards, run careering to the opposite end of its battery or leap in the air. Even with those that had been thoroughly tested, almost anything could happen. So, then, its mouth, its harness, and its rounded bronze flanks were carefully inspected. Charges of powder were placed at the base of the gun carriage, within the gunner's reach, but without being too exposed to the enemy's fire; cannon-balls were carried in hammocks from the gun-room; decks were sprinkled with wet sand; doors, tables, chairs, benches and anything else that fire could easily get a hold on, had been dismounted and stowed in the holds.

Thus prepared, there was nothing to do but to trust to luck, and to the wooden heart of the ship whose solid walls recalled the fairest forests of the homeland, and were, incidentally, more than three feet thick. Everywhere men were awaiting their trial of fire and steel with that stoical resignation which is sooner or later identified with the "quiet heroism" so beloved of historians.

In what was normally the midshipmen's quarters, the surgeon had set up his "clinic", lit his candles, and prepared his operating table—an ordinary table covered with a length of sailcloth. He laid out his delicate instruments, knives, scalpels, saws, and the sponges and lint to check haemorrhage, leather gags to be thrust into the patients' mouths by his assistants, rum to prevent fainting, and tubs to receive the amputated limbs or shreds of flesh from the wounded. The surgeon knows what a battle means. Soon he will not have a moment of respite, and it is lucky for him that the wounds vary little, and that his patients are not choir-boys!

All concerned here have long ago learnt how to suffer and how to make light of death. The officers entered the service from a love of danger and adventure; they have been tossed from ocean to ocean since boyhood. While still boys, they have known, in the course of their service, the heat of battle, of alcohol, of brothels, and the torments of tropical fever. As for

the crews, the only difference between them and the galley-
slaves at Lepanto is that they have no chains round their
ankles. But apart from that, they, too, are in a wretched state
of misery. They are the flotsam of society, vagabonds dragged
from prison at an Admiralty's behest, or else simply poor
wretches press-ganged in some monstrous round-up. Their
life on board is unimaginably frightful, from the discomfort
and filth of the ships themselves, and the rough conditions of
service, as much as from the iron discipline that grinds them
down.

A fine range of corporal punishments was in use: men
were flogged, chained in the bilge or hanged at the yard-arm
with carefree abandon. Hygiene was unknown, and food
abominable. On every voyage more casualties were caused by
dysentery, typhus and cholera than by gunfire. What, then,
did it matter to such men whether they were drowned or
killed by grape-shot, when they had abandoned all hope as
soon as they had taken service in the fleet?

All in all, they thought of battle, with its succession of
danger and adventure, as a means of escape—the best sport
possible. But the most astonishing thing was that these wretches
were always ready for any sacrifice to defend the flag of the
country that had enslaved them. It was their own peculiar way
of freeing themselves from their slavery; above all it was their
way of showing that, despite appearances, they had not wholly
lost pride in their manhood, that in their utmost misery they
still possessed not only a great deal of courage but a modicum
of honour.

*

It was nearly 11 o'clock.

There were still two miles to go before the English fleet
came within range; they had crowded all canvas, even to their
studding-sails—those small sails never used in battle—to
catch every breath of the feeble breeze. The crews of the
Franco-Spanish fleet watched the English ships grow larger

and clearer, and they saw their black hulls—also picked out with a double band of yellow—breasting the long swell of dark green water with their potent prows.

Nelson's column appeared to be heading for the advance-guard of the allied fleet, moving in line ahead, its formation somewhat irregular. Collingwood's column meanwhile was making straight for the rear-guard, and seemed to be moving in ill-formed line abreast. This had no suggestion of an attack on orthodox lines. It gave the impression rather of the approach of some ponderous and irresistible two-headed siege-engine. Behind the more forward ships the slower ones strove hard to keep up with the battering-ram which in less than an hour's time would be smashing into the wall of the French and Spanish navies.

Villeneuve stood on the poop of the *Bucentaure* in undress uniform, his hair freshly powdered, and calmly contemplated the spectacle. In the middle of the morning he had given orders to the leading ships to hug the wind and crowd on sail to prevent congestion of the line, and to the rear-guard to make all the headway they could, so as to be in a position to cover the centre, the most vital point. This was done, and the feeble-ness of the breeze and the sea-conditions rendered unnecessary any further manœuvre to "straighten out" the line. There was nothing more, then, for him to do, but to keep his eyes fixed on the enemy and await his chance to demonstrate that, in spite of what the Emperor had said, an admiral of France still knew how to fight and how to die. But how slowly the time passed! Within the enormous arena the two fleets seemed never to get any closer. All the same, at 11.15 Villeneuve felt that it was time to put an end to these elegant preliminaries, and at his order the signal "Open fire as soon as the enemy is within range" was run up on the *Bucentaure*, even before his own flag and the ensign.

It was as if the spirit of the fleet had been suddenly trans-formed. Above the noise of military bands and the shrill bosuns' whistles, a mighty roar passed along the line from end to end to greet with numberless cries of "Long live the Emperor!" and "Long live the King!" the tricolour standards and the banners of the two Castiles as they broke against the grey sky.

For a few seconds Villeneuve paused to listen to the fierce swell of the cheering as the sea breeze carried it in snatches towards the land. Then, accompanied by his chief of staff and preceded by two midshipmen carrying the imperial eagle, he made a last round of inspection of the batteries of the *Bucentaure*. As they passed slowly, almost as at a religious ceremony, the heavy drum-beats supplied a burden to the shrill music of the fifes, while seamen stripped to the waist, their heads tied in bandanas, and soldiers in uniform wearing their leather shakos, jostled one another to touch the hands of their Commander-in-Chief, shouting at the pitch of their voices "Long live the Emperor!" "Long live Admiral Villeneuve!"

Simultaneously the same ceremony took place on board all the other vessels of the fleet, with the same demonstrations of enthusiasm. The men seemed intoxicated. Forgotten were the gruelling passage to the West Indies, the disappointments of July 22, the comrades dropped overboard with iron weights at their feet, and the tavern brawls at Ferrol and Cadiz. Even the Spaniards had regained confidence under the protection of the Holy Cross displayed beneath their national flag.

It was at this time also that Nelson, oblivious alike to the clamour of the opposing fleet and to the cheering of his own men at the sight of St. George's flag, went down to his cabin, sank on his knees, and wrote in his diary this prayer: "May the Great God, whom I worship, grant to my Country, and for the benefit of Europe in general, a great and glorious Victory; and may no misconduct in any one tarnish it; and may humanity after Victory be the predominant feature in the British Fleet. For myself, individually, I commit my life to Him who made me and may his blessing light upon my endeavours for serving my Country faithfully. To him I resign myself and the just cause which is entrusted to me to defend. Amen. Amen. Amen."

This done, he put on his best uniform with his most glittering decorations, and locked away his portrait of Emma, so that it should not be found broken or stained after the battle. He then returned to the poop with a brisk step. Those that were there—Hardy, Blackwood (who had not yet rejoined his ship), the secretary, the chaplain, the surgeon—exchanged looks of dismay as he appeared. He was no longer a mere man, but a blazing sun of gold and silver. On his blue jacket, with the right sleeve, as ever, empty and folded over, the various orders and decorations shone with many-coloured fire, splendid, but an inviting target. His appearance was almost uncanny, as it were a challenge to the enemy and a glove flung in the face of death. But what could they do? Could they ask him, vain and headstrong as he was, to conceal his prodigious personality under a cloak of anonymity—especially when, only an hour earlier, he had emphatically refused to leave the dangerous decks of the *Victory* and direct the battle from Blackwood's frigate?

In any case, it was too late. The English squadron was bearing down close on the allied fleet, which had curved in upon itself like some monster that senses the approach of a storm. Clearly and more clearly still the English could hear the roll of the French drums, and the unceasing cries of "Long live the Emperor!" Nelson was radiant. Well, he thought, even if the manœuvre did not precisely conform to the "Memorandum", it had the general idea, and he could count on the dash of his men for the rest! Only the threatening, lowering sky worried him.

"Signal prepare to anchor at the end of the day," he said to Lieutenant Pasco a moment later.

He then adjusted his glass, and carefully observed the enemy fleet from which the *Victory* was now separated by less than half a mile. Next he turned his glass towards the second column that seemed to have almost made contact, and uttered a cry of admiration:

"See how that noble fellow Collingwood carries his ship into action!"

Immediately after this, as if struck by a brilliant idea, he lowered his glass, and asked Blackwood:

"Do you not think we should run up one more signal? Something like 'Nelson confides that every man will do his duty'?"

"It is an idea," replied Blackwood, who was obviously searching for words, "but possibly it might be better to say, 'England expects . . .' "

"You are right, Blackwood. Mr. Pasco, if you please— signal this message to the fleet: 'England expects that every man will do his duty!' "

A minute more, and the signal was flapping at the *Victory's* main top in a string of coloured flags, for all the squadron to see, and for posterity to acclaim.

Nelson seemed really relieved.

"Now," said he, "there is nothing more I can do! Signal No. 16 [close action], see that it is hoisted and made fast, and that it never comes down!"

The allied fleet was now at a range of no more than a quarter of a mile.

With a warm smile, Nelson offered his hand to Blackwood:

"I think the time has come for you to return to your *Euryalus*, my dear friend."

"Yes, sir. And when I come back, very soon, you will have captured twenty ships of the line!"

Nelson shook his head, gazed steadily at Blackwood, as if he would impart some important confidence:

"God bless you, Blackwood, I shall never speak to you again."

It was now a matter of minutes.

Collingwood's *Royal Sovereign* was pushing in like a wedge between the Spanish warship *Santa-Ana*, sailing seventeenth in the allied line, and the French *Fougueux* immediately behind her. On Collingwood's starboard were the remainder of his pack, the *Belleisle*, the *Mars* and the *Tonnant*, each making straight for one of the allied rear-guard.

There was an amazing silence over the sea. On board the *Royal Sovereign* the gunners held their breath as they lay flat on their stomachs, taking cover from the first enemy broadside. High up on the poop a quartermaster stood by the imperturbable officers, and was just deciphering the signal that flew from the *Victory's* main top, alongside Signal No. 16, which he called out in a loud voice: "England . . . expects . . . that . . . every . . . man . . ."

"I wish Nelson would stop signalling," exclaimed Collingwood. "We know well enough what we have to do!"

He was interrupted by a thundering flash of purple flame bursting with ferocious violence from the black hull of the *Fougueux*.

It was 11.55.

*

Fire now followed fire all along the line, rising to a crescendo of fury. Each ship in turn opened fire.

After the *Fougueux*, the *Santa-Ana* let fly; then the *Indomptable* and the *Monarch*, sailing close to starboard. Imperturbably, the *Royal Sovereign* pressed on. In the course of the next five minutes she came within musket range of Admiral Alava's flagship, opened fire, hauled close to the wind and bore down on her opponent with her full weight, yard against yard. Amid the whining of musket-balls and the yelling of men could be heard the dry cracking of woodwork and rigging as they were wrenched away. The *Fougueux* tried to crowd on sail to come to the aid of the *Santa-Ana*. Hardly had she got into action when a devastating broadside swept her poop; it came from the *Belleisle*, which was following the *Royal Sovereign* in cutting the allied line. After her came the *Mars*, firing at the *Pluton*. Meanwhile, the *Bellerophon* was coming alongside the

Aigle, bearing down directly on the bows of the French ship, whilst astern of the latter another attacker was looming up, the *Colossus*, trying to get to grips with the *Swiftsure*.

Within twenty minutes every ship of the allied line between the 17th and 24th found herself engaged by one of the leading vessels of Collingwood's column. But this was only a prelude, and an extremely slow one because of the light wind, for Nelson's column was not yet in action. Up to now it had been making for the head of the Franco-Spanish line, as if to cut off all possible retreat to Cadiz, but it now went on the opposite tack towards their centre, sailing parallel to the allied advance guard, but in the opposite direction. Six of Nelson's ships formed a more or less compact group. The *Victory* was still leading, with the *Temeraire* on her starboard side; behind her, and to port, came the *Neptune*, the *Leviathan*, and the *Conqueror*, and lastly, far out to port, the *Africa*, that had become separated from the main body during the night. The six other ships of the column, the *Orion*, *Britannia*, *Spartiate*, *Minotaur*, *Ajax* and *Agamemnon*, had fallen more or less to the rear, and were in any case not in a position to come quickly into action.

At 12.40 the *Victory* came within range of the Frenchman *Scipion*, sailing behind the *Neptuno*, and the second of the allied line. Suddenly a violent cannonade burst out, running from north to south as, following the *Scipion*, the *Intrépide*, the *Formidable*, the *Duguay-Trouin*, the *Mont-Blanc*, the *San-Francisco-de-Asis* and the *Héros* opened fire in turn on Nelson's flagship. To no avail. Undismayed by these broadsides that merely surrounded her with dozens upon dozens of jets of spray, the *Victory* swept majestically on her course towards her chosen objective, Villeneuve's *Bucentaure*, at the centre of the line.

From time to time Nelson was trying unsuccessfully to make out the tall silhouette of Collingwood's flagship through the curtain of smoke that engulfed the southern part of the battle. The *Royal Sovereign* was out of control, grappled to the *Santa-*

Ana, and raked by the fire of the *Fougueux*, the *Monarca*, and the *Indomptable*. She had lost her main and mizzen masts. Her gun-decks were strewn with dead and wounded. But she was not the only sufferer. Grape-shot was flying everywhere, mowing down, ripping, and slashing—taking an ever heavier toll as the men warmed to their work and as fresh English ships came into action against the enemy rear-guard.

As the *Fougueux* came to grips with Collingwood's flagship, being fired on at the same time by the *Belleisle*, a shot from the *Pluton*, following up behind her, had just killed Captain Duff, commanding the *Mars*. About half a mile behind them again, Magon's *Algésiras* was engaged with the *Tonnant*, the *Bahama* and the *Agile* were locked in a struggle with the *Bellerophon*, while the *Montanes* and the *Swiftsure* were occupied in holding up the *Colossus*. Further behind yet, at the rear of the line, the *Achille* closed with the *Argonaute*, while the former's French namesake had the *Defiance* bearing down upon her. The *Principe-de-Asturias*, Gravina's flagship, the *Berwick* and the *San-Juan-Nepomuceno* began to receive the fire of the *Revenge*, the *Polyphemus*, and the *Swiftsure*, to which would soon be added that of the *Prince*, the *Dreadnought* and the *Thunderer*; these latter had been held up, but were eager to get into action.

The battle had now lasted three-quarters of an hour, and the *Victory*, flanked, as ever, by the *Temeraire*, had just come within range of the guns of the *Santissima-Trinidad*, *Bucentaure* and *Redoutable*. The moment was critical. Bursts of fire ripped the sails of Nelson's flagship, tore away the shrouds, and beat upon the hull. The steering-wheel and the fore top were shot away, one after the other, while the admiral's secretary and eight soldiers were killed.

"This is too warm work to last long," remarked Nelson to Captain Hardy.

But the *Victory* was no more than 275 yards from the three enemy ships, and the question was, which of them would she attack? Nelson was naturally in favour of the *Bucentaure*, but Hardy felt more attracted by the lavishly gilded towering mass of the old *Santissima-Trinidad*, that seemed to symbolise the navy of days gone by. As it was, the three allied vessels were packed so tight together that any idea of cutting the line by passing between them was quite out of the question.

"I can't help it," exclaimed Nelson. "My good Hardy, it does not signify which we run on board of—take your choice!"

Hardy chose what happened to be the weakest of the three, the *Redoutable*, and in order to get to grips with her, steered for the stern of the *Bucentaure*.

Immediately the firing redoubled.

Their faces and hands blackened with powder, the allied gunners eagerly fired on the unconquerable ship which rode the long swell towards them like a ghost, wrapped in a pale grey pall of smoke from her waterline to the flag of St George. On board the *Bucentaure*, Villeneuve seized the imperial eagle and shouted to his men, "I am going to hurl it on to the Englishman's deck. We shall go in to recapture it, or die!"

He ran up signal No. 5:

"Any ship that is not in action is not at her post, and must take up whatever position will bring her most quickly into firing line."

On board the *Redoutable* her commander, Captain Lucas, a little man of extraordinary energy, held his boarding-party in readiness: like their ship, they were of the élite.

The expected clash came in two phases.

As she came upon the stern of the *Bucentaure*, towering over her with the full height of her three decks, the *Victory* swept her with a salvo of fifty guns firing double and treble charges. She passed so close that her yards crossed over the poop of the French ship, and then suddenly, pulling over to starboard, and losing at the same moment her mizzen-mast and her main-topgallant mast, fairly flung herself on the *Redoutable*, pouring in grape-shot at point-blank range.

It was now one o'clock in the afternoon.

The whole centre of the allied fleet looked like an erupting volcano. Behind the *Victory* and the *Redoutable*, locked in their terrible embrace, came the *Temeraire*. Not content with firing on the *Santa-Ana*, already at grips with the *Royal Sovereign*, she attacked the *Neptune* which had driven to leeward, but was herself swept by fire from the *San-Justo* and *San-Leandro*. Further north, the English *Neptune* rushed upon the *Bucentaure*, still reeling under the *Victory's* first broadside. At the same time, the *Leviathan*, supported by the *Conqueror*, had cut the allied line, and, despite opposition from the *Héros* and the *San-Agustin*, was proceeding to grapple with the *Santissima-Trinidad*.

This was no longer a "strung-out" battle, such as had been the practice for centuries, but a series of single combats of the most bloody ferocity. Eight of the allied ships alone were taking no part in the battle. They were the advance guard, that is, from the head of the column: the *Neptuno*, the *Scipion*, the *Intrépide*, the *Formidable* (flag-ship of Rear-Admiral Dumanoir), the *Duguay-Trouin*, the *Mont-Blanc*, the *San-Francisco-de-Asis*, whose place was immediately in front of the *Héros*, and the *Rayo* that had driven to leeward. These continued imperturbably on their way to Cadiz, as if Villeneuve had never run up his signal No. 5, which was, however, categorical and could still be clearly seen—as if nothing whatever were going on behind them.

We know what the confused fighting in the centre was like. But to the south, among the group formed by the *Royal Sovereign, Belleisle, Santa-Ana, Fougueux, Monarca* and *Indomptable*, the engagement was no less ferocious. Admiral Alava on the *Santa-Ana* had fallen seriously wounded; the *Belleisle* was docked of her mizzen-mast, the *Royal Sovereign* was covered with wreckage and looked as if she had been ravaged by some frightful storm; the *Fougueux* and the *Monarca* had neither sails nor yards left. . . . Not far from them the *Pluton* and the *Mars*, the latter with her quarter-deck stripped and her rigging in tatters, were drifting with the tide, engaged in a fight to the death. Lower down the line the last ships of Collingwood's

column had all made contact, and a few of them had begun
to double round the rear of the allied line. The ships fought
hull against hull, regardless of losses. The *Aigle* was combatting
the *Bellerophon*, locked to her bows, and her captain was struck
down by four successive wounds. The *Algésiras* was so tightly
locked with the *Tonnant* that her bowsprit was caught in the
main shrouds of the English ship, and only half of her officers
were still alive; on the *Argonaute*, grappled hard by the *Achille*,
men were fighting with cold steel.

But no decision had yet been reached. Shattered by the
English onset, and despite the blood already shed so plentifully,
the allied fleet was nevertheless holding its own with remarkable gallantry and boldness considering its sad lack of method,
cohesion and tactical manœuvre. Of this the admiral's flagship provided an astonishing example. Rallying round
Villeneuve, the men of the *Bucentaure* put up a resistance to
those of the *Neptune* that nothing could either shake or break.

It was to leeward of the line, round the indistinct mass of
Lucas's *Redoutable* and Nelson's *Victory* that the struggle now
reached its most dramatic height. Before grappling, the two
ships had exchanged a furious broadside that caused heavy
losses on either side. With their boarding-parties hanging on
to the shrouds or massed along the bulwark-netting, they
were pounding each other unmercifully, with grape-shot at
point-blank range. During this pitiless contest the *Victory* began
to show signs of exhaustion, despite her power. She had lost
her mizzen mast, her foretop, and her main-topgallant mast.
Her seamen were falling every minute under the showers of
musket balls and grenades poured in from the rigging of the
Redoutable.

Nelson paced the quarter-deck encouraging his surviving
men by voice and gesture. The ribbons on his jacket were a
blaze of colour, and his silver and gold decorations shone; he
could be seen from all sides.

The French took careful aim. They were excellent shots.

Suddenly Captain Hardy, who had felt the buckle of his

shoe torn off by an explosion a few seconds earlier, saw the admiral fall, face to the deck. A sergeant and two men sprang forward to raise him. A trickle of red stained the brilliant tunic.

"My back is shot through," said Nelson in a firm voice. "They have done for me at last."

On Hardy's order, his face and tunic were covered with a handkerchief, so as to conceal his features and decorations, and he was taken down to the casualty station, where the surgeon Beatty was working by candle-light. The stench of death filled the narrow place, mingled with the musty smell of vinegar and gin. Nelson opened his eyes:

"You can do nothing for me, Mr Beatty: I have only a very little time left."

He felt a paralysis creep into the small of his back (the ball had passed through the spinal column), and blood entering his lungs. He gasped.

"My backbone is shot through."

They laid his body out as well as they could, and Beatty began to undress him. The chaplain came running up.

"Do not forget Lady Hamilton nor Horatia. . . . Yes. . . . I leave them to my country. . . . Yes, Lady Hamilton . . . Horatia. . . ."

*

Above them the battle redoubled its fury, heedless of the death-agony of one of the greatest seamen of all time. The captain of the *Héros* collapsed, dead; the second-in-command of the *Achille* fell, mortally wounded; Admiral Gravina and Rear-Admiral Escano were among the wounded on board the *Principe-de-Asturias*, which had been overwhelmed by the *Revenge*, the *Defiance*, the *Prince* and the *Dreadnought*.

On every side grape-shot indiscriminately mowed down admirals, captains, seamen and everything else in its path. The *Bucentaure* could still be seen with a fiery tempest raging in her middle, while the *Santissima-Trinidad* was submerged in a whirlpool of smoke, from which orange flashes were bursting.

At the mast-head of the French flagship a new signal was flapping in the thick of the fight, confirming No. 5, and calling on the advance guard to "Come about all together". It was a final appeal to those who were continuing their flight to calmer waters, disregarding the sacrifices of their brothers-in-arms.

It was now 1.50 in the afternoon.

Despite their losses not one of the allied ships hauled down her flag. On the English side certain ships, such as the *Mars*, the *Royal Sovereign* and the *Victory*, had been reduced to a condition where it seemed impossible for them to survive another broadside. Victory (or defeat) hung by a thread. If Dumanoir continued his flight, the arrival of the five or six ships of Nelson's column that had not yet entered the battle would soon decide the fate of Villeneuve's exhausted fleet; but if on the other hand he came in with his eight fresh ships the case might still be altered.

Villeneuve, on board his half-destroyed *Bucentaure*, turned anguished eyes northwards.

Dumanoir was no coward, but his course of action, since the first shot was fired, remained inexplicable. He had no enemy to engage, yet he had neither attempted to cut Nelson's column, nor given the least sign of coming to the assistance of the stricken centre. He had not even acknowledged signal No. 5, run up at 1 o'clock, and flapping for a considerable period at the admiral's mast-head. ["Any ship that is not in action is not at her post and must take up whatever position will bring her most quickly into the firing-line."]

Had Dumanoir forgotten Villeneuve's charge, "Any captain who is not under fire is not at his post; a signal to recall him to action would be a stain upon his honour"?

To tell the truth, Rear-Admiral Dumanoir resembled an all too numerous group of officers of the Imperial Navy. Though adequate in ordinary circumstances, he had none of the qualities required to face the harsh realities of a Trafalgar. Such a situation revealed, instead of the distinguished theorist and the eminent and much-praised strategist, a creature of trepidation, blinded by his prejudices, stunned by his responsibilities and incapable of giving orders or exacting obedience.

Even so, when they saw Villeneuve's fresh signal, the advance guard finally executed the required manœuvre. The eighth man-of-war of the group, however, the *Rayo*, had driven to leeward and was unable to move; the seventh, the *San-Francisco-de-Asis*, though she had not seen the signal, still less understood it, came about on her own initiative, followed by the two ships leading the centre, the *Héros* and the *San-Agustin*. The remaining six, including Dumanoir's flagship, the *Formidable*, came about with the aid of their long-boats. During this manœuvre the *Mont-Blanc* and the *Intrépide* fouled one another, fortunately without causing any damage. But a certain amount of confusion ensued. As soon as he was ready Dumanoir began to beat to windward, heading west, while he waited for all his ships to get into position. He had barely covered half a mile on this course when he ran across the *Neptuno* and the *Intrépide*, headed southwards.

"Where are you going?" cried the Rear-Admiral to the captain of the *Neptuno*.

"Into the fire," answered the Spaniard drily.

As for the "pasha" of the *Intrépide*, a Provençal named Infernet, he merely replied in guttural tones with a strong flavour of oil and garlic:

"Headed for the *Bucentaure*!"

That was indeed the quarter, rather than to westward, in which the battle was playing itself out. Wedged between the *Neptune* and the *Conqueror*, Villeneuve's flagship continued to maintain her existence by dint of superhuman effort. It was miraculous to see how she managed to keep her three colours flying high at the masthead—a beacon to the whole fleet. It was not to be for long. One by one, like two gigantic ninepins, her mainmast and mizzen-mast, cut through by gunfire, crashed down to starboard, crushing everything in their path.

"Nail the tricolor to the mast!" yelled Villeneuve.

Three seamen seized the flag and fixed it to the stump of the mainmast.

"Long live the Emperor!"

There can be no doubt that the modest Pierre de Villeneuve had never so eagerly desired to meet death face to face. He sought it in the midst of his shattered ship—exposing himself to flying bullets and explosive charges as they burst in the air and descended in fiery showers. The captain and the navigating officer were both wounded, and there were three hundred casualties. But death would have none of Villeneuve, though it was now very near his rival, the fortunate Nelson, on board the *Victory*.

"What is Hardy doing?" murmured the Viscount of the Nile on his bloody couch. "Water! Air! . . . Is Hardy killed? Beatty, why does not Hardy come?"

Hardy did not come because the struggle between the disabled *Victory* and the riddled *Redoutable* was not yet over. Ten minutes before, the French seamen had tried to board the English ship. Five of them, including a midshipman, had succeeded in climbing aboard her by coming up the anchor cable. But at the same moment the *Temeraire*, hastening to the relief of Nelson's flagship, had come up and launched herself against the starboard side of the Frenchman. Caught thus between two fires, the *Redoutable* was approaching the end of her glorious career.

"Surrender!" cried the men of the *Temeraire* to Captain Lucas.

A pathetic "Long live the Emperor!" accompanied by a volley of shots was the only reply. Thirty seconds later the mainmast of the French vessel crashed down across the *Temeraire*, shearing off her two top-sail yards which smashed across the poop of the *Redoutable*, staving her in completely.

Things were now going badly for the allies.

In spite of their heroic resistance, and in spite of the approach of the *Intrépide*, the *Neptuno*, the *Héros* and the *San-Agustin*, all four of them striving to reach the vessels of Villeneuve and

Lucas, the technical superiority of the English was tipping the scale.

Thus the tail of the allied line had already been rounded by the *Dreadnought* and the *Polyphemus*, and the *Prince* also was threatening to round it. The two rearmost vessels, the *San-Juan-Nepomuceno* and the French *Berwick* were cornered between two fires, and suffered grave damage. Further up the line Gravina's flagship, the *Principe-de-Asturias*, was drifting eastwards with her admiral seriously wounded, dragging along with her the *Montanes* whose captain had just been killed. Yet further up were the *Argonaute* with her deck devastated, the *Argonauta* with her guns disabled, and the dismasted *Swiftsure* trying as best they might to get away from the English clutches.

Further up still desperate single combats were in progress between the *Aigle* and the *Defiance*, and the *Algésiras* and the *Tonnant*, while the *Bahama* and *Monarca* strove against the *Colossus* and *Bellerophon*. The first surrenders soon made these contests unequal by releasing more ships on the English side. Finally, near the centre, the *Santa-Ana* was growing weaker every minute, as the *Royal Sovereign* poured grape-shot into her, grappled to her side, and the *Belleisle* raked her with broadsides.

The *Santa-Ana* was a proud ship. She had been the first to come under fire, and had paid dearly for the privilege of leading off the dance of death. Her three masts had been stripped of sails and yards, but kept flying the banner of the two Castiles and of Christ on the cross above a horrifying mêlée of dead and dying, from which arose a chorus of gasps and groans. The ship's commander, Admiral Alava, and three hundred men were buried under this charnel. Over their mingled bodies the survivors kept up their fire to repeated cries of "Long live the King!" This hopeless and unequal struggle might perhaps have continued to the last man, had not the three masts been suddenly brought crashing down together, like a funeral salvo. It was the end. At 2.20 Collingwood received Admiral Alava's sword with its hilt of chased gold—the symbol of the first success of the English fleet. He received it on the deck of his own shattered ship, which he was soon to leave in order to direct subsequent operations from the frigate *Euryalus*.

*

The misfortunes of the Franco-Spaniards now began in earnest. Hardly had the *Santa-Ana* surrendered than the mizzen mast of the *Redoutable* toppled over, and thus, of its own accord, brought down the ship's flag. Never before had a French ship put up such a vigorous fight. For close on two hours this modest vessel of 74 guns had held her own against two of the finest three-deckers of the British fleet, each mounting 100 guns, and with a combined total strength three times her own.

Statistics give the measure of her heroism: seven officers killed and six seriously wounded (Lucas was one of these) out of 18; six midshipmen killed and five wounded out of 11; 450 seamen killed and 70 wounded out of a crew of 643.

The *Victory* and the *Temeraire* would, undoubtedly, have taken her in the end. But apart from the fact that she was too badly damaged to continue in action, the *Victory* had lost 132 men killed and wounded—including Nelson, now in his death agony—while the *Temeraire* had 123 casualties. The three ships firmly fixed in their own wreckage, and out of control, were drifting together. Clouds of acrid smoke poured from their port-holes, like the breath of some panting beast. Below decks, in the sick bay of the *Victory*, Nelson continued to gasp for air. Above, the *Temeraire* hesitated to take possession of the *Redoutable* which seemed on the point of sinking; on her deck there still stood stripped to the waist a handful of French lads ready to run through the first Englishman who dared to climb aboard.

Suddenly, as in a nightmare, a fourth phantom shape loomed up. It was partially dismasted and, unable to steer, was approaching across the bows of the *Temeraire*. This new arrival was the

Fougueux, which had been left to her fate by the *Mars*. On the instant, the *Temeraire* reopened fire. In the first few seconds Captain Baudouin, commanding the *Fougueux*, fell mortally wounded. Commander Bazin took his place, and launched what remained of the ship's company against the enemy boarding parties, who were already gaining a foothold. The English were at first checked at the point of the bayonet. They reformed. A sheet of solid iron, belching from the *Temeraire's* carronades, deluged the Frenchman's deck.

"Surrender!"

"Fire!"

The English returned to the attack, and this time gained a foothold. Bazin felt a warm trickle under his tunic; he was wounded. He called for his first lieutenant—he was dead; for the second lieutenant—he was dying; for the third lieutenant—he had a musket-ball through his leg. There were five hundred casualties. To continue the struggle would have been madness. Bazin gave the cease fire, went below to the captain's cabin as best he could, took the leaden box containing secret orders, threw it in the sea, and came up again on to the deck now swarming with Englishmen. He was made prisoner, and the flag of the *Fougueux* was struck.

The *Santa-Ana*, the *Redoutable*, and the *Fougueux*—the English could now count three prizes, and it was 3 o'clock.

North-westward, not far from the scene of the real battle, Dumanoir's division, now reduced to four ships headed south —the *Formidable*, the *Duguay-Trouin*, the *Scipion* and the *Mont-Blanc*—exchanged a few shots with the *Spartiate* and the *Minotaur* as the latter were rejoining the centre ahead of the *Ajax* and *Agamemnon*. Their task was assuredly easier than that taken on voluntarily by the *Neptuno* and, even more, the *Intrépide*. These had detached themselves from the advance-guard, and had now reached the nerve-centre of the battle among the pack of English ships hounding down the *Santissima Trinidad*, the *San-Agustin*, and the *Bucentaure*.

The *Santissima-Trinidad* had lost her masts, and two hundred men killed; she was now firing only at irregular intervals. The *San-Agustin* was shorn bare, like a hulk. Villeneuve's *Bucentaure*, as she plunged in agony, was drifting, and dragging on her drunken course the English *Neptune*, determined to destroy her.

Some way from these three doomed ships were the *Swiftsure*, shorn of her fore and main masts, the *Algésiras* that had also lost her fore-mast, the *Achille*, half on fire, the *Berwick*, three parts dismembered, and the *Argonauta* stricken to death. These were dying by inches. The hindmost ship of the allied line was the *San-Juan-Nepomuceno*, commanded by the explorer Churucca, the youngest officer in the Spanish navy. His leg had been crushed at the beginning of the action, and there were 250 casualties among his men. He had just surrendered to the *Dreadnought*, making the fourth victim of the day. But in actual fact the allied line had long ceased to exist—nothing but individual ships dutifully struggling against an enemy whose tactical superiority, mobility, rate of fire and dash were continuously in evidence. Already Gravina's flagship, the *Principe-de-Asturias*, rescued from a position of grave danger by the Frenchman *Neptune*, the *San-Justo* and the *San-Leandro*, was making north-westwards together with these latter, leaving the battle behind them. There were indications that the allied fleet, like a building undermined by rain, was about to collapse completely, and to be swallowed up in an irrevocable catastrophe.

It fell to the ill-starred *Bucentaure* to inaugurate this new phase—the last. Raked by the fire of the *Victory*, the *Conqueror* and the *Leviathan*, one after the other, and grappled by the *Neptune*, the admiral's flagship had suffered all and given her all. One hundred and thirty-seven of her men—seven of them officers—were dead. "The *Bucentaure* has accomplished her task: mine is not yet finished," murmured the despairing Villeneuve. He called for a long-boat to carry him on board some other ship. But not a single seaworthy boat was left, and no prospect of immediate assistance appeared. The *Redoutable* and the *Fougueux* were in the hands of the English; Gravina and Dumanoir were in flight; the nearest group of allied vessels, the *San Francisco-De-Asis*, the *Rayo* and the *Héros*, was also making for calmer waters. So all was lost. The imperial eagle itself lay shattered. Villeneuve gave orders for it to be thrown into the sea together with secret signals and documents. Then he surrendered. It was 3.30.

The same moment saw the capitulation of other allied ships. Northwards, not far from the *Santissima-Trinidad*—herself almost incapable of further action—the dismasted *San-Agustin*, with half her crew annihilated, surrendered to the *Leviathan*. Southwards the *Argonauta* yielded herself to the attackers that hemmed her in; the *Swiftsure* bowed before the *Colossus*; the *Aigle* submitted to the *Defiance* after losing her captain and second-in-command; the disabled *San-Ildefonso* and the *Bahama*, whose captain had had his head taken off by a cannon-ball, surrendered to the *Defence* and the *Bellerophon*.

Already the noise of battle was beginning to slacken. Aboard the *Victory*, Captain Hardy, who had not without difficulty succeeded in freeing his ship from the embrace of the *Redoutable*, could at last go below to Nelson's side. He took his hand affectionately.

"Well, Hardy," gasped the wounded man, "how goes the battle?"

"Very well, my lord," replied Hardy. "We have got twelve or fourteen of the enemy's ships in our possession, but five of their van have tacked and show an intention of bearing down upon the *Victory*. I have therefore called two or three of our fresh ships round us, and have no doubt of giving them a drubbing."

Indeed, he had no cause for misgivings. After finally making for the centre of the allied line and exchanging a few shots with the rearmost ships of Nelson's column, Dumanoir had decided that nothing further could be done to save the *Bucentaure* and the *Santa-Ana*. He had sheered off once more, this time for good.

"I hope," said Nelson, "that none of *our* ships have struck, Hardy?"

"No, my lord. There is no fear of that."

The admiral forced a twisted smile:

"I am a dead man, Hardy. I am going fast; it will be all over with me soon. Come nearer to me. Pray let dear Lady Hamilton have my hair and all other things belonging to me."

"You will see England again, my lord!" Hardy mumbled. Nelson slowly shook his head.

"Oh no! Beatty will tell you. The ball has passed through my back. You know that I am gone."

Then, gasping, "Yet, one would like to live a little longer, too. What would become of Lady Hamilton if she knew my situation?"

A sort of spasm in the battle made itself heard—the low roar of guns, and the crashing of grape-shot—and Hardy returned on deck.

There too the end had come. The allied fleet continued its collapse into a colossal defeat. Southward, the last signs of resistance were drowned, one after the other, in the huzzas of the English sailors.

The disabled *Algésiras* surrendered to the *Tonnant*. Rear-Admiral Magon had been wounded twice, and was finally killed by a bullet full in his chest. The captain of the ship had collapsed somewhere, gravely wounded; 300 men lay in their blood, dead, broken, mutilated. Half a mile away the *Berwick* struck her flag to the *Achille*. Her captain was killed and she had sustained 250 casualties.

Lastly, the Frenchman *Achille* was on fire, isolated like a leper. One after the other she had lost her second-in-command, Commander Montalembert, her captain, Captain Denieport, and Ensign Jouan, who had taken over command from them. When Jouan was struck by a bullet from the *Prince*, the fire simultaneously gained a hold on the foretop, which soon crashed down on to the deck, spreading the fire to the life-boats, and from the life-boats to the batteries. The *Achille* might thus have blown up at any moment, carrying with her in a terrible descent to the depths her unnumbered dead, her 200 wounded, and the soldiers and sailors so far unhurt. These latter, led by Ensign Cauchard, a young officer of 20, were fighting the fire, dowsing the powder, and working by relays at the pumps.

By 4 o'clock there were no more than 10 or 12 allied ships still in the battle. Certain of these, such as the *Héros*, the *Rayo*, the *San-Francisco-de-Asis*, the *Montanes*, the *Pluton*, and the *Argonaute*, were already pulling clear to join the *Principe-de-Asturias* from whose masthead was flying the signal for a general rally. Dumanoir's division was definitely out of the fight. To the northward the *Neptuno*, attacked by the *Minotaur* and the *Spartiate*, one behind the other, was still offering a courageous resistance worthy of all praise. So, too, was Infernet on the *Intrépide*, with four British ships on his flanks— the *Africa* (on which he had inflicted heavy damage), the *Orion*, the *Ajax* and the *Agamemnon*. It was nevertheless all too clear that the English fleet had gained the day.

On board the *Victory* Hardy was sure of this fact, and felt able to go below once more to Nelson's bedside where he found him in terrible pain; at sight of the captain of his flagship his livid face lit up.

"So far as we can judge, my lord," said Hardy gently, "fourteen or fifteen enemy ships have already surrendered."

"That is well," Nelson murmured. "But I bargained for twenty."

Then suddenly, raising his voice with a supreme effort, and with his mind on the coming storm that had haunted him since morning, he cried out:

"Anchor, Hardy! Anchor!"

Hardy was surprised, and demurred; suggesting that no doubt his second would now take upon himself the direction of affairs.

"Not while I live, I hope."

He tried to raise himself, only to fall back on his bed, exhausted, his face ghastly.

"No, do *you* anchor, Hardy."

"Shall we make the signal, Sir?"

"Yes, for if I live, I'll anchor."

He was clearly at his last gasp. His chest heaved like a blacksmith's bellows. Nevertheless, after a few moments he made a motion with his left hand, inviting Hardy to come near him, as if he had a confidence to impart.

"Don't throw me overboard, Hardy."

"No, no, certainly not."

"I should like to be buried near my parents . . . take care of my dear Lady Hamilton, Hardy. If she needs a protector, Hardy, I depend on you. . . . Kiss me, Hardy!"

His face pale, his eyes filled with tears, and with a lump at his throat, the commanding officer of the *Victory* sank to his his knees and planted a kiss on the forehead of the dying man. All around them wounded men babbled in delirium.

"God bless you, my dear Hardy . . . remember Lady Hamilton. . . . I wish I had not left the deck. . . ."

It was clear, despite his fixed stare, that everything was swimming before his eyes. But he recognised the chaplain:

"I have not been a great sinner, doctor."

This time, his eyes turned up.

"Water . . . air! . . . Remember that I leave Lady Hamilton and my daughter Horatia as a legacy to my country. . . . Water!"

Then, with his last breath:

"Thank God . . . I have done my duty!"

That was all. During the ensuing moments two joyous bursts of cheering could be heard across the water, greeting the surrender of the *Neptuno* and the *Intrépide*.

Then came a dull explosion from the south, as the *Achille* disappeared, going down in flames, but with her flag still flying. After that, silence—a huge silence that weighed heavily on the survivors, half-dead with fatigue, their legs giving way beneath them, and their mouths bitter with the nauseating taste of powder and blood.

*

The defeat of the allies could not have been more complete. Of 33 ships engaged, 17 had surrendered to the English: of the French, the *Bucentaure, Redoutable, Fougueux, Algésiras, Aigle, Swiftsure, Berwick* and *Intrépide;* and of the Spaniards, the *Santissima-Trinidad, San-Agustin, Santa-Ana, Argonauta, Bahama, San-Ildefonso, San-Juan-Nepomuceno, Monarca, Neptuno.* One ship, the French *Achille,* had sunk after blowing up.

Of the 15 ships that escaped safely from the action, four were in flight towards the open sea, under the leadership of Dumanoir: the *Formidable, Scipion, Duguay-Trouin* and *Mont-Blanc.* Eleven were withdrawing towards Cadiz with Gravina: the Spaniards *Principe-de-Asturias, San-Justo, San-Leandro, Rayo, Montanes* and *San-Francisco-de-Asis,* and the Frenchmen *Pluton, Héros, Neptune, Argonaute* and *Indomptable.* All the frigates got away.

Casualties among the men were without precedent in naval history. A preliminary count—for it was hard to give an accurate return—gave a figure of nearly 6,500 killed and wounded, of which more than 3,000 killed and more than 1,000 wounded were French. Rear-Admiral Magon and nine commanding officers were dead; Rear-Admirals Gravina, Alava, and Cisneros, and 10 commanding officers were more or less seriously wounded. Lastly, Villeneuve and several thousands of his men were prisoners in enemy hands.

As for the English, they had sustained no more than 1,600 casualties—to be exact, 449 killed and 1,214 wounded. True, they had lost the mighty Nelson, and in view of the damage suffered half their fleet had no choice but to run for shelter at Gibraltar. But the fact still remained that *in less than five hours the 27 British ships of the line had utterly defeated 33 French and Spanish.*

This resounding victory, with its far-reaching results, had

been won by the English at a very moderate price. Thus the *Colossus*, the most sorely tried of the whole fleet, returned no more than 200 casualties, of which 40 were killed, the *Bellerophon* 150 (27 killed), the *Royal Sovereign* 141 (47 killed), the *Victory* 132 (57 killed), the *Belleisle* 126 (33 killed), the *Temeraire* 123 (47 killed). Thirteen English ships were in the happy position of having less than 10 killed, and one, the *Prince* came away without a single scratch!

So, then, although the British fleet had suffered material damage to the extent of being barely able to navigate, it can be said that her strength in men remained virtually intact, whilst that of her opponents had been strained to its limits. Certainly, the English could congratulate themselves on not having had to face 33 ships of the calibre of the *Redoutable*, the *Santa-Ana*, the *Bucentaure* and the *Intrépide*. But still it was not due to them that Dumanoir had obstinately turned tail from the field of battle, and that some of the Spanish ships, like the *Rayo*, the *San-Francisco-de-Asis*, the *San-Leandro* and the *San-Justo* had taken practically no part in the engagement.

*

The day was quickly waning.

Villeneuve had been conveyed on board the *Mars* in an English long-boat after the taking of the *Bucentaure*, and from its deck he could gauge the extent of the disaster.

Clouds of smoke were still rolling skywards above skeletons of ships as they danced on the swell in a macabre measure, with their yards clashing against one another to beat time. Planks, corpses, barrels, oars and hats drifted, sinister and grotesque. To the north-east, the remains of the combined fleet of Their Majesties the Emperor Napoleon and King Charles IV were in flight with Gravina, whose flagship was being towed by the frigate *Themis*. To the south, four of the allied ships, now flying the English flag, were on their way to Gibraltar: the *Swiftsure*, the *Bahama*, the *San-Juan-Nepomuceno* and the *San-Ildefonso*. Westwards, Dumanoir had begun to

fade into the distance, his ships appearing no larger than the
rowing-boats that still cruised over the grave of the *Achille*,
crowded with half-naked men.

The night was terrible with the groans of the dying and the
moaning of the wind that blew more keenly hour by hour, as
the storm approached. "Cast anchor!" Nelson had said before
he died. But Collingwood was afraid of the inhospitable
Spanish shore, and preferred to remain at sea till morning,
turning his head to the wind.

At last day broke, pale and ominous. The English squadron
together with 13 captured ships were all that remained on the
scene, though the water still carried traces of the previous day's
battle. They now faced the rising storm. Not a sail was visible
on the horizon. Gravina and his escort had succeeded in
anchoring in the bay of Rota, at the approaches to Cadiz; the
convoy of French and Spanish prisoners, ordered to Gibraltar,
had gone to anchor off Cape Trafalgar, eight miles away;
Dumanoir was running for Cape Finisterre, in hopes of meeting Allemand's squadron there.

Collingwood had a fresh battle on his hands—to take in tow
and convey to Gibraltar in the most shocking weather ships
with neither masts nor sails. Surely no conqueror had ever
found his trophies such an encumbrance! The *Monarca*, the
Berwick, the *Santa-Ana* and the *Neptuno*, had been more or less
patched up during the night, and seemed unlikely to give
trouble, but some others caused serious apprehension. The
Bucentaure was adrift, the *Aigle* and the *Fougueux* were in
danger of sinking, and the *Redoutable*, with the English
Swiftsure beside her, was making water like a sieve.

During the afternoon, as the sea grew rougher the English
decided to abandon the *Fougueux*, the *Aigle*, the *Bucentaure* and
the *Algésiras*.

This was the beginning of a fresh series of incidents.

At 7 o'clock in the evening the stem of the *Redoutable* collapsed, and the gallant ship began to sink. The *Swiftsure's* boats
were able to rescue 169 men, of whom 70 were seriously

wounded, and 64 lightly. Four hundred and seventy-four had been lost during the battle and when the ship sank.

Simultaneously, on board the *Bucentaure* Capture Prigny and Lieutenant Fulcran Fournier summoned the English officers on board to hand the ship back to them. The Englishmen yielded perforce, a few sails were set, and the *Bucentaure* started for Cadiz. The crew of the *Algésiras*, led by Lieutenants La Bretonnière and Philibert, effected the same successful coup, disarming the three English prize officers with a cry of "Long live the Emperor!" and putting their ship back on its proper course—towards the allied port.

But the storm was blowing harder than ever, carrying the crippled ships towards the jagged coastline, as they strove against the furious squalls in their efforts to reach safety.

More dramatic incidents occurred. A pilot's error caused the *Bucentaure*, on arrival at the very entrance to the harbour, to hole herself on a reef and sink. The *Aigle* was obliged to drop anchor a league off shore, and two days later ran aground off Cadiz. The *Fougueux*, out of control, ran head-on against the boulders, and broke up. Only the *Algésiras* succeeded in anchoring near the light-house at Cadiz, saved by a miracle, but in a distressed condition. By dint of superhuman efforts she succeeded in entering harbour on the 25th.

So it was that on the morning of October 23, forty-eight hours after the battle, no more than eight of the allied prizes were still in Collingwood's hands as he brought his squadron back to Gibraltar: the *Santissima-Trinidad*, the *Argonauta*, the *Intrépide*, and *San-Agustin*, the *Monarca*, the *Berwick*, the *Neptuno* and the *Santa-Ana*. In the circumstances the admiral resigned himself to scuttling the first two, and setting fire to the third and fourth. Shortly afterwards the *Monarca* and the *Berwick* broke their tow-rope and drifted towards the coast, irrecoverably lost. So much for six of them.

There was more to come. Towards noon the English vessel towing the *Neptuno* and the *Santa-Ana*, which was sailing well ahead of the main body not far from the coast, was sighted through a break in the clouds by the *Pluton*, at anchor in the Cadiz roadstead. Without hesitation Captain Cosmao, a "tough nut to crack", hoisted the signal to set sail, and, followed by the *Héros*, the *Neptune*, the *San-Francisco-de-Asis*, and the *Rayo*, made straight for the enemy. The English vessel quickly let go her prizes and made off. Unfortunately, on the return to Cadiz, the *Rayo* stranded herself on the coast, where the English set fire to her during the night; the *San Francisco-de-Asis* and the *Neptuno* ran helplessly aground.

There remained the four ships that had been sent off to Gibraltar in the first place, and which had dropped anchor off Cape Trafalgar on the morning of the 22nd. One of them, the *Bahama*, sank on arrival at the Rock; two others, the French *Swiftsure* and the *San-Ildefonso*, were in such a hopeless state that they had to be destroyed; the fourth, the *San-Juan-Nepomuceno*, was the only one that could be preserved and incorporated into the British fleet.

And so, after all these adventures, the "credit balance" on the English side was reduced from the 18 allied ships captured or surrendered on October 21 to a single Spanish ship of 74 guns in serviceable condition. The remaining 17 were thus accounted for:

1 blown up (the *Achille*)

2 sunk (the *Redoutable* and the *Bahama*)

2 scuttled (the *Santissima-Trinidad* and the *Argonauta*)

2 deliberately set on fire (the *Intrépide* and the *San-Agustin*)

4 abandoned and wrecked on the coast (the *Monarca*, the French *Berwick*, the *Fougueux* and the *Aigle*)

2 got away, one to perish (the *Bucentaure*) and the other to make port (the *Algésiras*)

2 retaken by the allies off Cadiz (the *Neptuno* and the *Santa-Ana*, of which the former ran aground shortly afterwards)

2 taken to Gibraltar, found unserviceable, and promptly destroyed (the French *Swiftsure* and the *San-Ildefonso*)

However, the British were to make up for this destruction of the fruits of their victory, not only by burning the *Rayo*,

which, as we have seen, ran aground after her sortie from Cadiz
on October 23, but also by shortly afterwards scoring a fresh
success, as decisive as it was unexpected.

On November 2 Commodore Strachan with a force of four
ships of the line and four frigates off Cape Finisterre, having
been detached by Cornwallis to pursue Rear-Admiral
Allemand, sighted Dumanoir's division on its way to Aix. The
four French warships, *Formidable*, *Scipion*, *Mont-Blanc* and
Duguay-Trouin, had suffered 183 casualties (of whom 72 were
killed) at Trafalgar during their brief exchanges with the
Victory and, later, the *Spartiate* and *Minotaur*. They had also
suffered some material damage. The *Formidable* had no more
than 60 of its 80 guns in action, which reduced the total of
Dumanoir's armament to 280 guns, as opposed to 308 on the
English side. The latter had the additional advantage of support
from frigates.

The engagement did not begin till the 4th. Once begun, it
was of short duration. Dumanoir managed things badly, with
his customary irresolution, but Strachan attacked vigorously,
and the battle ended with the surrender of the whole of
Dumanoir's division. The French suffered 700 casualties, the
captain of the *Duguay-Trouin* was killed, and Dumanoir
himself was wounded in the hip and leg. His four ships were
conducted to Plymouth under close escort arriving a few days
later after an uneventful trip in fine weather.

So much for the naval epilogue to Trafalgar.

To sum up—we may perhaps be forgiven this succession of
statistics—out of the 33 ships of the line of the allied navies
that sailed out of Cadiz on October 19, 1805, only 10 returned
to port, having escaped both the English and the elements:

    5 Frenchmen (*Pluton*, *Algésiras*, *Héros*, *Neptune*, *Argonaute*)
    5 Spaniards (*San-Justo*, *San-Leandro*, *Santa-Ana*, *Montanes*,
        Principe-de-Asturias).

Five more had survived the battle, but were in English
hands, and 18 were no more, lost in the storm, sunk, destroyed,
or burnt by the enemy.

The final count of casualties shows that 4,530 sons of France and Spain had been killed or drowned (3,370 of them French), and 3,573 had been wounded (1,028 of them French).

Admiral Rosily learnt of the disaster on October 25 when he arrived at Cadiz to take over from Villeneuve. Instead of the 18 French ships of the line he expected to find, only 5 were present, all bearing the scars of the inferno through which they had passed.

Rosily ran up his flag on the *Héros*, in the hope that one day he might conduct this pitiful remnant back to Toulon or Brest.

But we have said that Trafalgar was to be an irreparable calamity for the French navy. The five survivors from the terrible battle were to fall into the hands of the Spanish insurgents on June 14, 1808, and so never more to return to their homeland.

*

The news of the battle ran through Europe like wildfire.

Napoleon was in Moravia, marching on Vienna, when he read the news on November 18. It came in a letter that Decrès had sent from Paris. He realised that people were watching him, and was well aware that his own responsibility for the tragic issue was not of the lightest. He therefore assumed a regal unconcern.

He replied to Decrès: "I await further details on what you have told me. Until then I am unable to form any opinion even upon the general nature of this affair (*sic*). . . . Meanwhile I hasten to inform you that it makes not the slightest difference to my plans for the cruising squadrons. Indeed, I am vexed that all is not yet ready. There must be no delay in their sailing. . . ."

Not a single word for the thousands of poor wretches who had died with the cry of "Long live the Emperor" on their lips! In reality, however, Napoleon could ill conceal his rage and resentment. What a navy! And that wretch Villeneuve! He was never to forgive the beaten admiral, who at that

moment, a prisoner on board the frigate *Euryalus* on his way
to England, was composing his report on the battle, and
informing Decrès:

"I am deeply affected by the extent of my misfortune, and
by the sum of responsibility that such a great disaster brings
with it. My greatest desire is an early opportunity to lay at His
Majesty's feet either a vindication of my conduct, or myself,
as the victim that must be sacrificed not to the honour of the
flag, which, I venture to say, remains untarnished, but to the
shades of those who have perished by my imprudence, my
lack of consideration, or my omission of some part of my
duty."

On December 2, in the presence of an immense and silent
crowd, and to the dull roll of crêpe-covered drums, the *Victory*
entered Portsmouth anchorage with her flag at half-mast,
bringing back to England the embalmed remains of Horatio
Nelson.

On that very day, too, Napoleon and the Grand Army
watched the sun gilding the battlefield of Austerlitz.

*

Four months passed.

On April 17, 1806 a naval officer with melancholy and tor-
mented face appeared at the Hôtel de la Patrie, 21 rue des
Foulons, Rennes. A servant walked beside him with his
baggage. It was Vice-Admiral Villeneuve, back from captivity
in England.

He was given a room on the first floor. He locked himself in,
and immediately wrote to Decrès to inform him of his return
to France and to ask for his instructions before pursuing his
journey.

On the evening of the 22nd came the dramatic dénouement.
The servant became uneasy. He heard no movement from his
master's room, though he had knocked on the door several
times. He gave the alarm in the hotel and informed the police.
The lock was forced. Villeneuve was lying at the foot of the

bed, half undressed and covered with blood, with a table-knife buried up to the handle in his chest. On his night-table was a letter addressed to "Madame Villeneuve, née Dantoine, at Valensole, Basses-Alpes."

"Rennes, April 21, 1806.
"My dearest love, how will you receive this blow? Alas! I weep for you more than for myself! All is over: I have come to the point where life is a disgrace, and death a duty. I am alone here, execrated by the Emperor, rebuffed by his Minister who was my friend, weighed down by the immense responsibility laid at my door for the disaster into which I was forced by fate. I know that you can accept no excuse for my action. But I crave your pardon—a thousand pardons. I must die. It is necessary and I am driven to it by the blackest despair. Live your life in peace, and draw your consolation from the sweet inspirations of religion by which you are upheld. My hope is that in them you may find the peace which is denied me. Farewell, farewell! Dry the tears of my family, and of all those to whom I may be dear. I wanted to close, but I cannot. How fortunate that I have no child to inherit this legacy of horror and to have the dead-weight of my name hung round his neck! Ah, I was not born to a fate such as this: it was none of my seeking: I was driven to it in spite of myself. Farewell, farewell!"

The autopsy was carried out the following day, and established that Villeneuve had died from six wounds, all inflicted with the same knife, whose blade had pierced the left lung and ventricle of the heart. It was suicide without a doubt. It seemed surprising that the admiral had killed himself after informing Decrès of his return, and before even learning his reaction. Was he afraid of arousing the wrath and contempt of his master? Of being condemned by his peers knowing that he would be unable to make free use of all necessary means for his defence? Had he sensed an atmosphere of hostility in small things he had only noticed since his arrival? Or was he simply at the end of his strength—haunted by some nightmare vision that would not leave him? Nobody knew then, and nobody will ever know now.

Be that as it may, public opinion was even less ready to accept the suicide theory since the Naval Ministry and Villeneuve's family, by common consent, had decided to suppress the admiral's letter to his wife. This document of major importance passed into the hands of the prudent Fouché on May 22. He had obtained it from Decrès "*so as to be in a position, if need be, to stifle the rumours that certain persons might try to spread concerning the manner in which this veteran general officer had met his end.*" Gossip continued none the less to spread through Paris and France. Napoleon decreed a pension of 4,000 francs a year to Madame Villeneuve on May 7, 1808 in consideration of her husband's services. But the widow of Bruix had received an honourable allowance of 6,000, so that his gesture settled nothing. Some thought that Napoleon had had Villeneuve murdered by his personal police; others that Decrès was the instigator, and that the murderer was Captain Magendie, who had formerly commanded the *Bucentaure*. Things reached such a point that in 1814 Magendie felt constrained to publish a statement stressing his close friendship with Villeneuve, and giving an account of the latter's death based on the findings of the inquest at Rennes.

When the Empire fell, the controversy took a fresh lease of life. It might still have died away for lack of fuel but for the appearance of two works, in quick succession, after the death of Napoleon on St Helena: *Napoleon in Exile*, by the Irish doctor O'Meara, and, more especially, the *Mémoires de Robert Guillemard*, a retired sergeant.

O'Meara states that one day on St Helena the Emperor declared to him: "Villeneuve took his defeat so hard that he began to study anatomy with a view to committing suicide and even bought a number of anatomical engravings of the heart. When he came back to France, I ordered him to stay at

Rennes and not to come to Paris. Villeneuve was afraid he might be tried by court-martial for disobeying my orders and afterwards losing the fleet. My orders were that he should not set sail nor give battle to the English. He was therefore resolved on suicide, and took his anatomical engravings, which he compared with his own chest. In the exact centre of the engraving he made a mark with a long pin, which he then drove into his chest, pressing it in right to the head. It penetrated his heart, and he died instantaneously. When his room was broken open he was found dead with the pin in his chest, and a mark on the engraving corresponded to the position of the wound. He should not have acted so; he was a brave man, though he lacked ability."

This extravagant story reopened the whole question. Since Napoleon himself had declared that Villeneuve killed himself with a pin, when the police had always maintained that he had stabbed himself with a knife, there could be no doubt that the truth lay elsewhere, to wit, in the sensational book of the "retired sergeant" Robert Guillemard, a witness of the murder.

This Guillemard was no ordinary man. According to his own account he was born at Six-Fours, near Toulon, and not only lived through the whole Empire saga from 1805 to 1814, but entered the navy six months before Trafalgar, and was directly concerned in the dramatic deaths of the two opposing admirals.

He was concerned as an actor in that he shot Nelson from the rigging of the *Redoutable* during her engagement with the *Victory*; and he was concerned as a witness as having been present—or almost so—at Admiral Villeneuve's murder at Rennes. He had volunteered as Villeneuve's secretary after the battle.

All these revelations are accompanied by a wealth of detail "in the service of History". At Trafalgar, when the fighting was at its hottest, Guillemard was on board the *Redoutable* looking down on the *Victory's* deck. He suddenly recognised Nelson by his decorations. He was a crack shot, and he did not miss. At Rennes, the day before Villeneuve's departure for Paris, five individuals with foreign accents, led by a fifth who appeared to be from Rouergue, had arrived at the hotel. During the night there were sharp cries and slamming of doors, and five dark forms were seen scurrying down the stairs. Guillemard sprang into the admiral's room. The latter lay on his bed, mortally wounded with no steel or weapon of any kind within his reach. Some weeks later Guillemard had returned to Paris and was strolling in the boulevards, when the leader of the Rennes gang crossed his path. To his surprise the man was wearing the uniform of a naval officer!

The sergeant's *Mémoires* appeared in 1825, and soon confirmed in their error those who believed Villeneuve had been murdered. A serious publication of 1828, *Annales maritimes et coloniales*, set against Guillemard's cock-and-bull story documents from the Rennes dossier, and, more particularly, Villeneuve's letter to his wife. But to no purpose; the sergeant's book continued to excite the man in the street and to appear on the bookshelves of the most serious readers.

The matter soon took a dramatic turn. On October 9, 1830, two years after the publication of his *Notice historique sur le vice-amiral Villeneuve*, the editor of the *Annales maritimes et coloniales* received a letter on the subject. It was from a certain Lardier, a former naval accountant, living at 20, chaussée Ménilmontant, Paris, and was of a most astonishing nature. Lardier said he had not heard of the *Annales* of 1828, and had only just come across the article on Villeneuve.

This is what he wrote: "The details given on the last moments of this officer prove conclusively that his death was a suicide, and give the lie to current rumours of his assassination.

"I have myself, perhaps, done something to spread this error (the assassination) by the publication of the *Mémoires de Robert Guillemard*. The circumstantial and detailed account of the admiral's death given there has been reproduced in a number of periodicals. But Guillemard is nothing but a fictitious character, and his alleged memoirs are an historical romance, in which I mingled my own personal recollections with certain little-known incidents which, by their obscurity, gave my material a dramatic interest. Therefore everything in my book that relates to this incident is purely imaginary. At the time of writing, I thought the admiral had been murdered, and, on the basis of this simple proposition, I grouped the incidents and characters I used to develop it. I have now got over my error, and it would be a pleasure to me to see my letter appear in one of the forthcoming volumes of your *Annales*, so that the truth may be known."

This was no joke. Lardier had been amusing himself at the expense of his contemporaries for five years, and here he was upholding the cause of truth. He was most certainly a real person; his father was a lawyer, and he was born at Ollioules (Var) on November 23, 1785. He entered Napoleon's armies in June 1806 as a quartermaster, and was transferred to the navy in May or June 1810 as an auxiliary clerk, 1st class. He had been well educated, and his imagination was above the ordinary. He began writing about 1824. He was said to have been a resident member of the Var Academy from 1811, which indicates that his talents as a joker had received early recognition. We may observe in conclusion that, with his natural turn for the sensational, he ended his days as a journalist in Algiers, in 1857.

*

Such was what we may term the grand farce of Trafalgar. The best part of it is that the celebrated Sergeant Guillemard survived the disavowal of his creator, and his exploits continue to appear in the most reputable historical works. Certainly the legend of Villeneuve's assassination gained little credence after this. But that of the death of Nelson was of a much hardier constitution, and, indeed, enjoyed a brilliant career as is shown in certain naval histories written in our own times. In June 1939 in the monthly bulletin of the French Navy M. André Vovard, in a spirited article, has jogged the failing memories of historians on the true origin of "Sergeant Guillemard". But, despite all, we can be quite certain that the incorrigible joker, even if he fails to carry the "murdered" Villeneuve to his grave, will, once or twice more, shoot down Nelson from the rigging of the *Redoutable*.

Little remains to be said.

On September 13, 1809 a committee of enquiry "charged with the task of taking cognisance of the conduct of Rear-Admiral Dumanoir at the Battle of Trafalgar" found that this officer had manœuvred "in conformity with signals received and with the promptings of duty and honour". This committee consisted of four men (Counts de Fleurieu and Bougainville, and Vice-Admirals Thévenard and Rosily) whose combined ages came to 288 years, and of whom not one had ever led a squadron into action.

On December 29, 1809 a second committee of enquiry made up of the same members, and "charged with the task of taking cognisance of the conduct of Rear-Admiral Dumanoir on November 2, 3 and 4, 1805" found that this officer "had lacked the quality of decision in all his manœuvres".

But at Toulon on March 8, 1810 a court-martial under the presidency of Admiral Ganteaume "charged with the task of passing judgment on the conduct of Rear-Admiral Dumanoir on November 2, 3 and 4, 1805", declared that this officer had "carried out his full duty", and that "no exception could be taken to his manœuvres", "honourably acquitted him", and further instructed the President to return Dumanoir his sword.

At St Helena Napoleon told General Gourgaud: "Nelson was a brave man. If Villeneuve at Aboukir and Dumanoir at Trafalgar had had any guts, the French would have won. I ought to have had Dumanoir's throat cut!"

We need only add that Rear-Admiral Dumanoir was appointed head of the navy at Danzig on August 1, 1811; he was captured when that city capitulated on January 2, 1814, and returned to France on July 1 following. Louis XVIII immediately made him a Knight of St Louis and, subsequently, a count, a grand officer of the Legion of Honour, a vice-admiral, and deputy.

*

On January 15, 1815 a woman died in a final fit of coughing in an unheated attic at No. 3 rue Française, Calais. She was emaciated and had lived for weeks on dogs' scraps brought her by a tender-hearted neighbour; a girl of pallid complexion watched over her.

Up to the end, the girl had asked her: "Who is my father?" But Emma Hamilton made no reply.

XIV
DEFEAT IS COSTLY

TRAFALGAR was the last great battle of the age of sail—four centuries of naval warfare. It closed the struggle for supremacy at sea upon which France and England had entered in the time of Louis XIV and whose last phase had begun in 1793.

After the battle of La Hougue in 1692 France had voluntarily withdrawn from this deadly rivalry and had abandoned the field to her opponent—not that her fleet had been defeated, but her morale had sunk. Later she recovered her spirit and after the American War she was clearly once more in a position to dispute with England the mastery of the seas. La Hougue, then, had been no more than an historical accident; its effects had certainly been serious, especially in view of the impression it made on the minds of contemporaries, but the damage was not irreparable.

Trafalgar, on the other hand, was the irrevocable disaster that finally settled the question. Even so, Napoleon did not leave the navy to its fate. He managed to overcome the distaste he felt for it since it had brought him nothing but disappointments. Under his orders naval construction continued to such effect that, in 1815, despite considerable losses, the fleet amounted to 103 ships of the line and 54 frigates, as against 79 ships of the line and 86 frigates in 1780. Improvements were carried out in the harbours of Toulon, Rochefort, Lorient and especially Cherbourg. New arsenals were established at Venice, Castellamare, Spezia and Genoa, and Antwerp was like "a loaded pistol at England's heart". Crews were reorganised on military lines and the seamen not only wore uniform and carried muskets like soldiers but underwent an advanced form of military drill. Finally, special schools were opened on board old ships in the roadsteads of Brest and Toulon to train young men who wanted commissions in the navy.

Alas! These efforts, genuine though they were, could only yield long-term results and came too late to alter the course of events. France had indeed reached the summit of Continental power; she was mistress of Europe, but was imprisoned by the sea and cut off from the rest of the world. She now had to bow to her rival, who with the inexorable power of naval supremacy was slowly but surely choking her to death.

It may be recalled that on the eve of Trafalgar Decrès had suggested to the Emperor a method of driving the enemy "to despair" by appointing squadron commanders and sending detachments far afield, strong enough to check the English cruisers and at the same time fast enough to get away from them. The first attempt of this kind ended in a complete failure. Two divisions sailed together out of Brest on December 13, 1805. The first consisted of five ships of the line and three light craft under command of Rear-Admiral de Leissègues; it was utterly crushed by the English off San Domingo. The second was commanded by Rear-Admiral Willaumez and consisted of six ships of the line and two frigates; it returned to France piecemeal, having lost one of its ships on the American coast.

In 1807 Rear-Admiral Allemand slipped through the net and miraculously succeeded in joining the Toulon squadron with his five line of battleships from Rochefort. But in 1809 Commander Troude lost a third of his force in an attempt to relieve Guadeloupe. In the same year a fleet of 12 ships of the line and three frigates that had been concentrated in the anchorage of the island of Aix for a projected expedition to the West Indies was boldly attacked whilst at anchor by Admiral Gambier; five ships (four of them of the line) were set on fire or captured by the English.

Soon it became almost impossible for French ships to venture outside their bases, except perhaps to sail from Brest to Lorient, or from Toulon to the Hyères Islands. The English had advanced their frontiers to the very coasts of the Empire. They made themselves at home at all the key-points. They refitted their ships at leisure in the bay of Douarnenez, sailed up the Rhone in their small boats whenever they felt so inclined, occupied the Hyères Islands, and even went so far as to enter the great Toulon roadstead to cage in once more the birds that were trying to fly.

What could Napoleon do to relax this deadly strangle-hold, maintained by nearly a thousand warships (969 in 1809, of which 764 were in full commission), that was tightening round his throat from day to day? After Trafalgar an aggressive campaign was out of the question; the cruisers' war had lasted no more than a season; all that was left was the privateering war —a poor man's expedient formerly advocated by Pontchartrain—and the Continental blockade.

Once more single ships detached from the fleet and privateers sallied forth in the steps of Jean Bart and Duguay-Trouin. Even the great Surcouf went to sea again in pursuit of the English merchantmen. The first results were meagre when set against the volume of English trade, but looked like a good beginning. Three hundred and eighty-seven British ships were captured in 1804, increasing to 519 in 1806, a level maintained until 1810. In that year 195 privateers were at sea. But the English reacted strongly, and France's credit balance rapidly diminished: only 470 captures in 1811, 371 in 1813, and 145 in 1814.

The Continental blockade had more considerable results. It was the supreme effort of the land power to overcome the sea-power. By the Berlin Decrees of November 21, 1806, the Empire closed its markets to British trade. Great Britain thus found herself shut off from the whole Continent in the space of twenty-four hours, and was thus threatened by bankruptcy on a vast scale. She ran the risk of sinking under the weight of merchandise, filling her warehouses and falling a victim, paradoxically enough, to her excessive prosperity.

But even so, France soon had to climb down. Thanks to the

Spanish insurrection of 1808, English trade regained a foothold on the Continent. Smuggling, made easy by a constantly growing number of import licences, and the vigorous assistance the British Government received from commercial concerns, did the rest. At this point Napoleon realised that the blockade could never produce a quick decision, and once again took up the idea of a war of aggression at sea. There was fresh talk of an invasion of England, of an expedition to Ireland, to the West Indies, to Egypt. One hundred and four ships of the line and 200,000 men were to be ready by August 1812.

But Spain had shown Europe that the French army was not invincible, thus preparing the way for a terrible reaction. And the French navy, condemned to idleness for seven years, grown into an enormous floating barracks tied to the shore, still unable to find a leader worthy of the name, and manned by crews who knew no more of the high seas than land-troops—that navy would no more sail out of its harbours.

It was condemned to serve as a final reservoir of manpower for the exhausted Grand Army.

*

When the Empire fell not a single colony remained to France. Those she still possessed in 1805 had fallen, one after another, into the hands of the English.

But that was not all.

Between 1802 and 1806 the French navy had lost 13 ships of the line, 14 frigates and 28 smaller ships. And there was Trafalgar.

Between 1806 and 1814 she lost, in cruisers alone or in the defence of her coasts and overseas possessions, 26 ships of the line, 49 frigates and 66 smaller ships.

In 1815, 120,000 French seamen were prisoners in England, as against 36,000 in 1806.

Finally, of the 1,500 ships of the merchant fleet engaged in foreign trade at the time of the Peace of Amiens, no more than 179 were still in commission in 1812. In ten years the English had captured 1,244.

During this period the number of merchant vessels flying the British flag had risen, despite the blockade and the privateers, from 17,885 in 1800 to 22,501 in 1805 and 23,703 in 1810. On the other hand, British naval losses in the course of hostilities amounted to 18 ships of the line, 45 frigates, and 202 smaller ships, as against 124 ships of the line, 157 frigates, and 288 smaller ships lost by France and her allies!

Such were the results of Trafalgar from the naval point of view.

But we must look beyond this. On October 21, 1805 England not only won control of the sea, but she became *ipso facto* the leading world power, the richest and the most prosperous. The French and Spanish navies were swept from her path, and her security was assured. She was thus able, by depriving France and her satellites of their outlet to the sea, to stimulate and, above all, to finance from the vast resources gained from her naval supremacy, the alliances which in the end brought the tottering French empire crashing down. It was useless for Napoleon to multiply his resounding victories. It was useless for his veterans, his light infantry, and his cuirassiers to amaze the world and to make history. The decisive factor was that he had not the time to forge and sharpen the one weapon that could have restored the balance and enabled France to breathe. Despite the blood shed so freely on the battlefields of Russia, Germany and France, the land still could not conquer the sea.

There was certainly Austerlitz, but then there was also Trafalgar, and Trafalgar was the prelude to Waterloo.

*

The question remains: did Napoleon really intend to invade England?

The Emperor once made an observation to Metternich that has often been quoted: "I should never have been fool enough to invade England unless a revolution had first broken out there. The army I concentrated at Boulogne was always destined to fight Austria, and you have reason to know how close Boulogne is to Vienna."

But these words were spoken in 1810, and at that period it was all too clear that they merely served to cover his disappointment. Later on, at St Helena, he confessed to Las Cases:

"People thought my invasion was nothing but an empty scare, because they could see no practicable means of carrying it out. But I had been smitten with the idea for a long time. . . . I was to have had 70 or 80 French and Spanish line of battle-ships in the Straits of Dover. . . . My army of 100,000 men were going through embarkation and disembarkation drill daily; they were full of eager good-will. . . . Once I had made my landing, I could think in terms of a single pitched battle: there could be no doubt of its result."

There can indeed be no possible doubt that in 1805 Napoleon was resolved on attempting the one enterprise that would have enabled him to make short work of England. He did not close his eyes to the risks. His decision at the end of 1803 to rely on the support of men-of-war shows that he had a very clear idea of the difficulties to be overcome. It also shows that, unlike the engineer Forfait and many other technical experts, he had no illusions about what the invasion fleet could do if left to its own resources.

We known now why he failed.

In conclusion, the reasons may be thus summarised:

1. First and foremost, the Emperor had no fleet capable of giving him control of the North Sea during the period necessary for the invasion fleet to make its crossing. All things considered, it would have been possible for a fleet of fast-sailing and well-trained ships, acting quickly, achieving surprise, and commanded by a man of energy, to give him this control for a short period. But the death of Latouche-Tréville put any such operation out of the question. The ships were still available,

but there was no longer a *man* capable of leading them.

2. The appointment of Villeneuve was a serious mistake, and to keep him in command of his squadron after his first sortie failed was a costly blunder. Ganteaume had his faults, but he would have been a better choice. Missiessy would have been better still. But his emigration in 1793 put him out of the running, just as Truguet's excessively republican views had done in his case.

3. Whilst admitting that Villeneuve bungled everything because he lacked character, we can plead in his defence that Napoleon did not make his task any easier for him. The French admirals commanding at sea were certainly no paragons, but the Emperor never revealed his plans to them (as in the cases of Villeneuve, Missiessy and Allemand). He made them spin round like weather-cocks, deprived them of all initiative, deluged them with cascades of frequently contradictory orders, and thus transformed them into robots, or else into men paralysed by diffidence.

The presence of Decrès at his elbow was no help at all. On the contrary, it merely confirmed him in his conviction that the navy was an incompetent rabble, who were not even prepared to fight, and that if it was to be managed at all, he was the only man to do it. This was the source of his lack of confidence in his admirals, of his obstinate habit of treating them like corporals on a field-day, and of his desire, against all reason, to think of his squadrons in terms of army corps. The navy always made him scream with impatience because it is an arm that can only be slowly built up and trained, delicate to handle, and dependent on twenty different elements against which man is helpless. He often invoked Suffren, but we may well ask whether the legendary character of the celebrated bailiff could have served such a master.

Furthermore, the English navy with its perfect efficiency, exasperated him and, for all his military genius, was to bring him down in the end. He forgot that this navy had been founded in the tenth century and that it was at once the source of England's life, the blood in her veins, and the cause of her prosperity.

When Napoleon was told that Villeneuve had taken refuge at Cadiz, he lost his temper, called him a coward, and, as we have seen, talked of bringing him before a court-martial. For thirteen days he nursed his anger, trying to think of a way to get this fleet out of its hole, when it refused to fight, though all France hung on its movements. Finally on September 15, 1805 he simultaneously relieved Villeneuve of his command without informing him, and gave him orders to sail for Naples, and, if he encountered the enemy in inferior strength, he was to attack without hesitation—with "spirit"—and to force "a decisive engagement".

Surely the "wretched Villeneuve" was too much of a "coward" to obey such an order!

But Villeneuve obeyed, and that was Trafalgar—Trafalgar, the last great battle of the second age of naval history, the age of sail.